Videotape Recording

LIBRARY OF IMAGE AND SOUND TECHNOLOGY

ACOUSTICS OF STUDIOS AND AUDITORIA
V. S. MANKOVSKY

BASIC MOTION PICTURE TECHNOLOGY
L. BERNARD HAPPÉ

WIDE-SCREEN CINEMA AND STEREOPHONIC SOUND
MICHAEL Z. WYSOTSKY

COLOR FILM FOR COLOR TELEVISION
RODGER J. ROSS

VIDEOTAPE RECORDING

Theory and Practice

JOSEPH F. ROBINSON

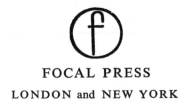

FOCAL PRESS

LONDON and NEW YORK

ISBN 0 240 50791 6

To
ANDREA, JOHANNE and KIRSTI

Text set in 10/11 pt. Monotype Times Roman, printed by letterpress, and bound in Great Britain at The Pitman Press, Bath

Contents

PREFACE   13

INTRODUCTION   15

1   TAPE RECORDING PRINCIPLES   19
    Hysteresis   19
    Sheared hysteresis   22
    Audio recording   23
    Erase process   24
    Record process   25
    Replay process   28
    Low frequency losses   31
    High frequency losses   31
    Other losses   32
    Head alignment losses   34
    Final response   36
    Distortion   36
    DC bias   37
    AC bias   38
    Equalisation   39
    Characteristics of recording tape   41
    References   44

2   BASIC REQUIREMENTS OF VIDEOTAPE RECORDING   45
    Elements of a videotape recorder   45
    Care of tape   48

Tape checking   49
Care of the tape deck   49
Degaussing   51
Tip projection   51
Care of the electronics   51

3   THE BROADCAST QUADRUPLEX FORMAT   55
Track width and spacing   56
Overlap   58
The purpose of longitudinal tracks   58
Position of field sync   61
Format data   61
Deck layout   63
Vacuum chambers   63
References   65

4   CCTV FORMATS   66
Two-headed wrap   67
One-headed wraps   68
Sync line-up   74
Stop-motion   75
The control track   75
References   76

5   FM THEORY   77
Basic FM theory   77
Frequency modulation used in video recording   82
Deviation frequency and modulation index   83
Distortion in FM Signals   84
Causes of moire patterning   87
Choosing centre frequency to combat patterning   89
Pilot tone and chroma pilot   91
Response requirements for the signal system   92
Specification of pre-emphasis   93
Conclusion   94
References   94

6   SIGNAL SYSTEMS   95
Record electronics   95
Frequency modulators   95
Automatic frequency control   99
Record driver   100
Optimisation   101

Playback 102
High input impedance amplifier 103
Low input impedance channel amplifier 104
Equalisers 104
The cosine equaliser 105
Switchers 107
Blanking switchers (quadruplex) 108
The stages of switching (quadruplex) 110
Switch waveform generation (quadruplex) 110
Generation of front porch switch 111
Demodulation 112
Methods of producing twice frequency pulses 113
Switch suppression and feedback clamping 114
Drop-out compensation 115
Auto-equalisation 116

7　SERVO-MECHANISMS 119

Velocity control methods 119
Servo elements 120
Phase comparators 121
The forward backward counter 123
Discriminators 124
Motor control 126
Ring counter 128
Amplitude and pulse width control of an a.c. supply 129
DC control 130
Practical quadruplex servos 131
Identification of frame pulse 138
Head wheel servo 138
Head wheel comparator 141
Auto tracking (capstan) 142
Practical helical servos 143
Playback modes 144
Instability 146
References 146

8　GEOMETRICAL ERRORS 147

Adjustments to quadruplex machines 147
Azimuth (preset) 148
Axial displacement (preset) 149
Quadrature displacement (preset) 149
Guide positional errors (adjustable) 150
Velocity errors 153
Guide radius 153
Tape transport topology 154
Temperature and humidity 156

Tape tension 156
Conclusion 156
Adjustments to helical machines 157
Head position 157
Tape path and interchange 158
Compatibility coefficient 159
Timing errors 162
Environmental changes 162
Tape tension 165
Auto tension 167
Conclusion 168
Reference 169

9   TIME BASE ERROR CORRECTION 170
Nature of timing errors 171
Methods of monochrome correction 171
Methods of applying delay 172
Binary delay switching 175
Determining the required delay 176
Fourth power law 177
The stable references 178
The quantised gate 179
Binary error detection 180
Colour correction 181
Sync feedback 184
Error dumping 185
Sync subcarrier lock 185
Velocity error correction (quadruplex) 186
Conclusion 193
References 193

10   COLOUR CORRECTION IN CCTV 194
Tolerant systems 194
Electronic stabilisation 197
Pilot tone 198
Burst locked oscillator 199
Methods of stabilisation 200
Bandwidth reduction 202
Pilot chroma carrier 204
Conclusion 206
Reference 207

11   CASSETTES AND CARTRIDGES 208
Broadcast cassettes 208
The helical cassette 211

Conclusion   214
References   214

12 EDITING   215

Physical editing   215
Electronic editing   217
Erase and RF turn-on   219
Playback and record phase   227
Editing color sequences   228
Electronic editing, general   229
Cue tone programming of edits   229
Time code addressing   231
Recording codes   231
SMPTE address code   234
Format of SMPTE code   235
Functions of sync word   239
Bit number 10 (the "drop frame flag")   239
Bit number 11 (standard binary groups)   240
Bits numbers 27, 43, 58, 59   240
Automatic editing   241
References   242

13 MAGNETIC VIDEO DISCS AND SLOW MOTION
    TECHNIQUES   243

Record and playback sequence   245
Stop-motion   246
NTSC chroma correction   247
Half line delay logic   248
Video disc signal path   251
PAL chroma correction   251
Slow and fast motion   253
Conclusion   254
References   255

APPENDIX   256

INDEX   301

Conclusion
References

12 EDITING

Physical editing
Electronic editing

The author wishes to thank the following organisations for help and permission to reproduce some of the diagrams in this book.

Ampex Corporation
Audio Engineering Society
British Broadcasting Corporation
Committee Consultative International Radio
European Broadcasting Union
International Video Corporation
Philips Electrical Ltd.
Plymouth Polytechnic
Radio Corporation of America
Society of Motion Picture and Television Engineers
3 M (United Kingdom) Ltd.
U.S. Department of Defence

Preface

The object of this book is to review the practice and underlying theory of videotape recording. For the reader with a basic engineering knowledge and some experience in television, the main body of the text should be practical, readable and informative, although owing to the complexity of the subject some effort is required toward the end of each chapter. For the student or engineer requiring a more precise treatment the complex analysis is included as an appendix. This should not deter the less academic reader, who should find plenty of information in the rest of the text.

The terminology used has been, where possible, that defined by the SMPTE, although in some cases a choice between two or more common terms has had to be made. A complete glossary, which contains most of the various terms used in VTR, is included at the end of the book. Trade terms, which have been avoided in the text, are also defined here.

The book fully explains the difference in VTR practice owing to the differing television line standards used throughout the world. This covers the 525 line 60 fields per second, NTSC colour, of the American continent and Asia, and the 625 lines 50 fields per second, PAL and SECAM colour of Europe, Russia, Africa and Australasia.

The choice of units was a difficult one, as most mechanical design work on VTR was based on the foot, pound, second (FPS) system, making dimensions in these units whole numbers or neat fractions of whole numbers. Today, however, there is an international drive to standardise on the metric system.

The metre, kilogramme, second (MKS), system of units has, therefore, been adopted, with the exception of mechanical dimensions where the FPS system is used with its metric equivalent in brackets.

The book is designed to be a useful reference work for the VTR engineer, because, where possible, the various standard formats have been described and analysed. These include the Broadcast Quadruplex 2 in wide, Ampex omega 1 in wide, IVC alpha 1 in wide, VCR $\frac{1}{2}$ in wide cassette, EIAJ $\frac{1}{2}$ in wide. Each chapter is well referenced and bibliographed for further reading.

13

Introduction

The achievement of magnetic recording has a long history of arduous struggle, inspiration, deep theoretical analysis and lucky breaks. Its evolution has been motivated by war and economic gain. Its progress can be followed for over 70 years in three main continents of the world, Europe, America and Asia. Sometimes the major steps were as a result of theoretical research but more often the theory followed the practical demonstration. The development did not result from international co-operation but as a result of an international engineering requirement to store or record information. The milestones in this development can be seen in Denmark, United States of America, Germany, United Kingdom, Holland and Japan.

Evidence of experiments in magnetic recording exists as early as 1880 but the first practical demonstration was given by Valdemar Poulson in 1898 when he patented, in Denmark, the Telegraphone.[1] The device used a continuous steel wire as the recording medium and produced a noisy, distorted low output signal. This poor performance did not deter Poulson and a colleague Pederson from forming the American Telegraphone Company in 1903 and later, in 1906, they patented d.c. bias, which improved the distortion and increased the output although the signal/noise ratio was still poor.

Apart from developments in electronic amplification very little improvement was made until the late 1920's when two major advances on opposite sides of the Atlantic created the improvements which, although not fully exploited until after the war, led to high quality recording and playback as we understand it today:

1. Research work in the US Navy by Carlson and Carpenter culminated in the first patent for the use of a.c. bias.[2] This improved the distortion and the signal/noise ratio on existing wire recorders considerably.

2. In 1928, Pfleumer[3] patented a method of coating and using paper tape

15

covered with magnetic powder. This idea of a tape was to overcome several problems associated with wire recorders, in particular that of the wire twisting and the difficulty of coupling the flux from the wire to the pick-up head. With improvements in tape oxide[4] and the increased use of plastics instead of paper, magnetic tape consisting of ferric oxide on a plastic base was to provide the future magnetic recording medium exclusively for at least 40 years. In 1935 the AEG Company in Germany demonstrated the Magnetophone[5] at the German Annual Radio Fair. It was this recorder that laid down the basic principles that are in use up to the present day. Many improvements have been made but the layout and concept is almost identical with that of modern 1/4 in reel-to-reel recorders.

In parallel with plastic covered tape, the use of steel tape was developed in the United Kingdom by the Marconi company with the Marconi-Stille[6] and in Germany with the Blattnerphone.[7] Such devices were limited by the recording medium itself where large reels over 60 cm in diameter containing 3000 metres of tungsten-steel tape lasted a little over 30 minutes. During World War II Germany developed the plastic tape medium while the Allies concentrated on wire and steel tape. In 1946 it was obvious which had advanced the most.

Further improvements in tape and heads brought the tape speed on high quality audio recorders from 30 inches per second down to $7\frac{1}{2}$, $3\frac{3}{4}$, and even $1\frac{7}{8}$ i.p.s., giving satisfactory performance. Since 1947 recorders based on the Magnetophone design have been produced in almost every industrialised country of the world. Audio cassettes now provide a quality superior to any recording device known before World War II with a packing density that enables a man to store in his pocket more information than it would have been possible for him to lift using steel-tape as the recording medium.

In the early 1950's the need to record measurement signals used in medical, physical, mechanical and electronic research led to recorders of similar design to audio recorders but with a much higher frequency response, multitrack facilities and a tighter specification on tape speed. The response of such machines can now exceed 3MHz with speeds up to 120 i.p.s.

It was thought that the answer to video recording was an extension of this stationary head and fast tape speed principle and in 1954 RCA demonstrated a longitudinal track recorder[8] operating at a speed of 360 i.p.s. It did not have the full bandwidth capabilities and three main problems were evident:

1. The quantity of tape used and the size of the spools became intolerable for any reasonable length of recording.

2. It was difficult to control the tape speed, in particular fluctuations in tape speed, to within the limits required for a television signal. A time-base error of $\pm$ 1 microsecond can be severe on a television signal and this would require the tape to be in the correct position at the correct time to within one millionth of a second.

3. The bandwidth of a video signal is at least 18 octaves and the theoretical limit for any tape system is 10 octaves, irrespective of head-to-tape speed.

An attempt to solve the last point was made in 1958 by the BBC with their Vision Electronic Recording Apparatus.[9] The video was band-split into two separate frequency bands, 0–100 kHz and 100 kHz – 3 MHz. The low-frequency components frequency modulated a 750 kHz carrier which was recorded on a separate track to the unmodulated high frequency components. A third track was used for the frequency-modulated audio signal.

The development of the longitudinal track recorder for video proved to be a cul-de-sac and the progressive step which was to provide the basis for further development, the quadruplex transverse track recorder, was demonstrated by the Ampex Corporation[10] in 1956 and was the result of two major solutions devised by Charles P. Ginsburg and Charles E. Anderson:

1. To slow down the tape and achieve the high head-to-tape speed by moving the head or heads. Two-inch-wide tape was used and the video heads were mounted on a 2 in diameter wheel and rotated at 240/250 r.p.s. to scan the tape transversely from edge to edge.

2. To devise a wideband, low deviation, low carrier f.m. signal with frequency components within the pass-band of the tape system.

All modern practical video recorders use both these principles although the original concept of the rotary head has been redesigned for CCTV applications.

The development costs and the complexity of early videotape recorders was so great that the obvious and only market was the broadcaster.

At over £50 000 each they were not expected to sell by the hundred. Their use as a simple record/playback device, however, soon became outmoded and their use as a production machine increased. Many thousands of broadcast VTR's are in use throughout the world and can be seen in almost every television network.

With the facility of instant playback, television producers wanted the flexibilities of film with editing, mixing and inlay techniques. Also high quality multigeneration dubs were required in colour. Alas, in the early days, even though the playback quality from Video-tape* recorders was good, at times imperceptible from the original, its stability was inadequate for monochrome mixing, never mind colour. Quality deteriorated rapidly with multigeneration dubbing. Physical editing was very tricky. Interchange between machines was also risky and it became quite common to send the record head assembly with the programme tape to ensure satisfactory playback. Some engineers likened the situation to Dr. Samuel Johnson's preaching woman. 'It is like a dog walking on its hind legs, it is not done well but you are surprised to find it done at all.'

Patents were held for several developments used in the first rotary head recorder. These obviously were not insuperable because RCA (USA), Rank-Cintel (UK) and Fernseh (W. Germany) soon developed machines to produce tapes of identical format. Rank-Cintel subsequently withdrew. Some credit must be given to bodies such as the SMPTE, EBU, CCIR and IEC for standardising tape format and general practice.

* Ampex trade mark.

At about 1960 the development split along two paths to satisfy two requirements, broadcast and CCTV.

The broadcast machine was developed to achieve playback synchronism and improved stability. Editing was improved first by precision physical cutting of the tape and then by electronic editing. This was further improved by developing cueing arrangements with rehearse and cue shift facilities and editing to one-frame accuracy. Even animation proved no obstacle for development. The art has now reached the sophistication of fully automatic editing with unique digital frame address codes for each frame on the tape and automatic fast search and edit. A-B roll techniques are possible.

Time-base stability was also improved, electronically, to allow for multiple generation of colour tapes.

The response of the system was increased to permit the high band standard with its improved signal performance, particularly for colour signals.

All this, coupled with automated controls to alleviate manual adjustment, has led to an extremely complex system.

However impressive the broadcast development may seem, the closed circuit television requirement of a low cost machine giving reasonable quality was a formidable problem of equal magnitude. In the early 1960's this task was undertaken in Japan, USA and Holland.

The solution was common, helical scan, but the number of separate developments meant a whole host of differing techniques and tape formats. Standardisation was impossible. The early 1970's brought hope of a European standard cassette, the VCR, and only time will tell of its success or failure.

The object of the following chapters is to detail the theory on which the practice is based. In many instances the practical solutions to any one problem are manifold, as in the case of CCTV colour recorders. An attempt is made to explain them all with emphasis on those in common use.

References

1. POULSEN, V., The Telegraphone, *Electrician*, Nov. 30, 1900. POULSEN, V., Steel Tape as a Recording Medium, U.S. Pat. No. 661,619.
2. CARPENTER, G. W. and CARLSON, W. L., A.C. Biasing, U.S. Pat. No. 1,640,881.
3. PFLEUMER, F., Powdered Recording Media, German Pat. No. 500,900.
4. KATO AND TAKEI, Preparation of magnetic material by mixing metallic oxide powders, JIEE of Japan 1933.
5. VOLK, T., A.E.G. Magnetophone, AEG Mitteilungen, Sept. 1935.
6. RUST, N. M., Marconi-Stille recording and reproducing equipment, *Marconi Review*, Jan–Feb. 1934.
7. HAMILTON, H. E., The Blattnerphone, *Electrical Digest*, Dec. 1935.
8. OLSEN, H. F., A system for recording and reproducing television signals, *RCA Review*, March 1954.
9. AXON, P. E., The BBC VERA, *EBU Review*, Part A Technical 49, May 1959.
10. GINSBURG, ANDERSON AND DOLBY, Video Tape Recorder Design, *JSMPTE*, Vol. 66, No. 4, April 1957.
11. ANDERSON, DOLBY, ROIZEN, GINSBURG, BEHREM, Ampex Videotape Recorder, *JSMPTE*, Vol. 67, No. 11, Nov. 1958.

1 Tape Recording Principles

Some of the problems of video recording are an extension of those found in audio recording and the basic limitations of both techniques are very similar. Several publications deal with the basic principles and are to be recommended to the complete novice.[1, 2]

A summary of the fundamental processes involved would not only help the reader to understand the underlying principles of video recording but might also counteract the growing neglect of the audio performance of VTR's. It should be remembered that all video recorders have at least one and possibly two audio tracks.

Hysteresis

It is the phenomenon of hysteresis that makes tape recording or any magnetic memory device a possibility.

Figure 1.1 shows the relationship between the applied magnetic force, $H(At/m)$, and the resultant flux density, $B(wb/m^2)$ in a magnetic material.

If no magnetic force is applied and the material is unmagnetised then: $H = 0$ and $B = 0$ (point 1).

Increasing H causes B to increase in a non-linear manner. The reason for the non-linearity is rather complex and beyond the scope of this book. One explanation for it is the Weiss domain theory[2] which, although not rigorous, does give a physical picture and produce quantitative results. An important factor is that the material saturates and any increase in H causes a minimal increase in B (point 2). If the applied force is now reduced, B does not follow the increasing curve. When H is reduced to zero the value of B is reduced to some value greater than zero. This value of B is said to be the remanence, its dimensions being that of flux density, Webers/square metre.

This remanence can be made to fall to zero by application of a force H in a negative direction from 3 to 4. The value of H required to achieve this is said to be the coercivity and is a measure of the ability of the material to retain its magnetism. Its units are the same as those of H in ampere turns/metre.

A further increase of H in a negative direction causes the material to saturate in a negative direction (4 to 5) and a reduction of H forms a curve similar to that obtained in the upper quadrants (5 to 6 to 7).

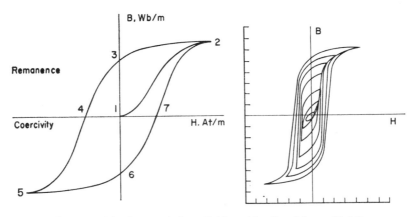

Fig. 1.1. Major hysteresis loop (left) *and family of loops* (right).

If the material is taken to saturation, the hysteresis loop is called a major loop and the values of remanence (sometimes called retentivity) and coercivity are the maxima obtainable and are those normally quoted by a tape manufacturer.

For different values of peak H we can obtain a family of hysteresis loops and a whole range of remanent flux densities.

These results can be transposed to form a new curve of remanent flux against applied force, Fig. 1.2. This curve is very non-linear at low and high values of H but exhibits a useful linear section between the two extremes.

A hysteresis loop is normally measured on a closed loop of that material. Its shape and dimensions give an indication of the usefulness in various applications. This can be seen if the characteristics of the tape oxide and the head material are compared as in Fig. 1.3. The desirable characteristic for the tape oxide is that it has high remanence for good signal to noise ratio and high coercivity so that the magnetic image is unaffected by stray fields. This means that a loop of large area is required. The head material should have a high $\dfrac{B}{H}$ ratio to provide a low reluctance path on playback. The material should also have a very low value of coercivity to reduce the possibility of the

20

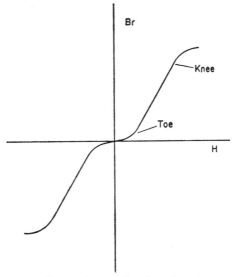

Fig. 1.2. Remanent flux against peak value of applied magnetic force.

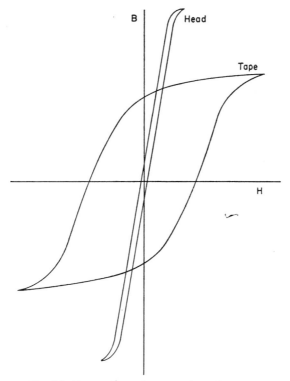

Fig. 1.3. Comparison of tape and head materials.

21

head becoming magnetised in a fixed direction. A small hysteresis loop area also indicates low loss which is desirable in a magnetic head.

Sheared hysteresis

It is possible to draw B-H characteristics for magnetic circuits. Figure 1.4 compares the loops obtained for two different circuits of similar material. From the curves it can be seen that the resultant remanent flux density is not

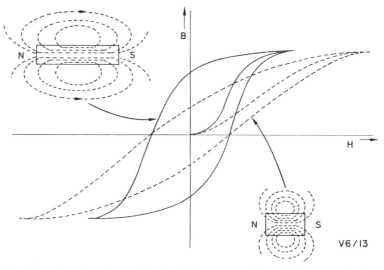

Fig. 1.4. Illustrating the sheared hysteresis loop caused by self-demagnetisation of a relatively short specimen.

only a function of the material and the applied magnetic force but also of the dimensions of the material. This is of importance in the resolution of magnetic tape. If the magnetic pattern on the tape is regarded as a series of bar magnets, then as can be seen from Fig. 1.4 the resultant magnetic flux density is higher for the longer specimen. This is due to the greater degree of self demagnetisation on the shorter magnet where the interaction between the poles is greater.

Typical values of coercivity and remanence for long wavelengths are as follows:

Coercivity

$$\gamma \ Fe_2O_3 \qquad\qquad \rightarrow 20 - 40 \times 10^3 \ At/m$$
$$\text{(Magnetite) } Fe_2O_4 \rightarrow 25 - 47 \times 10^3 \ At/m$$
$$\text{Nickel Cobalt} \qquad \rightarrow 60 \times 10^3 \ At/m$$
$$C_nO_2 \qquad\qquad\qquad \rightarrow 40 \times 10^3 \ At/m$$
$$\text{Head Alloys} \qquad\qquad 0\cdot5 \text{ to } 80 \ At/m$$

Maximum remanence (retentivity)

γ Fe$_2$O$_3$ → 0·06 to 0·09 wb/m^2
Nickel Cobalt   → 0·3 to 0·45 wb/m^2
C$_n$O$_2$ → 0·07 to 0·11 wb/m^2

Audio recording

As can be seen in Fig. 1.5 the audio recorder consists of a tape transport which passes the tape across a series of heads which:

1. Erase any information existing on the tape.
2. Record new information in the form of magnetic patterns along the length of the tape.
3. By means of these magnetic patterns, induce an e.m.f. by causing a changing magnetic flux around a replay head.

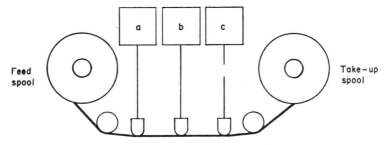

Fig. 1.5. Basic layout of an audio recorder: (a), *erase.* (b), *record.* (c), *replay.*

Sometimes, in cheaper equipment or where synchronisation is required, the same head is used for recording and subsequent playback. Record electronics are required to process the audio signal in a form suitable to cause linear magnetisation. Replay electronics are required to amplify very small level signal and compensate for losses in the process.

The three heads can be of similar construction but have some dimensional differences. Figure 1.6 shows a typical construction for audio heads. If a current is passed through the windings, a magnetic flux is produced proportional to this current (μr being constant).

The front gap is normally shunted by the tape oxide and forms a low reluctance path for this flux. This in turn causes the oxide to take up a remanent magnetism which changes in flux density along the length of tape.

The rear gap is a consequence of the method of construction of the head. However for the record head it is spaced with a magnetically inert material such as copper, paper, silica or polymer resin and is used to stabilise the reluctance of the flux path (see Appendix 1). This will stabilise resultant flux density, for a given current, against changes in μr or changes in head dimensions due to wear.

For the replay head the front gap is made smaller and the rear gap shunted with magnetic material for higher efficiency.

23

For the erase head, the gap is made very much larger and subsequently requires larger drive due to the increase in reluctance. To understand the reasons for this it is necessary to look at the basic functions in more detail.

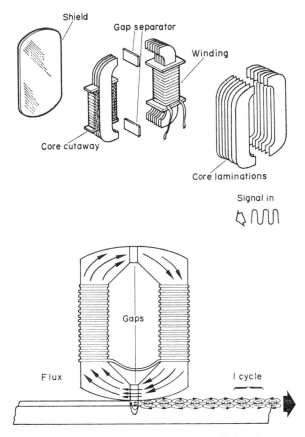

Fig. 1.6. The construction of an audio head.

Erase process

The object of erasure is to remove any remanent flux that may be on the tape. This could be done by applying a coercive force to oppose the flux. The difficulty arises in the fact that the force would have to be exactly that required to reduce B to zero.

An alternative approach is to apply a large saturating alternating flux which slowly reduces to zero. The effect can be seen in Fig. 1.7. If the rate at which alternating flux reduces allows the point to be erased to be subjected to several cycles of reducing flux, then as that point is taken around several reducing loops it subtends towards zero when the alternations reduce to zero.

The diminishing flux can be achieved with a standard head. Figure 1.10 shows the flux distribution across the pole pieces of a head. If a point on the

24

tape is pulled linearly across the head, it is subjected to, initially, an increasing flux taking the tape into saturation and then a decreasing flux reducing to zero. It is important that each point on tape is subjected to several cycles of reducing flux. This is achieved by increasing gap length and by using a high frequency erase current, 50 kHz – 100 kHz being typical.

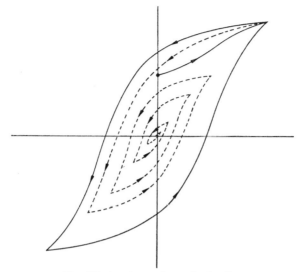

Fig. 1.7. An alternating reducing flux.

A more modern approach to erase head design can be seen in Fig. 1.8. The core is normally made of ferrite encapsulated in resin. This gives higher efficiency than metal alloys and the arrangement shown produces a smoother fall off in flux. A gaussian response is thought to be ideal.

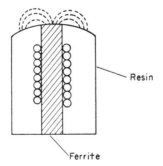

Resin

Ferrite

Fig. 1.8. A modern erase head.

Record process

Figure 1.9 shows the development of the magnetic record head. The simplest form is that shown in Fig. 1.9(a) where the tape is passed through a coil. The

25

tape is magnetised along its length according to the magnitude and direction of the current through the coil. For the instantaneous remanent flux to be proportional to the instantaneous current, the time taken for a point on tape to pass through the coil should be small compared with the periodic time of the signal frequency. At 15 i.p.s. tape speed and 15 kHz signal frequency, the coil would have to be somewhat less than 0·001 in long. Figure 1.9(b) shows the type of head used until 1950 in the Marconi-Stille steel tape recorder. Its main disadvantage is the difficulty in maintaining the tight tolerance required for the pole piece position.

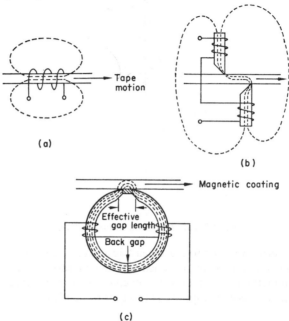

Fig. 1.9. The development of the record head.

The modern approach is that shown in Fig. 1.9(c). The face of the head is contoured to allow a smooth transition of the tape across the head. The tape is held in contact over the face either by use of pressure pads or by tensioning the tape across the head. The flux distribution across the pole pieces can be seen in Fig. 1.10. Some leakage flux occurs across the gap and through the non-ferromagnetic tape backing but most of the flux is through the oxide, the maximum flux density occurring between the pole pieces.

If the current and therefore flux, is changed sinusoidally, the remanent flux on tape varies in a similar manner. When the current is at a maximum the longitudinal flux density is also at a maximum. This can be seen in Fig. 1.11 where the resultant pattern on tape is shown diagramatically. When the current is positive, it causes a magnetic polarity from left to right from north to south. When the current reverses, the magnetic polarity also reverses. The net result can be regarded as a wavelength on tape from north to south

26

and back to north, or two bar magnets with like poles touching. This is somewhat over simplified and it must be remembered that Bx is changing sinusoidally.

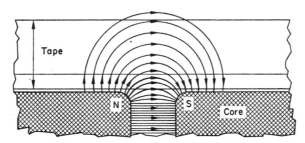

Fig. 1.10. The flux distribution across the pole tips of a conventional head.

The wavelength on tape is determined by the signal frequency and the tape speed. One wavelength is equal to the distance moved by the tape for the periodic time of the input signal.

$$\lambda = S \cdot \frac{1}{f} = \frac{S}{f}$$

1

λ = wavelength in inches
S = tape speed in inches per second
f = signal frequency

The higher the frequency the shorter the wavelength. The lower the tape speed the shorter the wavelength.

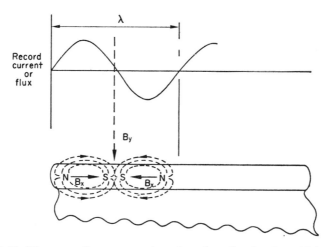

Fig. 1.11. Diagrammatic representation of resultant flux for sinusoidal current.

27

Replay process

Figure 1.12 gives a three dimensional picture of recorded pattern for a given wavelength. The three axes of flux density being *Bx* the longitudinal, *Bz* the lateral normally zero, and *By* the flux coming out of the tape. The useful

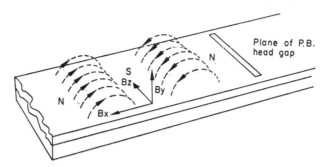

Fig. 1.12. A three-dimensional picture of magnetic pattern.

component is obviously *By* which is at a maximum when *Bx* is zero or *By* is shifted by 90° to *Bx*.

If one considers various wavelengths recorded on tape all having the same record current as in Fig. 1.13 then ignoring all losses *Bx* is the same for all wavelengths. By (flux density determined by density of lines of flux) however increases as wavelength reduces, or

$$By \propto \frac{1}{\lambda} \propto f$$

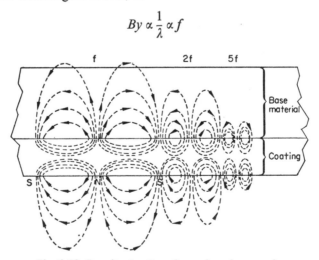

Fig. 1.13. Resultant pattern for various frequencies.

As the e.m.f. induced in the head windings is proportional to the rate of change of flux,

e.m.f. $\alpha By \alpha$ frequency

The mathematical calculations are:

During Record

$$i = I \sin \omega t \qquad\qquad 2$$

The longitudinal remanent flux density
$$bx \alpha i \text{ (For linear portion of transfer curve)}$$

∴
$$bx = K_1 I \sin \omega t \qquad\qquad 3$$

$$by \alpha \frac{dbx}{dt}$$

$$e \alpha by$$

∴
$$e = K_2 I \omega \cos \omega t \qquad\qquad 4$$

K_2 depends on head efficiency, number of turns, tape material etc. Formula 4 shows that:

1. The output voltage is proportional to the record current.
2. The output voltage is proportional to the signal frequency.
3. The output voltage undergoes a 90° phase change as indicated by the change from a sine term to a cosine term.

If all frequencies are recorded with the same peak head current, on playback, ignoring all losses, the e.m.f. increases at $6dB$/octave as shown in Fig. 1.14.

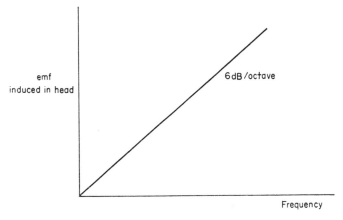

Fig. 1.14. A graph of head output against frequency ignoring all losses and assuming a constant record current for all frequencies.

Formula 4 may be written: $e = K_2 I \omega \cos \dfrac{2\pi x}{\lambda}$ $\qquad\qquad$ 5

where $\omega = 2\pi f, f = S/\lambda$ (from 1), $t = \dfrac{x}{S}$

∴ $\quad ft = \dfrac{x}{\lambda}$ $\quad x = $ distance moved in time t.

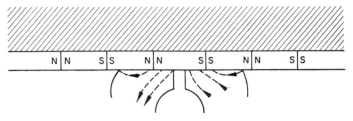

Fig. 1.15. Flux distribution, during playback, for medium frequencies

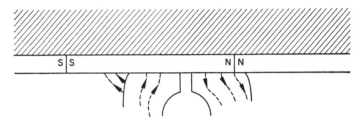

Fig. 1.16. Flux distribution for low frequencies.

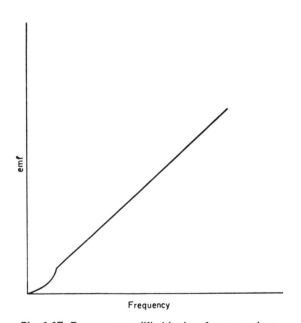

Fig. 1.17. Response modified by low frequency loss.

Low frequency losses

Figure 1.15 shows the flux distribution for the playback of medium frequencies. Medium frequencies can be defined as those that produce wavelengths greater than the gap length but smaller than the head face. The head can be regarded as providing a low reluctance path for the flux between the pole pieces and the head intercepts all the flux linkages between $\frac{1}{2}$ wavelength poles.

If the wavelength increases, as in Fig. 1.16, and becomes longer than the length of tape in contact with the head face, the head does not provide a low reluctance path for the total flux and an extra reluctance is introduced in the path of some of the flux.

High frequency losses

Increasing the frequency causes the wavelengths to become shorter. As the wavelength on tape becomes comparable to the gap length, a falling off of induced e.m.f. occurs. This can be seen in Fig. 1.18 where the gap length is equal to one wavelength. The resultant flux through the head is zero and as tape moves remains zero.

The frequency at which this occurs is called the 'extinction frequency' and depends on gap length and tape speed.

$$If \lambda = \frac{s}{f}$$

$$f = \frac{s}{\lambda}$$

$$fext = \frac{s}{gap\ length} \text{ where } \lambda = gap\ length$$

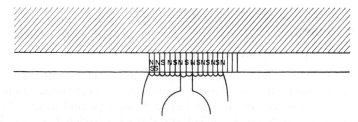

Fig. 1.18. Flux distribution where λ = gap length.

If the frequency is increased and wavelength reduces even further, output increases again. Except for special applications only the output below *fext* is used.

31

The response is similar to $y = \dfrac{\sin x}{x}$ function (Appendix 2) and is shown in Fig. 1.19(a). If this response is added to those obtained previously, a response as shown in Fig. 1.19(b) is the result. The frequency axis is normally logarithmic and a somewhat distorted view of the response may be obtained. Ignoring all other losses, the peak of the response is at $\dfrac{fext}{2}$, indicating equal pass band above and below the peak. The logarithmic scale tends to compress the upper response.

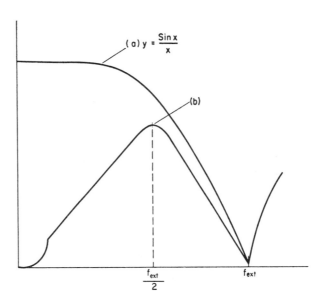

Fig. 1.19. Response modified by finite gap length.

Other losses

These are normally high frequency losses.

Spacing loss. The surface finish on tape is made as smooth as possible. However, it is not perfect and the tape tends to ride over the head on the peaks of the surface, causing an air gap between the tape and head. This high reluctance gap has a greater effect on shorter wavelengths than longer wavelengths, as can be seen in Fig. 1.20. The emergent flux spreads out farther from the surface for long wavelengths because the percentage increase in flux path is relatively small for long wavelengths as one moves out from the surface. For shorter wavelengths the same distance produces a proportionately higher percentage increase in the length of the flux path.

32

An empirical formula for the loss shown by R. L. Wallace[4]

$$\text{Loss in } dB = \frac{55\,d}{\lambda}$$

where d = distance from surface

λ = wavelength on tape

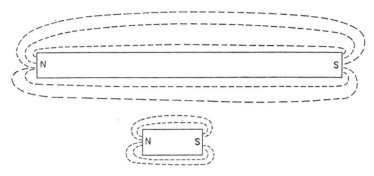

Fig. 1.20. Showing how emergent flux reduces more rapidly from the surface for short wavelengths.

Thickness loss. This follows from spacing loss. If one considers the oxide as being made up of discrete layers, the layer farthest away from the head has less effect at shorter wavelengths. At short wavelengths the surface of the tape produces most of the useful flux.

Demagnetisation. Demagnetisation can be caused by strong fields, temperature changes or physical vibrations. Shorter wavelengths tend to be affected to a greater extent owing to the self-demagnetisation effect previously mentioned. For this reason high coercivity tapes produce better high frequency response. All metal parts in the path of the tape should be degaussed at regular intervals to reduce this loss of high frequency components.

Eddy current. This is a similar problem to that experienced in transformer cores. Currents are induced in the core itself by the alternating flux. These can be minimised by forming the head in laminations insulated from each

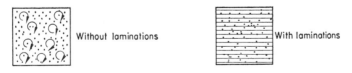

Fig. 1.21. Minimising losses in head due to eddy currents.

other, as shown in Fig. 1.21. Ferrite heads with high reluctance and low conductivity have negligible eddy current loss.

The relative effects of all these losses can be seen in Fig. 1.22.[4] The absolute

33

values of each loss depends upon many factors but the order of magnitude is typical for γ ferric oxide tape and a magnetic alloy head assembly.

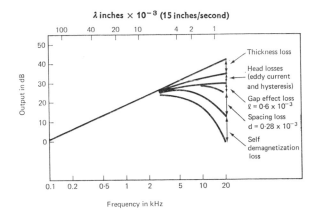

Fig. 1.22. HF losses in the tape process.

Head alignment losses

The head should be aligned to the tape correctly and losses should occur only when the head is mis-aligned. The five major positional adjustments are shown in Fig. 1.23.[3]

Tilt, tangent and contact. Misalignment of tilt, tangent and contact all affect the proper head to tape contact and accordingly upset the signal/noise ratio.

High frequency loss is also caused by the increased spacing loss. Drop-outs—which are mainly caused by stray particles, creases or buckles lifting the tape away from the heads—also become worse. If gross mis-alignment occurs, a complete loss of signal may result.

Height. Mis-alignment of height causes mis-tracking and may result only in a loss of signal level, but if adjacent tracks are close or the adjustment too far out, cross-talk from neighbouring tracks could occur.

On videotape recorders all these adjustments of the audio heads tend to be more critical than on $\frac{1}{4}$ in audio recorders, owing to the wide tape and the several heads contacting it. The audio tracks are in general on the edges of the tape and the tape does not readily form itself around a head, particularly in the presence of buckles. If the contact of a head is too great on an audio recorder, the effect is minor but on a video recorder the deformation may affect the contact of other heads. Edge damage may also result, causing audio drop-out at a later date.

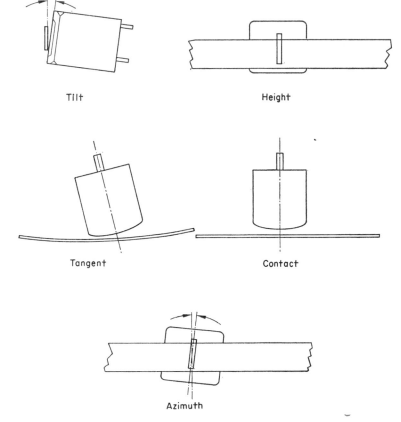

Fig. 1.23. The five major positional adjustments of an audio head.

Azimuth. The effect of azimuth can be seen in greater detail in Fig. 1.24. If a tape is recorded correctly,* but on playback the head is set at an angle θ then a phase difference occurs between the flux cut at the top of the gap and that at the bottom. θ is said to be the angle of 'azimuth' or 'static skew'. At long wavelengths the phase difference is slight and the loss negligible but as the wavelength falls the loss increases. The output would fall to zero when $\lambda = \alpha$.

At 7·5 inches per second with a $\frac{1}{4}$ in width track, an angle of 10 minutes would give an extinction frequency of approximately 10 kHz.

$$fext \text{ (due to azimuth)} = \frac{z\theta}{s} \qquad\qquad \text{Appendix 3}$$

* This is normally with the head gap at 90° to the longitudinal edge of the tape, although on some helical recorders this is not so.

35

z = track width
θ = angle of azimuth in radians
s = tape speed (same units as z)

An accurate line up is required for both the record and playback heads if compatibility and interchange is required. This is normally done using an alignment tape, accurately recorded, and adjusting the azimuth for a maximum output at a nominal high frequency.

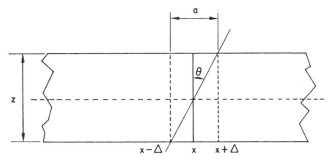

Fig. 1.24. The angle of azimuth.

Final response

The final response is shown in Fig. 1.25 and for an acceptable signal/noise ratio the system is limited to a dynamic range of about 50 dB.

This gives a bandwidth of about 10 octaves irrespective of tape speed. The upper frequency response is limited by the head to tape speed, gap width, tape resolution and tape finish.

A bandwidth from 25 Hz to 12·8 kHz is equal to 9 octaves.

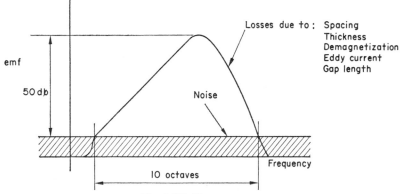

Fig. 1.25. Final response.

Distortion

It was shown that the curve of resultant remanence against applied magnetising force is very non linear, particularly at very low and high values. If a

36

sinusoidal current is the cause of the magnetising force, the resultant remanent flux density (*bx*) is far from sinusoidal, as can be seen in Fig. 1.26. On playback the e.m.f., which is proportional to the rate of change of flux, is rich in odd harmonics, predominantly third.

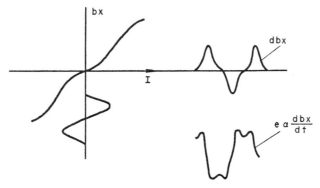

Fig. 1.26. Distortion without bias.

DC bias

If a d.c. current is added to the signal, as shown in Fig. 1.27, the signal can be shifted up on to the linear portion of the curve. This improves the linearity but has two main disadvantages:

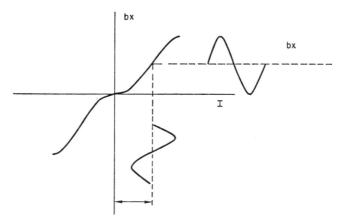

Fig. 1.27. Effect of adding d.c. bias to signal.

1. The full magnetic range of the tape characteristic is not being used; therefore the maximum signal/noise ratio cannot be realised.
2. Induction noise increases considerably. Any modulation of the surface contact causes a flux change in the head thus causing an unwanted e.m.f. The d.c. component always exists, therefore induction noise is always present.

37

AC bias

If a high frequency signal is added to the recorded signal during the record process, (see Fig. 1.28), it has the effect of lifting the record signal on to the linear portion of the curve. The high frequency is not amplitude modulated but consists of the simple addition of two signals.

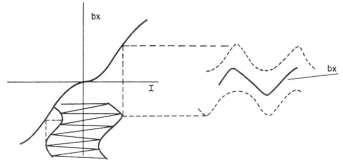

Fig. 1.28. Effect of adding a.c. bias to signal.

An element of tape crossing the gap is subjected to an h.f. signal whose average level depends on the audio signal. The effect is similar to erase except that the average level of the high frequency component is not zero but depends on the instantaneous level of the recording signal. The bias frequency is chosen to be at least three times higher than the highest record frequency to facilitate the averaging effect and to minimise any strange beat effects. It is normally the same frequency as the erase oscillator, 50–100 kHz.

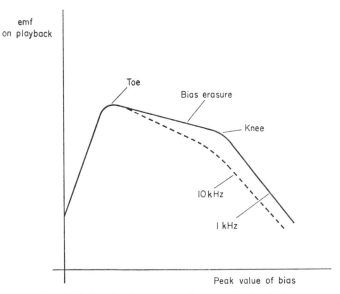

Fig. 1.29. Graph of output against amplitude of bias.

As can be seen in Fig. 1.28 non-linearity still affects the composite waveform but the average level of bias envelope, which determines the resultant flux, is sinusoidal.

If a curve of output level of signal on playback were plotted against bias level used in record process, the result would be similar to Fig. 1.29. The output is determined by the toe and knee of the remanence curve and also by erasure caused by the bias itself. The greater the bias amplitude the greater the degree of erasure. Also, because of self demagnetisation, previously discussed, shorter wavelengths are erased to a greater degree.

If a curve of distortion against bias is also plotted, any increase in bias has little effect once peak output is obtained.

The optimum setting for bias is about 1–2 dB over the peak; this gives the most stable results with oxide variations. Over-biasing tends to cause increased erasure of high frequencies and ultimately distortion due to the knee of the remanence curve. Under biasing tends to increase distortion.

Equalisation

Standards have been laid down by various bodies as to the record pre-emphasis and playback post de-emphasis for tape recorders to allow for the interchange of tapes between machines.

The important standards are:

NAB*   National Association of Broadcasters
BSI   British Standards Institute
CCIR   Committee Consultative International Radio
IEC†   International Engineering Committee

The technique is to specify high frequency boost response for record and high frequency cut response in playback. The amount required is difficult to determine but should be arranged to give the best signal/noise ratio and minimum overload distortion. It is the compromise between these factors and the desired spectrum for noise about which the various bodies disagree. CCIR, BSI, and IEC have recently agreed on a common standard for 15 i.p.s. and $7\frac{1}{2}$ i.p.s. but agree to differ on other speeds.

With reference to Fig. 1.25, the overall response without equalisation is quite complex and can be compensated for during playback or record In fact a combination of both is used. The increase in output proportional to rate of change of flux (6 dB/octave) is compensated for during playback. Tape noise, due to the random magnetisation of domains, has a flat spectrum (white noise) on tape. During playback noise e.m.f. increases at 6 dB/octave and by passing signal and noise through a circuit with a suitable response a flat spectrum for noise is obtained.

The losses due to thickness, spacing and demagnetisation etc. are compensated for before loss so that noise is not increased in obtaining a flat response.

* USA.
† International body of 40 countries including Europe and USA.

The record response and the playback response are *not* complementary. The combination of record equalisation, tape transfer response and playback equalisation should provide a flat response within the pass-band required.

In specifying a standard, either the record response can be defined from input to record flux or the playback response can be specified from induced e.m.f. to output. The latter is normally chosen because it is easier to measure and the record characteristic can be simply defined as that required to produce a tape which, when played back on a recorder with the specified response,

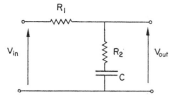

Fig. 1.30. Playback equalization circuit.

produces an overall flat frequency response. Such a response can be produced by the simple circuit shown in Fig. 1.30 Normally R_1 is larger than R_2. At very low frequencies X_c is large and

$$V_o = V_{in}$$

At very high frequencies X_c is small and

$$V_o = V_{in} \frac{R_2}{R_1 + R_2}$$

More rigorously

$$|V_o| = |V_{in}| \frac{\sqrt{R_2{}^2 + X_c{}^2}}{\sqrt{(R_1 + R_2)^2 + X_c{}^2}} \qquad 6$$

If $R_2 \ll R_1 < X_c$

$$|V_o| = |V_{in}| \frac{X_c}{\sqrt{(R_1 + R_2)^2 + X_c{}^2}}$$

Output falls by 3 dB $= \dfrac{1}{\sqrt{2}}$ when

$$R_1 + R_2 = X_c = \frac{1}{2\pi f C}$$

$$\text{or} f_1 = \frac{1}{2\pi C (R_1 + R_2)}$$

$$f_1 = \frac{1}{2\pi t_1} \qquad 7$$

$$\text{where } t_1 = C(R_1 + R_2) \qquad 8$$

At frequencies above f_1 output will fall at approximately 6 dB/octave until X_c is comparable in reactance to R_2. At very high frequencies $X_c = 0$ and

$$V_o = \frac{V_{in} R_2}{R_1 + R_2}$$

Output will be 3 dB up on this value at f_2 when $X_c = R_2$

From (6)

$$V_o = V_{in} \frac{\sqrt{2} \ R_2}{\sqrt{(R_1 + R_2)^2 + X_c^2}}$$

$$\text{If } R_1 > X_c \ (R_1 + R_2)^2 \gg X_c^2$$

$$V_o = \frac{\sqrt{2} \ R_2}{R_1 + R_2}$$

$$\therefore \ f_2 = \frac{1}{2\pi C R_2}$$

$$f_2 = \frac{1}{2\pi t_2} \qquad\qquad 9$$

where $t_2 = CR_2$ $\qquad\qquad\qquad\qquad\qquad\qquad\qquad$ 10

$$\text{Also } \frac{t_2}{t_1} = \frac{R_2}{R_1 + R_2} \qquad\qquad 11$$

which equals the attenuation at high frequencies. The complete curve therefore can be specified by quoting two time constants. This specifies two turnover frequencies at the 3 dB points and the attenuation of high frequencies relative to low frequencies.

The table on page 42 compares the various international specifications in use.

Characteristics of recording tape

Magnetic tape with all its virtues is, and most probably will always be, one of the imponderables in audio and video recordings.

A recorder will almost certainly use more in value of tape than the capital cost of the equipment itself. Its quality is variable and faults are normally disastrous. When the requirements for tape are investigated it is surprising that it is possible to manufacture at all.

The tape backing, consisting of 0·001 in* thick Mylar or acetate, is coated with 0·0004 in† of a gamma ferric oxide suspended in a binder. Some recent

* 0·0005 in sometimes used for 'long play', 0·0015 in used for increased strength in special applications.
† 0·0002 in coatings for extra long play.

41

TABLE 1

Speed i.p.s.	Standard	t_2 μsec	t_1 μsec
15 i.p.s.	CCIR	35	∞
	IEC 94	35	∞
	BSI (1970)	35	∞
	NAB (I.E.C. U.S.A.)	50	3180
$7\frac{1}{2}$	CCIR	70	∞
	IEC (GB)	70	
	BSI (1970)	70	∞
	NAB (I.E.C. U.S.A.)	50	3180
	IEC (France)	50	∞
$3\frac{3}{4}$	CCIR	140	∞
	BSI (1970)	90	3180
	IEC (GB)	90	3180
	IEC (EUR)	140	3180
	or	90	∞
$1\frac{7}{8}$	CCIR	280	∞
	BSI (1970)	120	1590
	IEC 94	120	∞

$t_1 = \infty$ signifies that $f_1 = 0$ Hz

development work is being carried out on chromium dioxide and nickel cobalt coatings and show promise of improved performance and new problems.

The tape can be used in various widths depending upon applications.

$< \frac{1}{4}$ in   domestic audio cassettes
$\frac{1}{4}$ in   professional or domestic audio
$\frac{1}{2}$ in   pro audio or CCTV video
1 in   pro audio, CCTV video or computer.
2 in   pro audio or broadcast video.

Base material. Several materials have been used as a backing material for the oxide. Cellophane, paper and PVC were used with varying success but have now been superseded by Mylar (Terylene), polyester and cellulose acetate. The ideal backing material should be:

1.   Flexible
2.   Inexpensive
3.   Non-hygroscopic
4.   Perfectly plane and flat surfaced
5.   Non-inflammable
6.   Resistant to fungus and mildew growth

It should also have

7. A tolerable temperature expansion*
8. A tolerable elastic elongation*
9. Good tensile and tear strength

The perfect backing does not exist but the two most suitable are acetate and Mylar with the following characteristics (based on 0·0015 in × 0·25 in tape):

TABLE 2

	Acetate	Mylar or Polyester
Cost	Inexpensive	Expensive
Thickness uniformity	Excellent	Good
Tensile strength	5·6 lb	11 lbs
Tear strength	4 grams	25 grams
Mildew resistance	Low	High
Coefficient of thermal expansion per 1°F change	30×10^{-6} in/in	15×10^{-6} in/in
Coefficient of Humidity expansion per 1% change of R.H.	150×10^{-6} in/in	11×10^{-6} in/in

The worst properties of acetate are its low tear strength and its high coefficient of humidity expansion. These are just tolerable for audio but prove to be inadequate for video transports. For this reason Mylar type backing is used for videotape.

Oxide. The oxide that is used on most tapes is the acicular (needle-shaped) form of ferric oxide called the gamma form. It has a particle length of 0·2 to 0·8 microns (1 micron = 10^{-6} metres) and a width one-half to one-sixth of its length.

Binder. The binder has many functions which can be seen from its ingredients:

1. Adhesive—to bind the particles to the backing.
2. Plasticiser—to keep binder flexible.
3. Wetting agent—to keep the oxide particles separate.
4. Lubricant—to minimise head and transport friction.
5. Anti-fungicide.

The oxide and binder are mixed in a ball-rolling process for several days to ensure the even dispersion of the oxide particles. After several sample tests it is coated on the backing material in 26 in wide reels. Before drying, the particles are oriented along a preferred direction depending on its intended application, i.e. longitudinal for audio and transverse for 2 in video.

After drying, the surface is polished to ensure a good and consistent head-to-oxide contact when used. The tape is then checked for the following parameters:

* It would be incorrect to state that these should be zero for VTR (see Chapter 7, Geometry errors).

43

Physical imperfections of backing material. Poor handling of the tape can cause creasing, stretching or buckling of the backing. The slitting process in particular is liable to cause edge damage.

Oxide and binder physical parameters. The oxide and binder consistency is critical. If it is too soft, oxide shedding can occur with the possibility of head clogging and oxide build-up on tape guides. If it is too hard, the tape may be abrasive, causing high head and guide wear.

Loose particles from the tape are also a major cause of drop-outs.

Consistency in width. The guiding of the tape is dependent on tight tolerances and the specification of a tape is typically nominal width $+0$, -0.004 in.

Ground noise. Random noise on virgin tape is caused by the slight magnetisation of oxide and their uneven dispersion. In practice ground noise is not absolutely random and does not quite produce a white noise spectrum. It is modified by the formation of agglomerates, surface finish and irregularity in coating depth.

Modulation noise. Noise in the presence of a signal is mainly due to surface imperfections causing amplitude modulation of the recorded signal. Mistracking caused by poor guiding due to deformed edges is a secondary source. Tape speed variations can also cause frequency modulation of the signal.

Output level variations. Long term variations are normally due to nonconsistency of the oxide or changes in thickness. Variations are normally less than ± 0.5 dB.

Drop-outs. A drop-out can be defined as a drop in signal level in excess of a determined amount, say 35 dB. It can be caused by a surface imperfection, a stray particle of dust or oxide or a complete loss of oxide on the tape. A drop-out count is normally specified as a maximum number of drop-outs per minute modified by a weighting factor dependent on the drop-out length and the time interval between them.[5]

Because of the precarious nature of drop-outs the exact record and playback conditions are performed for measurement.

Sensitivity. The sensitivity of the tape is measured to ensure that it takes up a given remanence for a given applied field. This is important to avoid resetting of record signal and bias levels to maintain constant output, distortion and response.

References

1. MCWILLIAMS, A. A., *Tape Recording*, Focal Press Ltd., SPRATT, H. G. M., *Magnetic Tape Recording*, Temple Press Ltd.
2. BROWN JR., W. F., *Magnetostatic Principles in Ferromagnetism*, North-Holland Co.
3. 3 M'S COMPANY, *Sound Talk*, Vol. II No. 3, 1969.
4. WALLACE R. L., JR., The Reproduction of Magnetically Recorded Signals, *Bell Systems Technical Journal*, Pt. 2, 30, 1145 (1951).
5. BBC RESEARCH DEPT. TECH. REPORT, No. E.L-6 1967/26. A meter for the assessment of drop-outs in video tape recording.

2 Basic Requirements of Videotape Recording

The recording of high frequencies requires high head to tape speeds and it is difficult to record a signal with a frequency range exceeding 10 octaves. The high head to tape speed, something normally in excess of 500 i.p.s. (12·7 m.p.s.), is achieved by moving the tape at a relatively slow speed, 5 i.p.s. to 15 i.p.s. (12·7 cm.p.s. to 38·1 cm.p.s.), and rotating the video record/playback head or heads, mounted on a wheel or drum at a high velocity to provide the necessary high head to tape speed. The action of the head is to scan the tape and the resultant track layout is called the record format. Formats in use are explained in detail in the following chapters but basically the tape can be held across its width and scanned transversely from edge to edge, as it is with the quadruplex format (Chapter 3) or it can be wrapped longitudinally around a drum in the form of a helix to produce an helical format (Chapter 4).

The problem of reducing the number of octaves can be solved by modulating a high frequency carrier and shifting the d.c. components up the band. If a video signal, with a bandwidth from d.c. to 5·0 MHz, modulates an 8 MHz carrier then, assuming a double side-band system, the modulated signal would have a bandwidth from 3 MHz to 13 MHz. This has a frequency span slightly greater than two octaves. Frequency modulation is nearly always used because of its tolerance to amplitude variations, which occur in tape recording.

Elements of a videotape recorder

The theory and practice of the individual elements of videotape recorders are covered later but it is worthwhile to obtain a picture of the general system shown in Fig. 2.1.

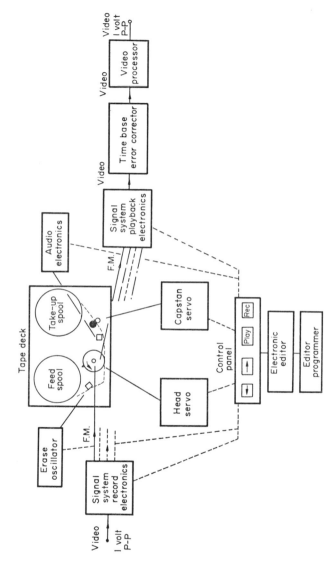

Fig. 2.1. Basic elements of a videotape recorder.

The tape deck. The configuration of the tape deck differs considerably between manufacturers and formats but the basic requirements are the same.

It must have a feed spool and take-up spool to contain the tape.

A capstan is required to control the longitudinal speed of the tape. This may have a pinch roller to provide traction or may simply depend on friction between itself and the tape.

A rotating head wheel or drum scanner with a separate motor drive is also required to provide the head speed. This assembly has some method of coupling the r.f. signal to and from the heads, either by using slip rings and carbon brushes or rotary transformers.

The audio heads are stationary and audio tracks are recorded longitudinally in the conventional manner with an audio erase head preceeding the record/playback head.

Erasure for the video tracks is also achieved with a stationary head upstream to the video heads.

Head servo. The rotational speed and phase of the video head(s) are electronically controlled by means of a servo mechanism on the head motor. The playback timing stability is a function of the velocity stability of the head.

Capstan servo. The tape speed and phase is controlled by means of an electronic servo on the capstan motor, although on some cheaper helical recorders the servo is eliminated. During record the servo determines the video track spacing whilst during playback it ensures accurate alignment of the video head with a recorded track.

Signal system record electronics. The record electronics produces the frequency modulated r.f. signal, from the input video signal, at a level high enough to saturate the tape. Individual adjustment of the drive to each head is normally provided which is set to the onset of saturation. This adjustment, called 'optimization', is important to obtain the best signal noise ratio.

Signal system playback electronics. The playback electronics amplifies the very low level induced e.m.f., equalises for playback losses, switches between heads and finally demodulates the f.m. signal back to video. Playback equalisation is normally adjusted for a flat video frequency response. Some sophisticated systems also provide automatic equalisation on colour signals and compensate for tape drop-outs.

Time base error correction. The video on the output of the signal system has timing instability owing to the mechanics of the head scanning process. These can be removed by further electronics and for complete removal the errors are reduced in three separate stages:

1. Monochrome correction
2. Colour correction
3. Velocity error correction

The monochrome correction is a coarse reduction of timing errors to give a playback stability suitable for monochrome signals.

The colour correction is a further reduction to improve the stability for colour signals.

Velocity error correction reduces the remaining error, after the above two processes. This error occurs during the line period if the rate of change of error is fast, i.e. it has a high velocity.

Video processing. This unit re-blanks and adds fresh synchronising pulses and colour bursts to the output video. It is only used in broadcast systems or in the more expensive CCTV installations.

Audio electronics. The audio electronics is similar to conventional audio recording with high frequency bias, pre-emphasis and de-emphasis. The audio quality is very often inferior to audio recorders of a similar standard owing to the proximity of stray fields, grain orientation being on the wrong axis, poor tape contact on edges of tape and reduced track width.

It is quite common to have more than one audio track.

Control panel. The control panel provides the normal control functions required by any recorder, fast spooling, forward or reverse, playback and record. The control logic needs interconnection to most of the elements described in order to switch individual circuits on or to switch their mode of operation.

Electronic editor. An electronic edit is a controlled switch from the playback of a previously recorded scene to the recording of a new scene. The edit should be synchronous so that a disturbance is not noticeable at the splice point. The editor logic therefore also needs interconnection to the individual elements via the normal controls.

Editor programmer. Once an electronic edit is made, some of the original scene is over recorded and destroyed, which can be disastrous if an error is made. An editor programmer enables edits to be rehearsed and edit points changed until the final result is achieved. The recorded edit can then be made as programmed.

Repeatable results can be achieved either by using cue tones recorded on the second audio track to initiate edit points or by using a digital address code (see Chapter 12).

Care of tape

The limitation of any recorder is normally the tape itself and meticulous care of the tape pays dividends in the final playback quality. The following are the more important points in handling videotape:

1.   Tape should be stored away from stray magnetic fields under moderate ambient conditions: 55–75°F (12–24°C) and 40–80% relative humidity.

2.   If tape has been allowed to go outside these limits, i.e: during transport, it must be allowed to normalise to moderate conditions for at least 24 hours before use.

48

3. Tape should be rewound under constant tension to avoid uneven wind and slippage. After rewinding, the tape pack should be examined for windows or cinching.

4. All physical contact with the oxide side of the tape should be avoided and, unless absolutely necessary, the tape should not be removed from the transport in the middle of a reel.

5. Physical splicing of the tape should be avoided whenever possible.

6. A reel of video tape should be handled and lifted from the centre hub, not the flanges, and storage boxes should always have a hub support.

7. Videotape boxes should be stored upright.

8. The wrinkled and damaged end of any tape should be cut off. Rapid wear results from its contact with the head.

9. Drop-out is caused by stray particles of dust or oxide on the surface of the tape. Contamination should be avoided, wherever possible, by keeping the recorder and the surrounding area clean.

Tape checking

Tape is expensive and the careful checking and selection of tapes also results in improved playback performance. The procedure however is time consuming, tedious and also costly so that the economic factors must be weighed against the final improvement. Several electronic devices with a tabulated readout have been marketed to check tapes although in practice the most reliable way is to view a tape from end to end.

The careful logging of the quality of all playbacks does give an indication of tape condition. The points to be noticed are:

1. Average drop-out count with an indication of areas and severity of excessive bursts of drop-out.

2. Noise.

3. Banding due to noise or response changes.

4. Tendency to clog heads or shed oxide.

5. Audio quality, with particular emphasis on level variations and drop-out caused by edge damage on the tape.

Care of the tape deck

Loose dirt on the videotape transport can eventually deposit itself on the tape surface and cause drop-out and increased head wear.

Fixed dirt, in particular tape oxide and binder, can cause tape scratch and misguiding of the tape path.

Cleaning solvents marketed for use on videotape recorders fall into two categories.

1. Tape oxide binder solvents such as xylene or MEK (methyl ethyl ketone) and

2. Non binder solvents such as freon, alcohol, petrol and carbon tetra-chloride.

Group 2 form the most widely used as they are relatively harmless and little damage can be done with careless use, although they are all toxic to some degree and should not be used in confined spaces. Their main disadvantage is that they are not very efficient at removing deposits of oxide, particularly in the corners of the guides.

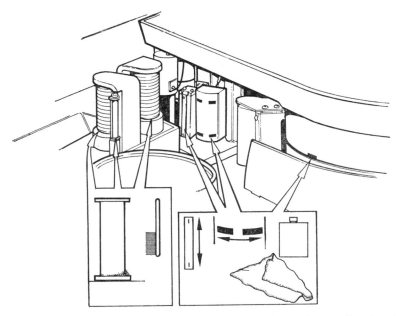

Fig. 2.2 Cleaning the recorder. A lint-free cloth should be used to apply solvent. An eyelash brush is useful for inaccessible corners.

Group 1 are better in this respect, although care must be used because these solvents *must not* come into contact with rubber, paintwork, plastic or Perspex. They must be used sparingly and allowed to evaporate before the tape is placed on the transport. The solvent removes oxide just as efficiently from the tape, causing deposits on guides and giving a high probability of a head clog.

A lint-free cloth provides the best general applicator for the solvent and all areas should be rubbed vigorously. A ladies eye lash brush is very useful for corners of guides and inaccessable niches. Cotton buds and conventional paper tissues should be avoided because they release fluff which can block vacuum guides and add to the general debris.

A tape deck should be cleaned after every recording or playback and it should be remembered that it is much easier to clean a transport just after a tape has been used rather than twelve hours later after the oxide and binder have had time to harden.

50

Degaussing

If the tape passes over any magnetic metallic parts of the transport including the heads, partial erasure of the short wavelengths can occur. A deterioration in the signal/noise ratio can also result, owing to modulation noise. It is good practice to demagnetise the transport at least daily and strictly every time the machine is switched on because surges can leave components magnetised.

The procedure is simple. A hand held degausser, producing an a.c. field from the mains supply, is brought near any metallic part. The field strength can be slowly reduced by physically moving the device away causing a cyclic reduction to zero.

Tip projection

The video head should penetrate and deform the tape by about 0·002 in as it scans. Over penetration can cause rapid head wear and tape damage while under penetration would give poor signal/noise ratio and increased drop-out.

On helical recorders the projection is adjustable and should be set to the figure stipulated by the manufacturer.

Gauges designed for particular machines are normally available and provide a useful way of measuring head wear.

Measurements should be taken over a period of time. Typically a head wear rate may be 5 micro inches per hour, therefore over 20 hours the head would wear 100 micro inches or 0·1 of a mil. If the maximum useful portion of a new head is 2 mil (from pole tip to the heel of the gap) then the expected life of that head, at the same rate of wear is 400 hours. The wear however may not be linear. If a lower projection is used, which may occur as the head wears, the rate of wear is less. It is a fact that a video head is at its peak performance during its last hours of life, owing to the leakage flux across the gap being at a minimum when the gap depth is zero.

On quadruplex machines the tip projection is fixed, although the tip penetration is adjustable by moving the tape vacuum guide. Because timing errors are caused by maladjustment of the guide (Chapter 8) the tip penetration reduces with the life of the head.

Care of the electronics

It is not good practice to make continual adjustments to the preset components of any electronic device. This causes unreliability as the component progressively becomes worn.

It is better practice to monitor and check performace continually. When any parameter falls outside the tolerable limit, the required adjustment should be made. These adjustments are dealt with in the following chapters but at this point the principle operational adjustments affecting performance are discussed:

1. Input video gain
2. Record optimisation

3. Playback tracking
4. Playback frequency response

On all but the cheapest recorders these are operational adjustments and ones that even the least technically minded must be conversant with if he hopes to obtain the best performance.

Input video gain. Most recorders are calibrated to accept a 1 volt peak–peak video signal. If the video amplitude is too low, the modulator is not fully deviated and the playback signal/noise ratio is poor. If the video amplitude is too high, the modulator is over deviated and sidebands, which cannot be reproduced, are lost, resulting in a video playback signal suffering from line tearing with a tendency to break-up.

The input video gain is either set on a meter to 100% or an oscilloscope to a set level.

Record optimisation. This adjustment sets the amplitude of the r.f. drive to a video head. If the r.f. amplitude is too low, the playback is noisy and if it is too high, self erasure occurs, particularly of the short wavelengths, giving noise in the high frequencies. As a video head wears, the r.f. drive required to saturate the tape becomes less and re-optimisation is continually required.

The basic technique is simple, although for broadcast colour the technique is refined and described later in Chapter 6.

A recording is made with the r.f. gain initially turned to zero and then increased in discrete steps. During the recording the r.f. level is monitored on an oscilloscope or on a meter if provided, and a commentary is recorded on the audio track indicating the r.f. level at each step. If the recording is now played back and the e.m.f. is monitored, for each increase in r.f. record drive, the playback e.m.f. should increase up to a point where no further increase is noted, followed by a slight decrease. The r.f. record level giving the onset of saturation is optimum and a new recording should be made with the r.f. level adjustment set to this value. This should be repeated for all heads and the playback checked for noise.

Playback tracking. During playback the video head should be aligned exactly to the track it is scanning. Failure to do this results in the partial scanning of the guard band or eventually the scanning of two tracks with a beat pattern between the two signals. A tracking control is provided which should be adjusted for the maximum r.f. on playback, which is normally indicated on a meter.

This adjustment should be made at the start of every playback and checked periodically throughout the reel.

Playback equalisation. The setting of the playback equaliser determines the high frequency response of the output signal and therefore effects the fine detail of the displayed signal. On NTSC and PAL colour signals it also effects the saturation of the displayed colours. Equalisation should be set at the start of every playback tape because its setting depends on the type of tape used, the head condition and its penetration and the record optimise settings when the programme was recorded. It is convenient to record a leader lasting at least a minute with test signals suitable for making this adjustment. For monochrome recordings the most useful signal is the line multiburst consisting of four or more discrete bursts of frequency up to the maximum response of the recorder.

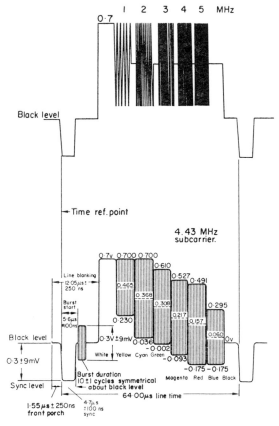

Fig. 2.3. (Top) *The multiburst signal.* (Bottom): *75% amplitude 100% saturated colour bars (EBU).* Note: *on 525/60 Hz standard, the line time is 63·5 μs and the colour subcarrier is 3·58 MHz.*

The setting of the equalisers also effects the signal noise ratio and a recording of black level provides a useful signal to assess the amount of noise in the picture, particularly for the quadruplex format where noise banding can occur. For monochrome playback a compromise is sometimes reached between the setting which gives the best response and that which produces the minimum noise.

For colour signals it is better to assess playback response on a recorded video signal of colour bars. This is particularly useful if a large area of one colour is also displayed to highlight banding between heads and beat moiré components produced in the FM system.

The adjustments described are normally operational ones, except on the very cheapest of machines where they are at least pre-sets under cover. It is important that they are familiar to even the casual operator if the best is desired from a recorder.

3 The Broadcast Quadruplex Format

The format or record track layout of videotape recordings used for broadcasting is in most cases substantially the same as that used on the early quadruplex (fourheaded) recorders.[3] Standards have been adapted for the various line standards in use, specifications tightened up here and there and recommendations for the particular use of tracks altered, but basically the format is the same. This standardisation has been the result of considerable effort throughout the world and has enabled the world wide interchange of tapes (see Appendix 20, Standards).

The broadcast concept is to mount 4 record/playback heads at 90° with respect to each other on a head wheel which has a nominal diameter of 2·06405 in, see Fig. 3.1. This wheel is rotated at 250 r.p.s. (5 × field frequency)

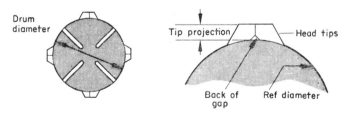

Fig. 3.1. The quadruplex head wheel.

on 625/50 Hz standards or 240 r.p.s. (4 × field frequency) on 525/60 Hz standards.

The resultant peripheral speed is:

$$S = \pi DN \qquad\qquad 1$$

where D = Nominal diameter

N = Rotational speed

S = peripheral speed

On 625/50 Hz systems

$$S = \pi \times 2{\cdot}06405 \times 250 = 1620 \text{ i.p.s.}$$

On 525/60 Hz systems

$$S = \pi \times 2{\cdot}06405 \times 240 = 1560 \text{ i.p.s.}$$

Two-inch wide tape is held across its width, by means of a vacuum, in a guide to form it into an arc of nominal radius $1{\cdot}03315$ in (see Fig. 3.2). During

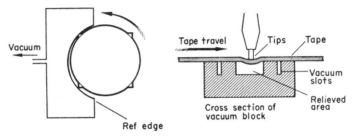

Fig. 3.2. The vacuum guide.

record or playback the guide presents the tape to the rotating heads causing the heads to penetrate up to $0{\cdot}003$ in into the tape as it scans the tape from edge to edge. The tape is also pulled longitudinally past the heads by means of a capstan. Its nominal speed is $15{\cdot}625^*$ i.p.s on 625/50 Hz standards or $15{\cdot}0$ i.p.s on 525/60 Hz standards.

The net result can be seen in Fig. 3.3 where a series of transverse tracks, at almost 90° to the tape edge are formed.

Track width and spacing

The track width (K) is simply determined by the video head width and with a nominal width of $0{\cdot}010$ in a 10-mil wide track is produced.

The centre–centre track spacing (L) is a function of the longitudinal tape speed and the head rotational speed. Both of these differ between line standards but this does not produce a different track spacing dimension between standards.

* There is also a half-speed standard of about 7·5 i.p.s although it is seldom used.

56

A new track is formed for each 90° rotation of the head wheel. The centre–centre track spacing is determined by the distance moved by the tape for 90° rotation of the head:

On 625/50 Hz

$$360° \text{ rotation takes } \frac{1}{250} \text{ sec} = 4 \text{ msec}$$

90° rotation takes 1 msec

The longitudinal speed = 15·625 i.p.s.

$\therefore$ Dimension $L = 15\cdot625 \times 10^{-3} = 15\cdot625$ mil

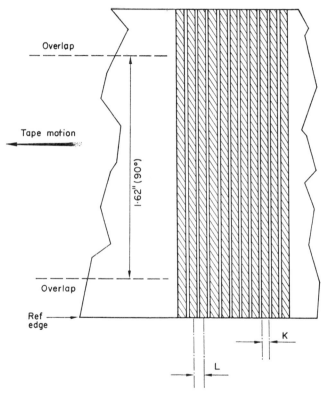

Fig. 3.3. The video tracks.

On 525/60 Hz

$$360° \text{ rotation takes } \frac{1}{240} = 4\cdot167 \text{ msec}$$

$$90° \text{ rotation takes } \frac{1}{960} = 1\cdot0415 \text{ msec}$$

The longitudinal speed = 15 i.p.s.

57

$$\therefore \qquad \text{Dimension } L = \frac{15}{960} = 15\cdot625 \text{ mil}$$

This similarity is not surprising when the mechanism of pulling the tape is understood. The rotation of the capstan, the device that pulls the tape, has a locked relationship with the rotation of the head wheel. This means that for every revolution of the head the tape moves the same amount irrespective of the head speed.

Overlap

During record, the frequency-modulated video is coupled, via slip-rings or rotary transformers, to all four heads simultaneously. The two-inch wide tape forms an arc well in excess of 90° wrap around the wheel. This means that at certain positions of the head wheel two heads are in contact and are recording the same information on the tape. Some of this overlap is erased to accommodate three longitudinal tracks giving the tape the format shown in Fig. 3.4.[6] It is important that video tracks representing at least 90° head rotation are left on the tape.

The track length representing 90° is:

$$\frac{\pi D}{4} = 1\cdot62 \text{ in}$$

It is practice to allow an excess of this to permit the occasional use of a scan greater than 90° on subsequent playback. During playback a switch is made from a head leaving the bottom of the tape to a head starting at the top of the tape. A switching transient during the picture period can be avoided by delaying the switching action until the line blanking period. For this reason the length of the video tracks is nominally 1·82 in (46·1 mm). From Fig. 3.4, length of video track = $G - E$.

The purpose of longitudinal tracks

Main Audio. This track is placed at the top of the tape and is used to record the main programme audio.

The audio record/playback head is placed downstream from the video heads by 9·25 in (235 mm). This means that the audio is physically in advance of the video and this distance, which represents about 0·6 sec, creates some problems when physically editing.

A typical specification for the track is:

Frequency response 50 Hz to 15 kHz ± 2 dB
Signal: noise ratio = 55 dB w.r.t. 3% harmonic distortion point.

Cue. This is a second audio track of narrow width and inferior quality which can be used for commentary, production information or second language sound. It is placed just below the video tracks and the head is positioned in

58

vertical alignment with the audio head, 9·25 in downstream. The track can also be used for cue marks in the form of 1 kHz and 4 kHz bursts of tone for initiating electronic edit functions or remote start of external operations.

Its third use is to record an 80 bit per frame digital address code; 23 bits are used to detail the frame address in the hour, minute, second and frame

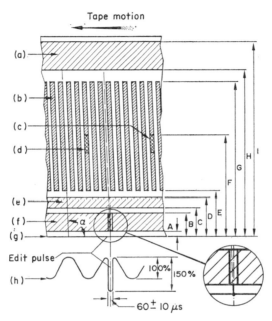

Fig. 3.4. The record track. Format for quadruplex from C.C.I.R. recommendation 469. The dimensions are as shown in Table 3. (a), Audio track. (b), video tracks. (c), start of field synchronising signal, 625 lines—50 fields. (d), start of field synchronising signal, 525 lines—60 fields. (e), cue track. (f), control track. (g), reference edge of tape. (h), wave form of the record current in the control track head.

Notes: *1. The magnetic coating of the tape faces the observer.*
2. Audio and cue records lead corresponding video record by 235 mm ± 2·5 mm.
3. Periodic time of control track signal:
   525/60 Hz—4·167 ms
   625/50 Hz—4 ms
4. Position of edit pulse is indicated for 625/50 Hz standard for position on 525/60 Hz (see Appendix 5).

of the twenty four hour day: 32 spare bits can be used for production idents and the remaining bits are used for synchronising information.

The facility of having unique frame addresses for every frame on the tape enables automatic search, cue, synchronisation and edit functions. A typical analogue specification for the track is:

Frequency response 60 Hz to 8 kHz ± 3 dB.
Signal/noise ratio 45 dB w.r.t. 5% harmonic distortion point.

Table 3

Dimensions	Millimetres	Inches
A	0·00 min.	0·000 min.
	0·10 max.	0·004 max.
B	1·02 min.	0·040 min.
	1·24 max.	0·049 max.
C	1·47 min.	0·058 min.
	1·57 max.	0·062 max.
D	1·98 min.	0·078 min.
	2·16 max.	0·085 max.
E	2·21 min.	0·087 min.
	2·39 max.	0·094 max.
F	29·2 ± 1·3	1·15 ± 0·05
G	48·31 min.	1·902 min.
	48·62 max.	1·914 max.
H	48·79 min.	1·921 min.
	49·02 max.	1·930 max.
I	50·50 min.	1·988 min.
	50·70 max.	1·996 max.
K	0·240 min.	0·0095 min.
	0·265 max.	0·0105 max.

Control Track. The control track is required as a synchronising signal by the VTR itself. During the record process a 250 Hz sine wave (240 Hz on 525/60 Hz systems) is recorded longitudinally on this track, one periodic cycle representing four video tracks. On playback the control track signal is used to control the tape position and ensure that the video heads re-scan the existing tracks exactly. Its full use is discussed in the section dealing with the capstan servo. The phasing of the video tracks relative to the control track is critical and the control track record/playback head is therefore placed as close to the video heads as possible to minimise the effect of longitudinal tape stretch.

A frame or edit pulse is added to the control track sine-wave signal, the purpose of which is twofold:

1. It acts as a reference mark indicating a position from which the video tracks containing the vertical blanking can be found. The frequency of this pulse depends on the standard:

Line standard	Frequency standard	Frequency of frame pulse
525/60 Hz	Low band and high band	30 Hz
625/50 Hz	Low band	25 Hz
625/50 Hz	High band	$12\frac{1}{2}$ Hz

The reason for the difference between 625 low band and high band is that the high band standard is normally used for PAL or SECAM colour signals which both have a four field sequence and a pulse identifying one field in four is required.

Figure 3.4, Note 4, shows that the pulse is in different positions, with respect to the track with the vertical sync, on the European standard and the USA standard. The reason for this is that the control track head cannot be placed directly underneath the video heads. On the USA standard it is placed almost three fields downstream. Because of the different field time this does not correspond to an integral number of fields on the European standard. Its exact position is as calculated in Appendix 5.

2. It phases up the VTR signal on playback. The control track pulse is used as a reference of the tape position and the capstan speed adjusted accordingly.

Position of field sync

The field synchronising period of the recorded video is positioned in the centre of a given track. This central position is chosen to avoid any switching transient occurring during the field sync period. This would be difficult to remove. Its position is also defined to within close limits to enable physical splices to be made between separate recordings. It is thought that the tolerances indicated are a little wide in this respect. The tolerance allowed depends on the required stability over the splice.

If a stability to within 5 μsec is required, each recording must be held to within 2·5 μsec therefore:

$$2\cdot5 \ \mu\text{secs at } 1560 \text{ i.p.s}$$
$$\text{displacement } (\Delta I) \ 1560 \times 2\cdot5 \times 10^{-6} = 0\cdot004 \text{ in } (0\cdot1 \text{ mm})$$

This does not allow for physical errors when joining the splice.

The exact mechanism for aligning the vertical sync on a track is shown in Appendix 4.

Format data[2]

General transverse tracks

Tape width	=	2 in
Arc of contact $= \dfrac{2}{1\cdot03315}$ radian	=	111°
Overlap $= 111° - 90°$	=	21°
Track spacing	=	$15\cdot625 \times 10^{-3}$ in
	=	0·397 mm
Tracks per longitudinal inch	=	64
Tracks per longitudinal cm	=	25·2

General longitudinal
Programme audio

Erased track width	90×10^{-3} in
Recorded track width	70×10^{-3} in
Guard band	20×10^{-3} in

61

Cue Audio
 Erased track width   40 × 10⁻³ in
 Recorded track width   20 × 10⁻³ in
 Guard band   10 × 10⁻³ in
 Control track width   50 × 10⁻³ in
 Total width of longitudinal tracks =   180 × 10⁻³ in

625/50 Hz Transverse
 Angular velocity = 360° × 250   = 90° per msec
 Angle per T.V. line = 90° × 64 × 10⁻³   = 5·76°
 TV lines per 90°   = 15·625
 TV lines per lateral inch = $\dfrac{15\cdot625 \times 10^3}{1620}$ = 9·7
 TV lines per lateral cm   = 3·8
 Tracks per field   = 20
 Tracks per second   = 1000

525/60 Hz Transverse
 Angular velocity = 360° × 240   = 86·4° per msec
 Angle per TV line = 864 × 63·5 × 10⁻³   = 5·49°
 TV lines per 90°   = 16·4

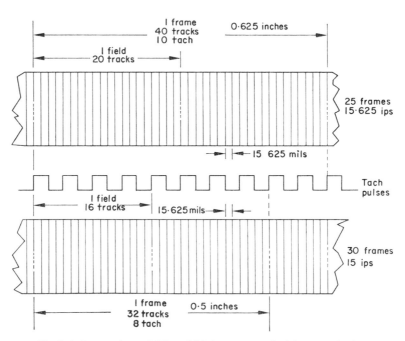

Fig. 3.5. Comparison of 25 and 30 frame rate television standards.

62

$$\text{TV lines per lateral inch} = \frac{15 \cdot 75}{1560} \qquad = 10 \cdot 1$$

TV lines per lateral cm $= 3 \cdot 98$
Tracks per field $= 16$
Tracks per second $= 960$

Fig. 3.5 compares the track spacing for both standards. One cycle of tach is produced for every revolution of the head.

Deck layout

The transport of two-inch wide tape past the various head assemblies requires an accurate, though simple, deck layout as can be seen in Fig. 3.6. The technique is very similar to that used on audio recorders where the longitudinal tape traction is provided by a capstan rotating at a constant speed. A pinch roller is used to hold the tape against the capstan spindle during play or record.

The supply spool provides a slight holdback torque to tension the tape as it is pulled past the erase head assembly (A). This head erases only the portion of the tape assigned for the video and control track areas with the provision for the control track section to be separately inhibited during some electronic edit functions. By not erasing the full width of the tape, video-only recordings can be made over existing audio or cue material. The tape is next formed into a canoe by the vacuum guide around the rotating video head wheel (C). On the bottom edge of the tape, just after the video heads, is the control track head. There is no erasure between the video heads and the control track head. For this reason and because bias is not used, the playback signal is distorted with a large amount of interference. The 250/240 Hz fundamental component is selectively filtered on playback.

The next head assembly provides the erasure of the audio and cue tracks followed by the record/playback heads, sometimes followed by a monitoring head. After the capstan the tape is passed around a linear measuring device calibrated in time.

The compliance arms after the supply spool and prior to the take-up spool act as buffers on the high inertia tape spools and avoid the rapid accelerations and tape snatch likely to cause tape damage.

Vacuum chambers

A more modern approach[5] in tape transport design is to isolate the two reels even further by means of two vacuum chambers as shown in Fig. 3.7.

The pinch roller can be eliminated and the contact force against the capstan provided by vacuum suction holes around the capstan roller. With the reduction in inertia, extremely fast lock-up times can be achieved without the danger of tape stretch because it is possible to accelerate the tape rapidly for short periods by using up the reservoir of tape stored in the chambers.

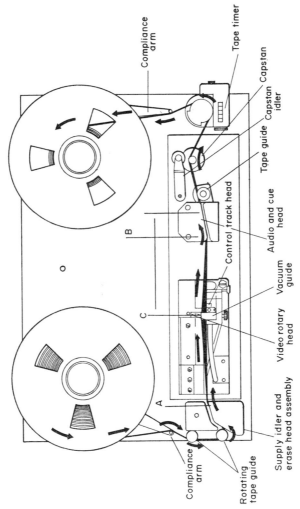

Compliance arm

Tape timer

Capstan idler

Capstan

Tape guide

Audio and cue head

Control track head

Vacuum guide

Video rotary head

Supply idler and erase head assembly

Rotating tape guide

Compliance arm

B

C

A

Fig. 3.6. The deck layout.

In the chapter on geometry errors the importance of tape tension is discussed and with the reels completely isolated it is easier to keep this tension constant as the reel diameters change.

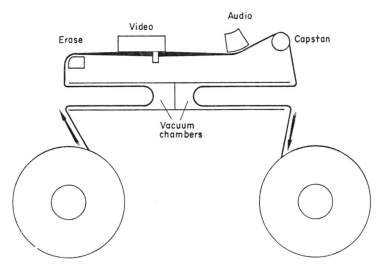

Fig. 3.7. Deck layout with vacuum chambers.

The control of the reel motors is more complex because each spool motor must be activated to keep the quantity of tape in the chambers to within the required limits. This can normally be done by monitoring the maximum and minimum limits of the tape with a light and PEC sensor which is blocked by the tape. The reel motor can be activated in either direction to add or remove tape and keep it within the limits.

References

1. ROIZEN, J., Television tape techniques today, *Broadcast Engineering*, Nov. 63 April 64.
2. BBC, Technical Instruction V. 6, Video-tape Recording, BBC Engineering Division.
3. GINSBURG, C. P., ANDERSON, C. E., DOLBY, R. M., Video tape Recorder Design, *SMPTE*, Vol. 66, April 1957.
4. EBU, EBU Standards for television tape recordings, *EBU Tech 3084-E*, April 1967.
5. WHITEHEAD, S., *Design consideration of tape transports for quadruplex Videotape Recorders*, Ampex Corp., Redwood City, California.
6. CCIR, *Standards for the international exchange of television programmes on magnetic tape*. CCIR Recommendation 469.

4 CCTV Formats

The object of designing a specific format for CCTV purposes is to make an economic saving on the amount of tape used and the number of heads, with associated electronics, required to scan the tracks. A saving in tape can be made by reducing the head to tape speed and the track width. Reductions in bandwidth and signal/noise ratio inevitably result but are considered tolerable for most closed circuit applications.

The number of rotating heads can be reduced only if the tape is wrapped further around the periphery of the head assembly. A 180° wrap would allow a minimum of two heads while a full 360° wrap would allow a single head.

Timing errors due to geometry changes occur on any recorder at track scanning frequency and the perceptibility of these fixed errors becomes less if they repeat themselves at a field rate and not multiples or sub-multiples of field rate. For this reason it is an advantage to make one track contain one television field.

The simplest method of wrapping the tape around the head wheel is to form the tape into a helix around a drum assembly causing the tape to rise as it moves around the head or heads. The method gives rise to the term helical scan or wrap and can be adapted for any number of heads although normally only one or two heads are used.

Two-headed wrap[1,2,3]

This is the simplest arrangement and can be seen in Fig. 4.1. The angle of wrap is made slightly greater than 180° to allow a slight overlap of information. The distance the tape moves up the drum, over the 180°, must always be less than the width of the tape to allow a space along the edges of the tape for

66

longitudinal tracks. The video heads, which can either move in the same or opposite direction to the tape, traverse almost from edge to edge producing a track length nearly equal to the peripheral distance between the heads. If the tape and head motion oppose each other, the resultant track length is increased. Similarly it is reduced if the tape and head move in the same direction.

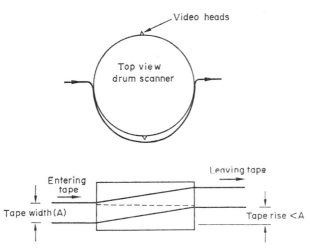

Fig. 4.1. Two headed wrap.

The track angle is determined by the rise and is slightly modified by the tape motion (see Appendices 4.1 to 4.4).

The rotational speed of the head must be half that of the field rate so that one video track contains one field.

The diameter of the head drum scanner determines the head to tape speed:

For a 50 Hz field rate

Rotational speed $= 25$ r.p.s.
Circumference of the drum $= \pi D$

where $D =$ drum diameter

$$\text{Head speed} = 25\pi D$$

If the required head speed is 600 i.p.s.:

$$D = \frac{600}{25\pi} = 7\cdot 64 \text{ in}$$

The angle of the track is very small so that to a first approximation the final head to tape speed = head speed + tape speed.

When the tape and head motion oppose:

If the tape speed = 7 i.p.s.,

$$\text{Track length} = \frac{607}{50} = 12.15 \text{ in}$$

For a 60 Hz field rate

For same diameter drum,

Head speed = $30 \times \pi \times 7.64 = 720$ i.p.s.

$$\text{Track length} = \frac{727}{60} = 12.1 \text{ in}$$

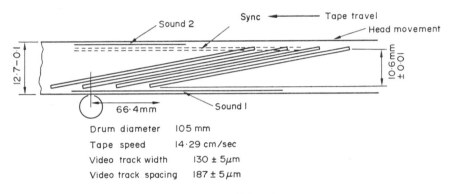

Drum diameter   105 mm
Tape speed   14.29 cm/sec
Video track width   130 ± 5μm
Video track spacing   187 ± 5μm

Fig. 4.2. Phillips V.C.R. format.

One-headed wraps[5]

On one-headed wraps the head rotates 360° for one field period which allows, for the same head to tape speed, the drum diameter to be reduced to half that required for two-headed configurations. The problem of aligning the heads with respect to each other is eliminated, although the problem of a long drop-out is created by the loss of information after ending one track and starting the next. The difficulty is in trying to get tape contact around the full 360° of the drum.

There are three basic methods of forming the tape around the drum: omega wrap, alpha wrap and conical wrap. Of these only the first two are in common use.

Omega wrap. If this wrap is viewed from the top of the drum scanner it forms the Greek letter Ω as shown in Fig. 4.3. Because of its shape it permits the

68

lower edge of the tape leaving the drum to be below the upper edge of the tape entering the drum. This produces the overlap, dimension 'd', which allows room for the longitudinal tracks. In a similar way to the two headed format the space left unrecorded is determined by the tape rise over 360° and is equal to the difference between the tape rise and the tape width. The overlap should be large enough to allow sufficient width for at least one

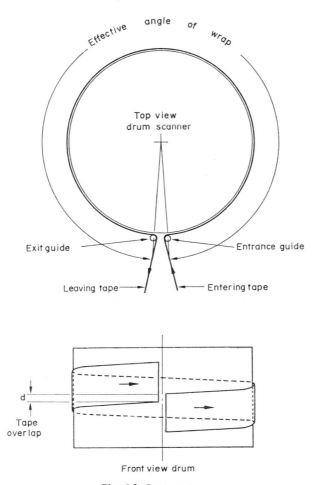

Fig. 4.3. Omega wrap.

audio and one control track and some formats leave room for a second audio track.

It is not possible to achieve tape contact over the full 360° because a small exit and entrance clearance is necessary for the tape.

This gap seldom exceeds 10° drum angle although even this creates a large drop-out.

On 625/50 Hz

1 revolution (360°) records 312·5 TV lines

$$10° = \frac{1}{36} \text{ revolution contains } \frac{312·5}{36} = 9 \text{ TV lines.}$$

On 525/60 Hz

360° records 262·5 TV lines.

$$10° \text{ contains } \frac{262·5}{36} = 7 \text{ TV lines}$$

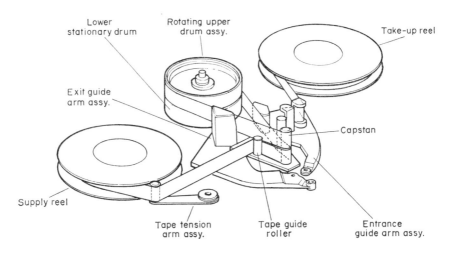

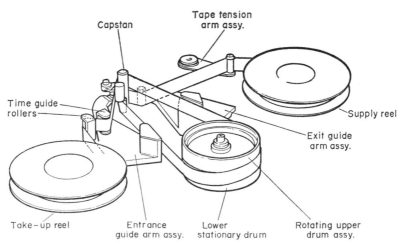

Fig. 4.4. Tape deck layout of an omega wrap with the arms in a retracted state.

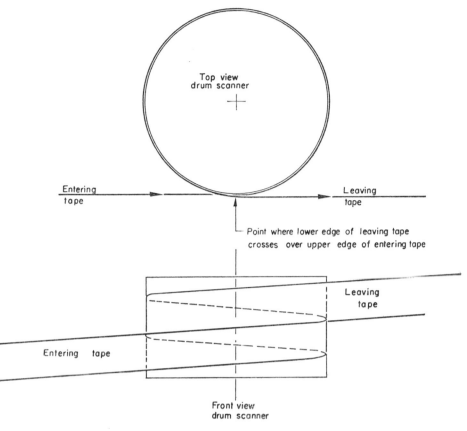

Fig. 4.5. Alpha wrap.

The tape path becomes quite tortuous for the omega wrap and some method to make the lacing of the tape easier is required. This can take the form of retractable guide arms which are only moved in during play and record. Figure 4.4 shows one arrangement which despite its simplicity still requires dexterity on behalf of the operator.

The drop-out lines lost are normally chosen to be those at the bottom of the picture. The start of a scan therefore would be the field synchronising period.

Alpha wrap. This wrap, as the name implies, forms the Greek letter α when viewed from the top and is shown in Fig. 4.5. It is a simpler form than the omega and is somewhat easier to produce operationally. Because the lower edge of the tape leaving the drum must be slightly higher than the upper edge of the tape entering the drum the tape rise must be at least equal to the tape width. With no overlap the tape is scanned from edge to edge with the minimum of drop-out from the end of one track and the start of the next.

71

A deterioration of the signal at the edges of the tape can easily result if the tape is in any way damaged. With the full width of the tape used up there is little room for the audio. If a portion of the tape width is erased, a second drop-out is created which, for a reasonably wide audio track, is quite large.

For an audio track width of 0·040 in on one-inch wide tape the proportion erased is:

$$\frac{0\cdot040}{1} \times 100\% = 4\%$$

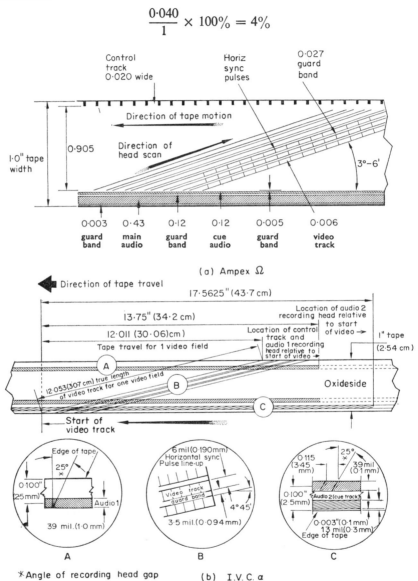

(a) Ampex Ω

(b) I.V. C. α

*Angle of recording head gap

Fig. 4.6. Typical one-inch formats for omega wraps (top) *and alpha wraps* (bottom).

This is equal to 12·5 TV lines on 625/60 Hz systems and 10·0 TV lines on 525/60 Hz systems. If a second audio track and control track are required, third and fourth drop-outs are created.

A compromise can be made if a poorer audio performance can be tolerated. Either a reduction in track width can be made or the audio signals can be recorded up-stream prior to the video. The action of the overscanning video head is to cause an amplitude modulation of the audio signal at the track or field frequency.

The effect of this distortion can be minimised by low frequency rejection filtering on playback and by placing the audio gap at an angle. The distortion of the audio on the video signal is minimal. Although beat components can be produced, the order of magnitude is low.

Figure 4.6 shows typical one-inch formats for omega and alpha wraps. The distinctive feature of the omega format is the positioning of the audio tracks

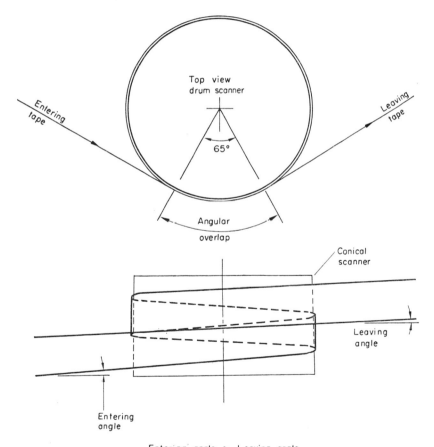

Fig. 4.7. Conical wrap.

on the extreme edges with the video tracks stopping short of the edge. The alpha format has video tracks extending to the edges of the tape with overlapping audio. If a new audio track is recorded over existing video then obviously the additional drop-out will be produced.

Conical wrap. The conical wrap is a form of alpha wrap which is not of practical use but it is of interest to see why a wrap with such apparent advantages cannot be used.

The form of the wrap can be seen in Fig. 4.7 where the entering angle of the tape is slightly greater than the leaving angle thus allowing an overlap where the entering tape is underneath the leaving tape. To achieve this the drum assembly needs to be slightly conical. The method seems to have the simplicity of alpha with the unrecorded section of the omega. Unfortunately the technique suffers from one major disadvantage. Because of the cone angle, as the tape moves up the drum its angle changes, thus causing the video track angle to change. The cone angle is determined by the required space for the audio tracks and the permissible angle of overlap. If the angular overlap is limited to 65° and the required width for the audio tracks is one tenth of the tape width, the track angle doubles over its length (see Appendix 7).

The recorded tracks are now no longer straight lines but form arcs with a centre–centre track spacing that varies. The capstan speed is chosen so that the line syncs on each track align themselves (sync line-up) to each other. As this is a function of track angle, sync line-up is impossible on this format.

Sync line-up

On all the formats described, one important design feature is that the distance the tape moves during one field time is such that the horizontal syncs on adjacent tracks 'line-up'. For this to occur the distance moved should be a whole number of lines plus half a line to take into account the horizontal sync phase at the start of a new field (see Fig. 4.8). This precise distance depends on the length of a horizontal line on a video track and the track

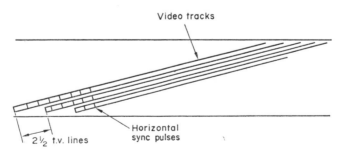

Fig. 4.8. Sync line-up.

angle. The exact number of lines moved depends on the format, but in general it is between 2½ to 4½ TV lines depending on the head/tape speed and line standard used (see Appendix 6). This feature very often results in rather odd values of linear tape speed which alter slightly between standards.

The advantage of sync line-up is apparent if the scanning of adjacent tracks is considered. This occurs during still frame, slow motion or simple mis-tracking during playback when the head crosses the guard band on to another track. If sync line-up was not designed into the format, a horizontal sync phase change would occur, causing the monitor picture to break-up and re-lock. Sync line-up ensures sync continuity over such disturbances.

Stop-motion

One advantage of helical scan is that stop motion playback is possible by stopping the tape and keeping the head rotating at field rate. The scan angle is now slightly different owing to the lack of tape motion. If the scan starts on the centre of a track, it ends on the centre of an adjacent track, a longitu-dinal distance equal to the distance the tape has moved. In crossing the guard band a noise bar is produced in the centre of the picture. A slight adjustment of the track position moves the bar to the top or bottom of the picture, thus starting the scan in a guard band and ending, in an adjacent guard band (see Fig. 4.9). The same recorded field is repeated on playback giving the effect of still frame.

Scan path

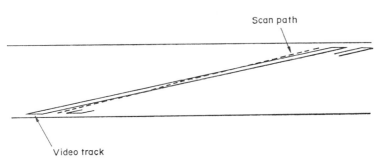

Video track

Fig. 4.9. Scan path of head when tape stationary.

A field by field inspection, sometimes misquoted as slow-motion, can be achieved by slowly moving the tape, but a noise bar drifts through the picture until the track presentation rate matches the scanning rate of the head at normal speed.

The control track

The object of the control track is to provide an identification mark for the start of each track. This can be used in playback to synchronise track and

75

scanning rate. It is normally derived from field sync and can be a single or multiple pulse placed on the tape by a separate head upstream or downstream from the video drum scanner.

References

1. SAWAJI YOSHIO, EIAJ Standards for half-inch videotape recorders, *JSMPTE*, Vol. 79, Dec. 1970.
2. EBU, *Different Types of non-standard television tape-recorders*. Technical Information Sheet No, 2, July 1967.
3. FOERSTE, G., *Technical Aspects of the Phillips VCR System*, Montreux TV Symposium 1971.
4. EBU, *Video player and recorder systems for home use*. Tech. 3093, March 1971.
5. JOHNSON, D., *Video record format of helical scan recorders*, Ampex Educational Division, Illinois.
6. BBC SPECIFICATION TU250, Outline specification for a Colour Helical Scan Video Tape Recorder.

5 FM Theory

The frequency response of a television signal is

> 0 to 5·5 MHz for System I 625 line system
> 0 to 5·0 MHz for System II 625 line system
> 0 to 4·2 MHz for   525 line system

Assuming that the d.c. component could be restored and that the minimum frequency required to be transferred through the tape recorder is 10 Hz, a pass band of up to 20 octaves would be required for the full bandwidth recording of the above standard signals.

To produce a record signal of less than 10 octaves some form of modulation of the video is required.

Frequency modulation is the most suitable, owing to its relative simplicity and ease of production compared with the more complex pulse code modulation techniques, and owing to its tolerance of amplitude variations compared with amplitude modulation.

Frequency modulation as used in VTR differs in two respects from most other systems in common use:

1. The centre frequency is very close to the highest modulating frequency.

2. The modulation index $\left(\dfrac{fd}{fm}\right)$ is lower than in most other systems.

Basic FM theory

A simple FM modulator system is shown in Fig. 5.1. where the input signal, called the modulating frequency (fm), controls the reactance circuit of an oscillator tuned to a centre frequency (fc). The system is assumed to be a linear one, whereby the oscillator frequency deviation is proportional to the amplitude of the input signal.

The output of the modulator therefore would be of the form

$$f = (fc + fd \cos 2\pi fmt)$$

$$\text{or } w = wc + wd \cos wmt \qquad\qquad 1$$

where fd = maximum deviation of instantaneous frequency from centre frequency

$$fm = \text{frequency of the modulating signal}$$

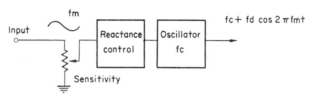

Fig. 5.1. The F.M. modulator.

The resulting waveform is shown in Fig. 5.2, with the modulated signal advancing and retarding in phase with respect to an unmodulated centre frequency.

If a phasor diagram is constructed as in Fig. 5.3(a), the modulated signal can be seen to advance and retard to a maximum angle θ. The magnitude of this angle is a function of the maximum deviation and the rate of deviation and is equal to

$$\theta = \frac{wd}{wm} = \frac{fd}{fm} \qquad\qquad 2$$

See Appendix 8.

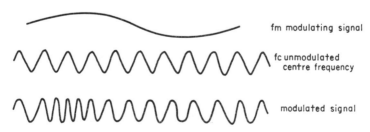

Fig. 5.2. The modulated signal.

This is not unreasonable to expect because it shows that, if the deviation is increased, θ will increase. Also if the rate at which the centre frequency is deviated is reduced, by reducing the modulating frequency, the resulting angle increases.

78

This is analogous to the phase difference between two cars on a circular race track, both averaging the same speed. If car A remains at a consistent speed of, say, 60 m.p.h. and car B accelerates to a speed of 70 m.p.h. and then decelerates to 50 m.p.h., the deviation can be said to be ±10 m.p.h. Increasing the deviation increases the angle between the two cars. Increasing the rate of deviation reduces the angle.

The analysis of the spectral or sideband distribution is complex and is shown in Appendix 9.

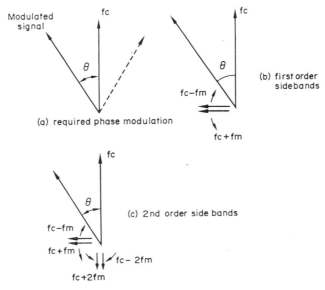

Fig. 5.3. Phasor diagrams showing the synthesis of F.M. side-bands.

From the phasor diagram in Fig. 5.3(b) it can be seen that, as a first order approximation, two sidebands at $fc + fm$ and $fc - fm$ would produce the required phase modulation assuming that the angle θ is small, i.e. $<45°$. The presence of only two, first order, sidebands do not quite produce the classical picture of an FM wave. Amplitude modulation exists because the resultant vector is larger in amplitude when the sidebands add in quadrature to the centre frequency. However if θ is small the effect is minimal and higher order sidebands can be ignored. To reduce the effect of AM, two extra sidebands can be postulated as shown in Fig. 5.3(c). These subtract from fc when $fc + fm$ and $fc - fm$ add to fc in quadrature. To achieve this, the second order sidebands must rotate through 360° for 180° rotation of the first order sidebands. In other words twice as fast or equal to $fc + 2fm$, $fc - 2fm$. It can be shown that third, fourth indeed an infinite number of SB's are present in an FM wave. The amplitude of these sidebands initially increases as θ increases. A graphical representation of the sideband amplitudes against θ are shown in the Bessel functions in Fig. 5.4. From the graph

79

it can be see that if θ is less than 1 radian (57°), most of the energy is in the first order sidebands.

The sideband distribution can also be shown as a spectral distribution as in Fig. 5.5 and it is interesting to note that as the modulating frequency reduces, θ increases, causing greater energy in the higher order sidebands. The bandwidth however remains substantially the same.

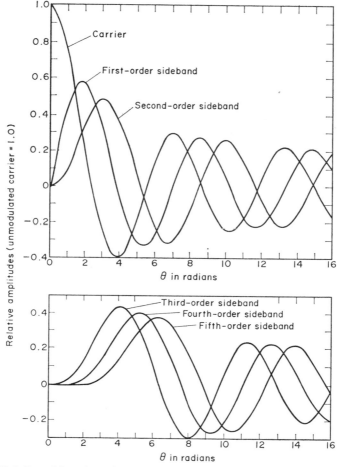

Fig. 5.4. Bessel functions showing the relative amplitudes of F.M. side-bands.

Frequency modulation used in video recording

Centre frequency. The term centre frequency, when referred to video signals, is not easy to define. As the limits of the system response are reached by the high frequencies of the modulating signals, it is convenient to regard the centre frequency as the modulator frequency at the mean level of these components, i.e. the low frequency luminance level.

Figure 5.6 shows the range over which the centre frequency can change for the various systems in use with peak white giving the highest frequency and sync tip the lowest. The choice of upper and lower frequency limit is set by the response of the *FM* path, the highest sideband being created by a high frequency component at peak-white and the lowest sideband by a high frequency component at black level.

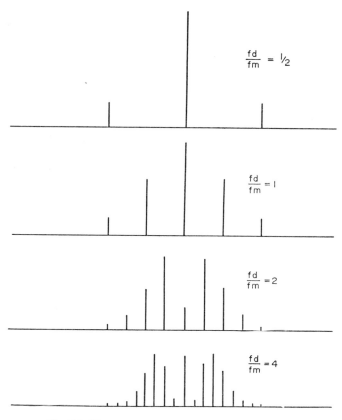

Fig. 5.5. The spectral distribution of an F.M. wave.

In VTR the maximum permissible centre frequency is limited by the upper frequency response of the tape transfer process and the highest video frequency. The response must be high enough to pass the highest first order upper sideband. In general this is limited by the head and the resolution of the tape. The maximum resolution of the gamma-ferric oxide tape is about 80–100 micro inches (2 microns). High energy tapes are improving this figure with possibilities of three to four times the resolution of gamma-ferric oxide. The lowest permissible centre frequency is limited by the low frequency response because it is required that the first order lower sideband is passed

81

by the system. The lowest centre frequency therefore must be higher than the highest video frequency plus the low frequency limit.

Table 4

T.V. System	Video Level		
	A Sync Tip	B Black Level	C Peak White
625/50 Low Band	4·95 MHz	5·50 MHz	6·80 MHz
625/50 High Band	7·16 MHz	7·80 MHz	9·30 MHz
525/60 Low Band	4·28 MHz	5·00 MHz	6·80 MHz
525/60 Colour Low Band	5·50 MHz	5·79 MHz	6·50 MHz
525/60 High Band	7·06 MHz	7·90 MHz	10·0 MHz
Typical 1″ Format (Video −3·0 MHz)	3·5 MHz		5·5 MHz
Typical ¼″ Cassette (Video −2·7 MHz)	3·0 MHz		4·2 MHz
625/50 Super High Band (9000)	9·0 MHz	9·9 MHz	12 MHz

Quadruplex. With a head to tape speed of 1570 i.p.s. and a resolution of 100–80 μin.

$$f\max = \frac{1570 \times 10^6}{100} \text{ to } \frac{1570 \times 10^6}{80} = 15\cdot7 \text{ MHz to } 19\cdot5 \text{ MHz}$$

$fc + fm$ must be less than 15·7 MHz

or $fc < 15\cdot7$ MHz $- fm$

where fc is the centre frequency

and fm is the highest modulating frequency

for 625/50 Hz with $fm = 5\cdot5$ MHz $\quad fc < 10\cdot7$ MHz

for 525/60 Hz with $fm = 4\cdot5$ MHz $\quad fc < 11\cdot2$ MHz

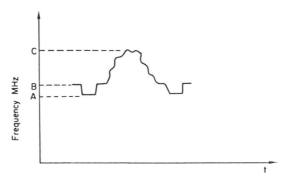

Fig. 5.6. *The deviation standards of the F.M. signal. The relevant figures are shown in Table 4.*

With a low frequency limit at about 200 kHz

$fc > 5.0 + 0.2 = 5.2$ MHz for system II 625/50 Hz

$fc > 4.2 + 0.2 = 4.4$ MHz for 525/60 Hz

For Helical. Typically the bandwidth of the video signal is limited to 3 MHz, and the tape speed is of the order of 800 i.p.s.

$$f\,\text{max} = \frac{800 \times 10^6}{100} \text{ to } \frac{800 \times 10^6}{80} = 8.0 \text{ MHz to } 10.0 \text{ MHz}$$

(With high energy tape, the head to tape speed can be reduced, owing to the higher resolution. Typically 320 i.p.s. would give the same maximum frequency of 8.0 MHz with cobalt doped or chromium dioxide compound tapes.)

$$fc < 8.0 - 3.0 = 5.0 \text{ MHz}$$
$$fc > 3.0 + 0.2 = 3.02 \text{ MHz}$$

The centre frequency of a video modulated *FM* signal is difficult to define but if a peak-white signal or a black-level signal has a high frequency component on it, it would be required that both the first order upper and the first order lower sidebands produced are passed by the system. The frequency produced by the average level of the video signal can therefore be defined as the instantaneous value of the centre frequency and this is a variable quantity between peak white and black level. The output frequency of the modulator therefore should not go beyond the limits calculated for an input video signal excursion from black level to peak white.

Broadcast standard frequencies have been internationally agreed but CCTV practice is as varied as the number of manufacturers. Table 4 shows the main standards in use.

Deviation frequency and modulation index

The maximum sinusoidal deviation that can occur would be for a video signal with an average mid-grey level and a frequency component with a peak value from peak-white to black level. In monochrome signals such a situation is rare although black to white transitions contain large amplitudes of high frequency components. In colour signals where the chrominance information is transmitted on a high frequency sub-carrier large amplitudes of high frequency are more common.

Assuming the worst case of 100% amplitude, 100% saturated bars, the maximum peak–peak sub-carrier amplitude is always less than 0.9 of the peak–peak excursion from sync tip to peak-white. On this basis the maximum peak–peak deviation and the resultant modulation index due to colour sub-carrier can be calculated from the frequency standards given in Fig. 5.6.

Where

$$\text{peak–peak} fd = (C - A) \times 0.9 \text{ (Without pre-emphasis)}$$

$$\text{peak} fd = \frac{C - A}{2} \times 0.9$$

This is modified by the amount of high frequency boost applied to the video signal prior to modulation and this is determined by the pre-emphasis characteristic which is discussed later.

However from Fig. 5.15

After pre-emphasis

$$fd = \frac{C - A}{2} \times 0{\cdot}9 \times \frac{\tau_1}{\tau_2}$$

The modulation index $(\theta) = \frac{fd}{fm}$

where fm is the colour sub-carrier frequency.

For 625/50 high band (colour sub-carrier = 4·43 MHz)

$$fd = \frac{9{\cdot}3 - 7{\cdot}16}{2} \times 0{\cdot}9 \times \frac{600}{240} = 2{\cdot}4 \text{ MHz}$$

$$\theta = \frac{2{\cdot}4}{4{\cdot}43} = 0{\cdot}54 \text{ radians} = 31°$$

For 525/60 Hz high band (colour sub-carrier 3·58 MHz)

$$fd = 10 - \frac{7{\cdot}06}{2} \times 0{\cdot}9 \times \frac{600}{240} = 3{\cdot}35 \text{ MHz}$$

$$\theta = \frac{3{\cdot}35}{3{\cdot}58} = 0{\cdot}935 \text{ radians} = 53°$$

These are maximum values and show, with reference to the Bessel functions (Fig. 5.4), that most of the energy is in the first order sidebands. With smaller amplitudes of colour sub-carrier the small second order sidebands become proportionally smaller. In all instances they can be ignored and their loss causes negligible distortion.

Distortion in FM Signals

An *FM* signal is tolerant of amplitude variations but it is important that the modulation index (θ) is preserved.

Several distortions can cause θ to deviate from its correct value, the most important being:

1. Non-flat frequency response
2. Non-linear phase response
3. Random noise
4. Moire (unwanted sideband components produced by harmonic distortion and folded sidebands).

Non flat frequency response. If a modulated signal is passed through a network with a frequency response as shown in Fig. 5.7, the upper sideband $(fc + fm)$

is attenuated with respect to the centre frequency (fc) and the lower sideband ($fc - fm$). One result of such distortion is to cause amplitude modulation, although this is of little consequence because it can be removed by limiting. A more important factor is that θ has been reduced which will result in a reduced amplitude demodulated signal. Low modulation frequencies would

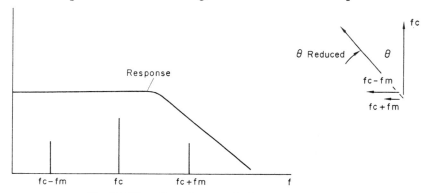

Fig. 5.7. The effect of a non-flat frequency response.

be less affected due to a greater proportion of the energy being in the sidebands close to the centre frequencies. The result is that of high frequency loss on the demodulated signal.

For colour signals differential gain occurs due to the higher luminance levels producing an increased shift of fc, $fc - fm$ and $fc + fm$ thus causing the upper sideband to be attenuated still further. A similar effect occurs if the lower sideband is attenuated.

Some differential gain correctors produce a slope in the upper sideband region to compensate for differential gain distortion.

Initially it would seem that it is important to have a flat response. It has been found however that some improvement in signal/noise ratio and unwanted beat interference can be made by having a linear fall off in response. If the response is linear, as shown in Fig. 5.8, $fc + fm$ is reduced relative to

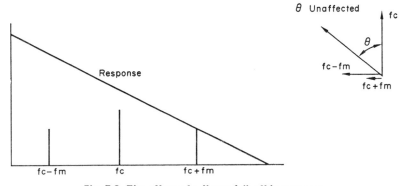

Fig. 5.8. The effect of a linear fall-off in response.

85

fc, and *fc − fm* is proportionately increased. The net result is that although amplitude modulation occurs, θ remains constant. The advantage gained in using such a response is that less of the upper sidebands are used and as these tend to be noisier, owing to compensation of high frequency loss and the presence of unwanted beat components (harmonic distortion), an improvement in overall signal/noise ratio and moire is made.

The process is sometimes called 'vestigial sideband'[2] *FM*, but both sidebands are used even though the lower sideband is used to a greater extent than the upper sideband. No saving in bandwidth is made and the term is a misleading one.

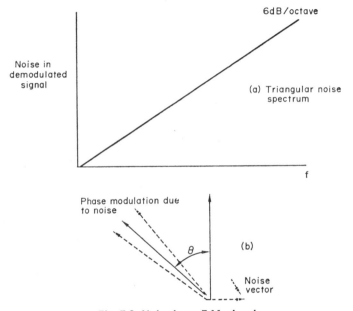

Fig. 5.9. Noise in an F.M. signal.

Non-linear phase response. In order to preserve θ, a linear phase response or constant group delay is required by the system. This involves complex equalisation to compensate for some playback losses.

Random noise. If random noise with a uniform spectrum is added to an *FM* signal, the frequency spectrum of the noise has a triangular distribution as shown in Fig. 5.9(a). This shows that the higher frequencies are noisier than the lower frequencies, which arises from the fact that in a simple *FM* modulation system:

$$\theta \propto \frac{1}{wm}$$

i.e. the greater the modulation frequency, the smaller the value of θ.

If a noise component is added to the spectral components of an *FM* wave, its effect as an added phase modulation to θ depends on the magnitude of θ itself. From Fig. 5.9(b) it can be seen that if a given amplitude of noise component modulates a signal with a modulation index (θ) of 20° by ±2°, the noise modulation is ±10% of the signal modulation. If θ is increased to 100°, the same noise modulation is only ±2% of the signal modulation. As θ reduces for higher modulating frequencies the effect of the noise increases, causing a triangular noise spectrum increasing at 6dB/octave.

The problem can be minimised by pre-emphasis of the higher video frequencies before modulation and an *HF* boost of 6dB/octave would cause θ to remain constant. If the modulating frequency were doubled in amplitude, *fd* would double, thus causing $\dfrac{fd}{fm}$ to remain constant. This is sometimes referred to as phase modulation.

In VTR practice, phase modulation would cause too high a value of θ for high video frequencies, thus producing energy in the higher order sidebands. A compromise is reached and about 8dB of boost is applied above 1 MHz before modulation. An equal and opposite de-emphasis is applied after demodulation.

Moire. The presence of large amplitudes of high frequencies, particularly sub-carrier, on the video signal cause beat components in the *FM* system. These appear on the demodulated video as objectionable patterning. On colour signals they amplitude and phase modulate the colour subcarrier causing saturation and hue errors. The subjective effect is similar to a beat or moire between two gratings and the unwanted components are called moire components.

Causes of moire patterning

The unwanted components described in the previous paragraph are created in two ways:

1. *Folded sidebands.* Energy in second order sidebands due to colour subcarrier is low and the loss does not cause a noticeable distortion. The

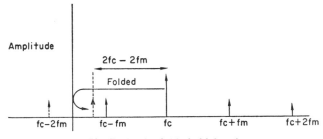

Fig. 5.10. The folded sideband.

second order lower sideband however is not lost and can be folded back into the pass-band (see Fig. 5.10).

For 625 Low Band
$fm = 4.43$ MHz
$fc = 5.5$ MHz (Black level)
2nd order lower sideband
$fc - 2fm = -3.36$ MHz
After demodulation $5.5 - 3.36 = 2.14$ MHz

For 525 Low Band
$fm = 3.58$ MHz
$fc = 5.0$ MHz (Black level)
2nd order lower sideband
$fc - 2fm = -2.16$ MHz
After demodulation $5.0 - 2.16 = 2.84$ MHz

For 625 High Band
$fm = 4.43$ MHz
$fc = 7.8$ MHz
2nd order lower sideband $fc - 2fm = -0.06$ MHz
After demodualtion $= 7.8 - 0.06 = 7.74$ MHz (Out of Band)
3rd order lower sideband $fc - 2fm = -4.49$
After demodulation $= 7.8 - 4.49 = 3.31$ MHz

For 525 High Band
$fm = 3.58$ MHz
$fc = 7.8$ MHz
2nd order lower $fc - 2fm = +0.74$ MHz
3rd order lower $fc - 3fm = -2.84$ MHz
After demodulation $7.9 - 2.84 = 5.06$ MHz (Out of Band)
4th order lower $fc - 4fm = -6.42$ MHz $= 1.48$ MHz

The negative sign has little meaning in terms of frequency and the sideband appears as a positive frequency, which after demodulation appears as a spurious frequency equal to the difference between the unwanted sideband position and the centre frequency.

2. *Harmonic distortion.* If an *FM* signal is passed through a non-linear device, harmonics of the fundamental are produced. Even harmonic distortion can be minimised by good design but odd harmonic distortion, predominantly 3rd, is inherent in the saturation record process, lack of *HF* bias and the limiting action of the demodulator.

If the centre frequency is 6 MHz, the 3rd harmonic would be at 18 MHz. If the centre frequency is deviated, the harmonic would also deviate. The harmonic therefore appears as a separate *FM* signal with its own sidebands. Although the harmonic is outside the fundamental passband, the lower sidebands of the harmonic can appear within the passband of the system and became a moire component.

The problem is further aggravated by the fact that the modulation index increases by the order of the harmonic. If a 6 MHz carrier is deviated by

88

1 MHz to 7 MHz, the third harmonic deviates from 18 MHz to 21 MHz—a deviation of 3 MHz.

$$\theta = \frac{fd}{fm} \text{ for the fundamental}$$

$$\theta_3 = \frac{3fd}{fm} \text{ for the third harmonic}$$

$$\therefore \quad \theta_3 = 3\theta$$

This higher modulation index increases the energy in the higher order sidebands of the harmonics and appear in the pass band as shown in Fig. 5.11.

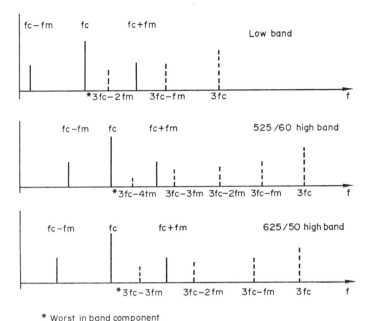

* Worst in band component

Fig. 5.11. Moire components due to third harmonic distortion.

Choosing centre frequency to combat patterning

High band. A reduction in the energy of unwanted components, within the pass-band, can be made by increasing the centre frequency thus causing the folded sideband to reduce in frequency and the sidebands of the harmonics to increase in frequency out of the passband.

The advent of colour, with its large amplitudes of high frequencies, and the improvements in the upper frequency limit of tape systems, led to the development of the highband standard where the centre frequency was chosen as high as possible within the limits of the system.

It has been seen from calculations that for the lowband standard the worst interfering folded sideband is the second lower sideband of the fundamental

89

while for the highband it is the third lower on 625/50 with a 4·43 MHz sub-carrier and the fourth lower on 525/60 with a 3·58 MHz subcarrier.

The energy decreases with the order of the sideband (see Appendix 10).

It can also be seen from Fig. 5.11 and the following calculation that for the lowband standard the worst interfering sideband (due to the third harmonic) is the second lower sideband of the third harmonic. On highband the worst sideband is the third lower of the third harmonic on 625/50 systems and the fourth lower of the third harmonic on 525/60 systems.

3rd Harmonic component
625/50 Hz Colour subcarrier 4·43 MHz

Low Band
$fm = 4·43$ MHz
$fc = 5·5$ MHz (Typical)
$3f = 16·5$ MHz (3rd Harmonic)
1st lower SB of $3fc = 16·5 - 4·43 = 12·07$ MHz (6·57 MHz†)
2nd lower SB of $3fc = 16·5 - 8·86 = 7·64$ MHz (2·14 MHz*)

High Band
$fm = 4·43$ MHz
$fc = 7·8$ MHz
$3fc = 23·4$ MHz
1st lower SB of $3fc = 23·4 - 4·43 = 18·97$ MHz (10·9 MHz†)
2nd lower SB of $3fc = 23·4 - 8·86 = 14·54$ MHz (6·47 MHz†)
3rd lower SB of $3fc = 23·4 - 13·29 = 10·11$ MHz (2·04 MHz*)

525/50 Hz Colour subcarrier 3·58 MHz
Low Band
$fm = 3·58$ MHz
$fc = 5·0$ MHz
$3fc = 15·0$ MHz
1st lower SB of $3fc = 15·0 - 3·58 = 11·42$ MHz (6·42 MHz†)
2nd lower SB of $3fc = 15·0 - 7·16 = 7·8$ MHz (2·84 MHz*)

High Band
$fm = 3·58$ MHz
$fc = 7·9$ MHz
$3fc = 23·7$ MHz
1st lower SB of $3fc = 23·7 - 3·58 = 20·12$ MHz (12·22 MHz†)
2nd lower SB of $3fc = 23·7 - 7·16 = 16·54$ MHz (8·64 MHz†)
3rd lower SB of $3fc = 23·7 - 10·74 = 12·96$ MHz (5·06 MHz†)
4th lower SB of $3fc = 23·7 - 14·32 = 9·38$ MHz (1·48 MHz*)

Frequencies on demodulated signals in brackets.

Shelf Working. It was shown by Felix[1] in 1965 that there is an optimum value for the centre frequency. This can be seen in Fig. 5.12. If fc is increased, the

† Out of video pass-band.
* Worst in-band interference component.

moire due to the third harmonic has a descending step function, reducing as each lower sideband falls outside the pass-band, thus causing the next lower sideband to be the worst interference. Before an unwanted component drops out of the passband its effect becomes greater due to the triangulation noise spectrum, thus causing an increase in moire prior to a rapid decrease. The net result is that fc should be chosen as high as possible and then reduced to

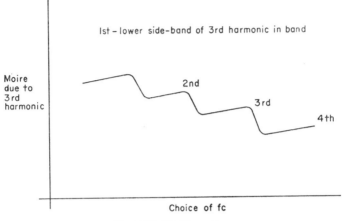

Fig. 5.12. Shelf working.

a minimum trough. This is called 'shelf working' and the 625 High Band standard operates on the third shelf with moire components about 32dB down on the peak–peak subcarrier. From previous calculations it can be seen that, owing to the lower frequency subcarrier of 3·58 MHz the 525/60 Hz standard operates on the fourth shelf with moire components about 40dB down.

Pilot tone and chroma pilot

An additional requirement in video recording, and in particular in colour video helical recording, is to record a colour subcarrier reference as a pilot tone or chrominance information on a pilot carrier with the *FM* signal. So that the pilot tone does not interfere with the *FM* signal, it must either be placed above the *FM* band or below it. It has already been shown that it is important to place the *FM* band as high as possible, so it is expedient to place the pilot below the *FM* signal. If a pilot is added to the *FM* signal, it must be ensured that cross-talk between the two signals is minimal. A typical example is shown in Fig. 5.13 where the chrominance signal modulates a 562·5 kHz pilot and is added to the *FM* signal. To keep the two signals separate, the chrominance signal is bandwidth restricted to 0·5 MHz allowing the upper sideband to extend to about 1·1 MHz. The black-level centre frequency is 3·36 MHz allowing space for a luminance frequency up to 2·26 MHz. In practice, owing to the low energy in the luminance signal above

91

2 MHz, the bands can overlap slightly allowing a luminance bandwidth up to 2·7 MHz. The chrominance information can be an *AM* signal and distortion is minimised by the presence of the *FM* signal which acts as an *HF* bias.

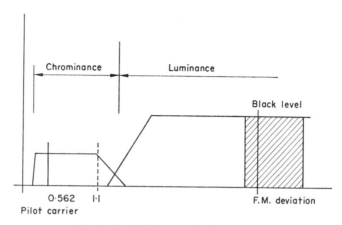

Fig. 5.13. Addition of pilot frequencies.

Response requirements for the signal system

The EBU define the ideal recording chain as:

1.   A modulator having a flat frequency response with respect to the modulating video frequencies.

2.   An *RF* section having a transfer characteristic such as to produce constant amplitude alternating flux emanating from the video head pole tips when driven by an alternating signal from the modulator having constant amplitude.

3.   A video pre-emphasis network inserted before the modulation stage.

The playback chain should contain:

1.   A compensator for phaseless high frequency losses due to resolution of the tape, spacing loss, thickness loss, self-demagnetisation and gap effect.

2.   A compensator for losses due to head and pre-amplifier reactive components.

3.   A low pass filter with a linear fall-off in frequency response (noise reduction).

4.   A demodulator with a linear response, producing an output amplitude proportional to frequency deviation.

5.   A video low pass filter to remove out of band components.

6.   A de-emphasis circuit following the demodulator.

The ideal signal path is shown in Fig. 5.14 and the frequency response from the output of the modulator to the input of the linear filter should be flat. The phase response should also be linear.

92

Specification of pre-emphasis

Equalisation has already been covered in the section on fundamentals and the requirements for pre-emphasis are very similar. The circuits should be simple, passive and easy to specify.

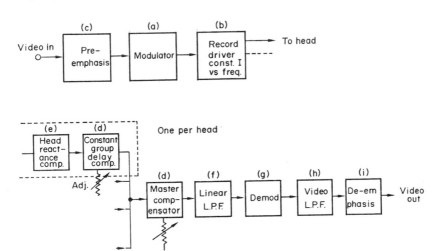

Fig. 5.14. The ideal signal path for a V.T.R.

The pre-emphasis is defined by the frequency and phase characteristics of a network such as that shown in Fig. 5.15, fed from a low-impedance source and feeding a high impedance load. The components can be specified by

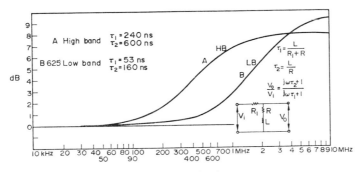

Fig. 5.15. Pre-emphasis curves.

two time constants and the attenuation can be calculated from the following relationship:

$$v_i = v_0 \frac{R + j\omega L}{R_1 + R + j\omega L}$$

93

$$\frac{v_0}{v_i} = \frac{j\frac{\omega L}{R} + 1}{\frac{j\omega L}{R + R_1} + 1} \times \frac{R + Rl}{R}$$

$$\frac{v_0}{v_i} = \frac{j\omega T_2 + 1}{j\omega T_1 + 1} \times \frac{T_1}{T_2}$$

For low frequencies $\omega \to 0$

$$\frac{v_0}{v_i} = 1 \times \frac{T_1}{T_2} = \frac{R}{R_1 + R}$$

For high frequencies $\omega \to \infty$

$$\frac{v_0}{v_i} = \frac{j\omega T_2}{j\omega T_1} \times \frac{T_1}{T_2} = \frac{T_2}{T_1} \times \frac{T_1}{T_2} = 1$$

The high frequencies therefore are boosted by a factor of $\frac{T_2}{T_1}$.

If the output is specified referenced to the low frequency attenuation then

$$\frac{v_0}{v_i} = \frac{j\omega T_2 + 1}{j\omega T_1 + 1}$$

Conclusion

The technique of *FM* in recording has evolved to a stage where most of the limitations are in the choice of deviation, centre frequency, modulating frequency and pre-emphasis. These have been chosen to provide the minimum distortion. Further improvements can be gained only by a further change in standards when the system limits will allow. A pulse code modulation may provide the answer or possibly a super high band. An improvement in heads and tape will allow either an increase in centre frequency with its moire improvements or a reduction in head speed for the same response capabilities. The market has accommodation for both improved quality for the broadcaster and greater simplicity, packing density and economy for the educational/domestic user.

References

1. FELIX, M. O., WALSH, H., FM systems of exceptional bandwidth. *Proc IEE*, Vol. 112, No. 9, Sept. 1965.
2. CHERRY, E. C., The transmission characteristics of asymmetric-sideband communication networks. *JIEE*, 1942, 89, Pt. III, p. 19.
3. TOOMS, M. S., Moire effects in the reproduction of TV signals by VTR machines. *RTS Journal*, vol. 13, No. 1, Jan. 1970.
4. FAGOT AND MAGNE, *Frequency Modulation Theory*. Pergamon Press.
5. VAN DER POL, B., The Fundamental Principles of FM. *Proc IEE*, 1946, 93, Pt. III.

6 Signal Systems

The signal system of a VTR is the section of electronics which modulates the video signal and provides enough drive current for the video head(s). During playback it amplifies the small e.m.f. induced in the head, compensates for losses or deficiencies in the signal and demodulates the *RF* signal back to video. It does not constitute the complete signal path but just the part that is the minimum requirement in any recorder.

The system has three modes of operation: Record, Playback and Standby, sometimes referred to as Electronic-Electronics (E-E).

During standby and record, the playback electronics are switched to the output of the modulator. This is useful as a visual check on the major portion of the record electronics and can also be used in alignment of the modulator and demodulator. During playback the input to the demodulator is switched to the output from the playback head(s).

Record electronics

The main elements of a record section are shown in Fig. 6.1. The AFC is optional and is a requirement only for colour signals. An adjustment of input video level determines the frequency deviation whilst the clamp potential, changing the d.c. level of the video signal, sets the black level frequency. The pre-emphasis circuit is a simple CR network composed of high tolerance passive components.

Frequency modulators

The centre frequency of the modulator is chosen to suit the line standard and the response of the record-playback process. It normally, however, lies

95

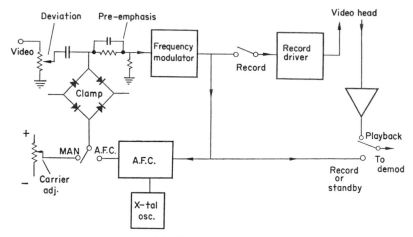

Fig. 6.1. The record electronics.

somewhere between 3·5 MHz and 8·5 MHz. The deviation from centre frequency is also a design variable which is of the order of 1 MHz. The problem therefore is to design an oscillator which can be deviated by at least 12%. The deviation frequency should have a linear relationship with input voltage up to the highest input frequency. Conventional 'reactance oscillator'

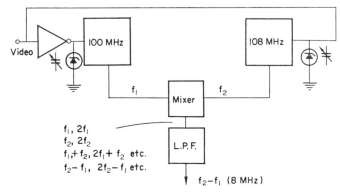

Fig. 6.2. The B.F.O. modulator.

circuits produce a linear deviation only when the change in oscillator frequency is less than 0·5%. Two methods of modulation are most commonly used: the beat frequency reactance oscillator and the A-stable multivibrator.

Beat frequency reactance oscillator. The arrangement of two reactance oscillators shown in Fig. 6.2, can be used to produce the required deviation linearly.

The two modulators are off-set by the required centre frequency and deviated in opposite directions. When the input voltage is zero volts the

96

wanted intermodulation product, $f_2 - f_1$, would be 108 MHz − 100 MHz = 8 MHz, in the example shown. An increase in voltage causes f_1 to reduce and f_2 to increase. If the sensitivity of each oscillator is 1 MHz/volt then an increase of 0·5 volts causes

$f_2 - f_1 = 108·5 - 99·5 = 9$ MHz.
a deviation of 1 MHz.
For a decrease of 0·5 V.
$_2 - f_1 = 107·5 = 7$ MHz.

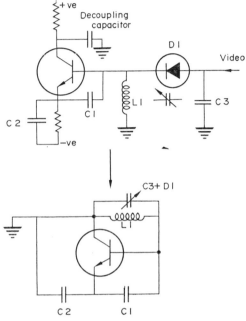

Fig. 6.3. The Colpitts modulator.

Linearity is good, owing to the low deviation, only 0·5% of the oscillator frequency. It is also improved by the cancellation of square law non-linearities. The output of each oscillator can be represented by

$$f_1 = K - \alpha v + \beta v^2$$
$$f_2 = K' + \alpha v + \beta v^2$$
where $K = 100$ MHz
$K = 108$ MHz
$\alpha = 0·5$ MHz/volt
$\beta =$ square law coefficient.
$$f_2 - f_1 = K' - K + 2\alpha v$$
cubic and odd law coefficient add
square and even law coefficient cancel

A Colpitts oscillator with a varactor diode as a reactance control, Fig. 6.3, forms an excellent modulator for one of the two required. The second modu-

97

lator can be made to operate in the opposite direction by reversing the varactor diode. It is important that the two modulators are identical in all other respects so that the magnitude of the square law coefficients are equal. The a.c. equivalent diagram shows the varactor diode shunting the inductive element that is connected between the collector and base.

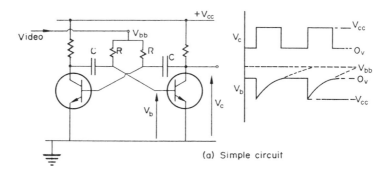

(a) Simple circuit

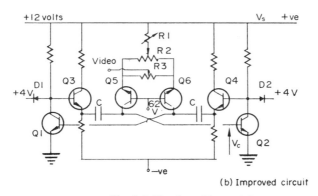

(b) Improved circuit

Fig. 6.4. The A-stable modulator.

A-stable multivibrator. This form of modulator provides an extremely popular method of producing *FM*, particularly in CCTV applications, as it has a small number of components compared to the BFO.

The multivibrator shown in Fig. 6.4.(a) has a frequency of oscillation dependent on the time constants CR and the aiming potential Vbb. If the modulating signal is Vbb, the instantaneous frequency of oscillation is a function of the amplitude of the modulating signal. The simple circuit however has two main drawbacks. First, the frequency deviation is not proportional to the voltage Vbb but has an exponential relationship, as seen in the waveform on the base of either transistor. Secondly it is difficult to produce the ideal fast rise times on the collector waveforms owing to the integrating effect of the coupling *C*, discharge resistor and the base input impedance of the opposite stage. This also is a limiting factor on the highest frequency of oscillation.

The problems are solved by modifying the simple circuit to that shown in Fig. 6.4.(b) involving 6 transistors. Q1 and Q2 are the multivibrator transistors. The coupling however is via the emitter followers Q3 and Q4, which provide a high input impedance to the collectors of each transistor and a low output impedance to the base circuits. This greatly improves rise times. The rise times are further improved by limiting the collector excursion to $+4$ volts by means of diodes D_1 and D_2. Linearity is improved by providing constant current sources to discharge the coupling capacitors. The value of this current determines the rate of discharge and hence the frequency (see Appendix 13). The standing current is determined by adjustment of R_1 (frequency). To compensate for differences in transistor and component values R_2 (static balance), is adjusted for an equal mark space ratio at the centre frequency. This ensures minimum second harmonic in the resulting waveform. R_3 (dynamic balance) ensures that symmetry is maintained at extremes of frequency deviation. R_4 adjusts the sensitivity of the modulator in terms of the frequency deviation caused for an input voltage change. The output is taken as a push–pull signal from the two emitter followers thus ensuring a symmetrical loading. To align the symmetry of a multivibrator as accurately as mentioned creates a condition where, on switch on, the device will not commutate. Both transistors come on and stay on. Safety circuits are sometimes added to momentarily unbalance the device should this occur. A second method of achieving symmetry is to design the modulator to operate at twice the centre frequency and dividing down by two to produce the correct frequency.

Automatic frequency control

Automatic frequency control of the modulator can be used to control the black level frequency to within very close limits. The AFC control voltage can be used to adjust the clamp reference and alter the d.c. level of the video before modulation.

The control voltage can be derived by comparing the frequency of the modulator, produced during the back porch time of the input video, with a reference crystal oscillator tuned to the correct black level frequency. One method of comparison is shown in Fig. 6.5. The black level crystal oscillator output is passed except at back porch time when the modulator output is gated through. This signal is then demodulated. If the crystal frequency and back porch frequency are the same, the demodulator output would be a fixed d.c. level. If the back porch frequency is high, the demodulator output would be a pulse whose amplitude would be a measure of frequency difference. The polarity of this pulse is arranged to be negative and is applied as a clamp reference potential reducing the d.c. level of the video and thus the back porch frequency. A positive pulse would result from a low back porch frequency.

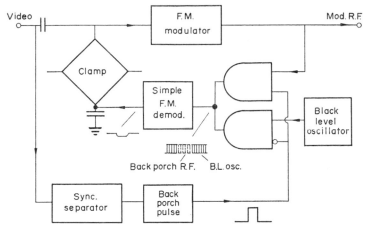

Fig. 6.5. Automatic frequency compensation.

Record driver

The record driver is required to switch on the *RF* to the video heads when required, pre-equalise to compensate for the head inductance and losses, provide for individual adjustment of the *RF* to each head (if there is more than one), and provide enough head current to saturate the tape. During normal record the same *RF* is applied to all heads simultaneously and no attempt is made to switch the *RF* to individual heads. The arrangement shown in Fig. 6.6 illustrates how the major portion of the record driver can be common to all outputs. The optimisation controls and all circuitry following are separated to allow for individual adjustment of record level. This will vary with the efficiency of each head. Adjustment is normally made to just saturate the tape. Full advantage of the tape remanence would not be made if a level below this optimum were used and any level above it would tend to demagnetise short wavelengths on tape.

The record equalisation is quite complex and is designed to produce a constant current over the complete frequency spectrum. The video head is basically inductive which means that if the final output stage has a low output impedance (a constant voltage source) the current through the head will tend to fall off at high frequencies. A simple equivalent circuit is that shown in Fig. 6.6. The shunt capacity has been ignored which is permissible if the source impedance is low compared with Xc (see Appendix 11).

The series resistance Rh represents the winding resistance and losses due to hysteresis and eddy currents. Its value is complicated by the fact that it increases with frequency. The high frequency fall off is compensated for by an equivalent high frequency boost. It is achieved in the circuit shown by selective feedback in the form of an emitter impedance. The adjustments are normally pre-set. The gain approximates to:

$$\text{Gain} = \frac{Rc}{Ze} \text{ where } Ze \text{ reduces with frequency}$$

Optimisation

The record current can be set to optimum most simply by increasing the level during record and noting the level on the audio track. On playback the e.m.f. from the head can be monitored and the point where any increase in record current fails to cause an increase in playback e.m.f. must be the onset of saturation which is optimum. The technique is simple but time consuming particularly if more than one head needs adjustment. The current also needs regular adjustment as the head wears.

Multiheaded machines can be arranged to make the process easier by allowing a combination of record and playback as in Fig. 6.7.

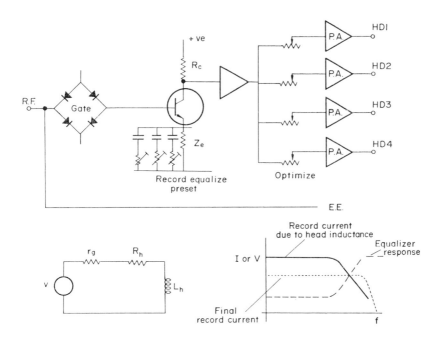

Fig. 6.6. The record equalizer.

If the record is only gated on when one head is in contact with the tape, the following head can be allowed to play back that track. This permits continuous monitoring of a record current and saves time in rewinding and replaying. Record current can then be adjusted until the e.m.f. induced in the following head reaches optimum. The capstan speed obviously needs reducing to allow the playback head to scan the recorded track. For a quadruplex machine the speed is reduced to $\frac{1}{4}$ while for a two-headed machine it is reduced to $\frac{1}{2}$ speed.

101

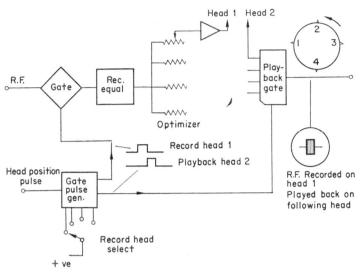

Fig. 6.7. The record current optimize mode on multi-headed V.T.R.'s.

Colour optimisation. On colour recordings optimisation is more critical owing to the importance of the frequency response on differential gain. A vernier adjustment is sometimes made in the following way.

1.   A standard recording is made to which all other recordings are made to match.

2.   The playback adjustments are made on the playback of the standard recording to obtain the best frequency response and differential gain.

3.   A recording is made on the blank tape and the frequency response and differential gain are checked.

4.   Record current is then adjusted (*note*: playback settings must not be readjusted) to obtain the best response and DG.

If this is done and checked regularly all recordings should be consistent.

Playback

The equivalent circuit for a head during playback can be seen in Fig. 6.8. By good design Lh and Ch are made low enough to produce a resonance well above the frequency limit of the system. Resonance between Lh and Cin, the input capacity to the pre-amp, however will occur between 8–12 MHz. If Rin, the input impedance to the pre-amp, is high, this series resonance produces a peak within the passband. If Rin is low compared with $\dfrac{1}{jwCin}$ then the effect of Cin can be ignored and the circuit will have a fall off at high frequencies due to Lh.

102

In the resonant case Lh varies from head to head and also on the same head as it wears so that if high impedance pre-amps are used the resonance must be compensated for and operational controls must be provided for alignment.

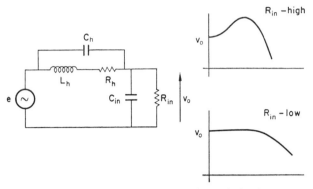

Fig. 6.8. Head equivalent circuit in playback.

High input impedance amplifier

Compensation for the head constants is achieved in two separate circuits (see Fig. 6.9). The high frequency fall off is first improved with a simple CR differentiating network. The resonant peak is then cancelled using a tuned circuit in the emitter of an amplifier. At resonance the gain of the stage is

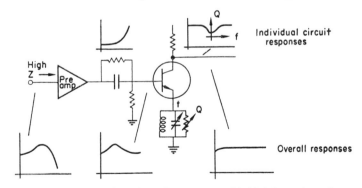

Fig. 6.9. Compensation of head constants with high input impedance.

sharply reduced as the emitter impedance increases. The f and Q are operational adjustments to exactly cancel the resonance in amplitude and frequency. As the video head wears then a re-adjustment is required. The method of adjustment involves sweeping the head and playback electronics by inducing RF into the head windings using a small coupling loop and adjusting the f and Q controls. The Q is sometimes later adjusted for best differential gain. The advantage of the high impedance pre-amp is this ability of differential gain compensation. Its disadvantage is the extra sweep alignment.

103

Low input impedance channel amplifier

The low input impedance channel amplifier has the advantage of being less dependant on the head constants. A single differentiating circuit is all that is required to compensate for high frequency fall off (see Fig. 6.10). This can be constructed of fixed passive components, with no requirement for operational adjustment. Such a simple arrangement does not allow for slight

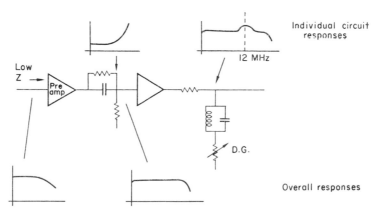

Fig. 6.10. Compensation of head constants with low input impedance.

corrections that may be required for differential gain matching. For colour operation therefore a peaking circuit tuned to resonate at around the upper sideband due to colour subcarrier at black level is used to create a slope at higher luminance levels. The amplitude of the peak is used operationally to provide the best differential gain.

Equalisers

The object of the playback equaliser is to compensate for high frequency losses due to finite gap length, tape resolution, spacing loss and tape thickness loss. These losses are different from head constant compensation because the frequency response does not have an accompanying non-linear phase response. High frequency boost therefore must have a linear phase response or constant 'group delay' for frequencies within the pass band. For optimum performance it is desirable to have control of the amount of equalisation to allow for variations from tape and also an individual control for each head. The simplest arrangement, for a quadruplex recorder, is that shown in Fig. 6.11(a) where five equalisers are used. One is used for each head and one as an overall adjustment affecting all four outputs which is adjusted to obtain a flat response. For a two headed machine such an arrangement would require three separate equalisers. A more economical method is that shown in Fig. 6.11(b) where advantage can be taken of the fact that only one head output is being used at any time. The first equaliser affects all outputs similarly, but the second equaliser has its adjustments switched as each head is selected in turn. Only two equalisers are therefore required irrespective of the number of heads. Such systems are in use but suffer from increased switching transients due to the additional switching of the equaliser control voltage.

For quadruplex recorders a third alternative, using three equalisers as shown in Fig. 6.11(c) overcomes the switching transient problem. The first

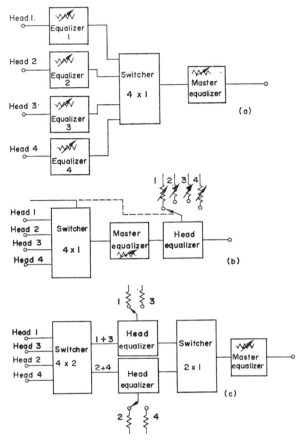

Fig. 6.11. Multi-head equalizer arrangements.

switcher combines opposite heads in a 4 × 2 operation. Two equalisers can now be used with an arrangement to switch the control between two adjustments for each equaliser. The final switcher combines the signal in a 2 × 1 operation. The third equaliser operates on all head outputs to adjust overall frequency response.

The cosine equaliser

The circuit shown in Fig. 6.12 has all the parameters required to equalise for losses in the tape transfer process. It has a constant group delay which is

105

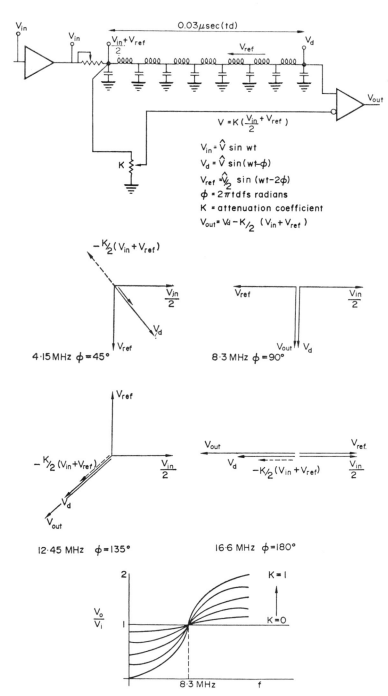

Fig. 6.12. The cosine equalizer.

constant for all settings of the potential divider K. It operates about a turnover frequency, determined by the length of the delay line. Frequencies above the turnover frequency are amplified by an amount determined by the setting of K while those below the turnover frequency are attenuated. The delay line is unterminated at its output and correctly terminated at its input.

The output of the delay line is the input signal delayed by the line (V_D). This is applied to one input of the differential amplifier, the other input being a fraction of the combined input and reflected signal. The length of the delay line depends on the frequency characteristic required but typically for a high band standard it would be 0·03 μsecs giving a turnover frequency of 8·3 MHz. The delay line being a $\frac{1}{4}$ wavelength or 90° at this frequency. The phasor diagrams at various spot frequencies are shown in Fig. 6.12(b). At 8·3 MHz, the turnover frequency, the reflected signal is in anti-phase with Vin causing complete cancellation at the input of the delay line. The output of the equaliser at this frequency equals Vin delayed by the line with the potentiometer having no effect.

Examination of the phasor diagrams at other frequencies shows that above the turnover frequency the output is greater than Vin, increasing with K and below the turnover frequencies the output is smaller decreasing with K. Further examination will show that the group delay is constant and equal to the delay of the line, irrespective of the setting of the potentiometer. This is important to avoid mis-timing similar to quadrature error. The final response is that shown in Fig. 6.12(c) which gives a cosine shaped response. Appendix 12 shows the full analysis. The adjustment of the potentiometer (K) becomes the operational control for individual equalisers and is adjusted for best response on the demodulated signal when playing back. The variable resistance on the input to the delay line is set to remove further reflections up and down the line.

Switchers

On multiheaded video recorders, the outputs from the heads can simply be added. If this is done, however, a deterioration in signal/noise ratio results because only one head contributes a useful signal and all heads contribute noise. Also if two FM signals are mixed during the overlap period, any phase differences result in a beat pattern between the two signals. A hard switch therefore is preferable allowing only one output to pass at any instant in time.

The action of switching inevitably produces a transient which can be objectionable if allowed to occur during the picture period. It is normally arranged to switch during the blanking period to avoid this. On two headed machines the vertical blanking period of 25 lines (625) or 20 lines (525) allows more than enough time for switching between heads. For quadruplex machines several switches per field are required, which means the use of the horizontal blanking period with increased complexity.

Blanking switchers (quadruplex)

If, on a four headed machine, switching is made every 90° rotation of the head wheel, a transient every 15·625 lines (625) or 16·4 lines (525) would result. This means that a switch must occur during the active line period. This can be avoided by making use of the small available overlap and delaying the switching action until the horizontal blanking period. The time for a particular head playing back is therefore always a whole number of lines. It must however average the number of lines for 90° rotation of the head, as in Table 5.

TABLE 5

Line Standard	Head number								Average
	1	2	3	4	1	2	3	4	
625	15	16	16	15	16	15	16	16—	15·625
525	17	16	16	17	16			—	16·4

For 625 lines with a required average of 15⅝

$15\frac{5}{8}$ lines per head pass = 125 lines per 8 head passes.

For 525 line system with a required average of 16⅖ lines

$16\frac{2}{5}$ lines per head pass = 82 lines per 5 head passes.

The sequence therefore repeats itself every 8 head passes for 625 line/50 field systems and every 5 head passes for 525 line/50 field system.

The next problem is where to switch during the horizontal blanking period. Figure 6.13 shows the blanking period for the two main standards. It would initially seem feasible to switch at the bottom of sync. This would be away from the colour burst with an interval greater than 4 μsec to position the switch time. This part of the waveform however cannot be used if electronic correction of the signal is to be used later on in the system.

Electronic correctors measure the timing error by comparing the leading edge of sync on the tape signal with a stable reference. This necessitates the sync edge being a timing reference for the following line. If a switch is made at the bottom of sync then the leading edge of sync is from the head preceding the following video. The trailing edge of sync could be used as a reference but this is somewhat unprofessional and can cause residual timing errors on signals from some sync pulse generators. Two solutions are possible:

1. Separate sync demodulation.
2. Front porch switching.

Separate sync demodulation. Figure 6.14 shows an arrangement with two switchers and two demodulators. One switcher for the video path switches in the bottom of sync and the other for the sync path switches in the middle of the active line period, during the previous line. After demodulation two signals are available, one with an unwanted transient in the sync and the

108

other with an unwanted transient in the picture period. The wanted sections of each signal are separated and combined to form a composite, transient free signal.

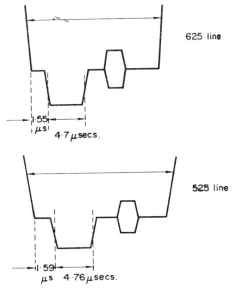

625 line

1·55 μs

4·7 μsecs.

525 line

1·59 μs

4·76 μsecs.

Fig. 6.13. Horizontal blanking.

Front porch switching. A more economical method, although one requiring more precision in timing, is to switch during the front porch period which can be as short as 1·2 μsecs. Care must be taken in order to avoid distortion of the leading edge of sync, and front porch switching is normally followed by transient suppression clamping on the demodulated video.

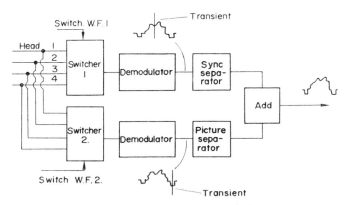

Fig. 6.14. A transient free switcher.

109

The stages of switching (quadruplex)

The operation of switching can either be achieved in one stage or made in two attempts to provide the required continuous *RF*. A switching stage is generally described in terms of the number of inputs and outputs, a 4 by 2 switch having 4 inputs with 2 outputs. Figures 6.11a and c show two methods of achieving the same result with b having a single 4 × 1 switch and c having two separate switches of a 4 × 2 followed by a 2 × 1. The switching wave-forms required by both methods are very similar and are derived from the head position pulse and a front porch clock pulse.

Switch waveform generation (quadruplex)

Basically three waveforms are required to perform the switching between four heads. Combinations of the three waveforms are sometimes derived for the various switching configurations and inverted versions of the waveforms maybe used. The head position pulse is formed into a 250 Hz (240 Hz on 60 Hz systems) square wave with transitions when heads number 1 and 3 are in the centre of the tape. This waveform can be used in a slow switch to combine heads 2 and 4. The second waveform is a delayed version of waveform 1 and is used to combine heads 1 and 3.

The slow switch requirements are quite modest because the switching action takes place during the 1 msec space between the opposite head outputs. The final switch waveform is the fast switching action which must occur during the front porch period with the minimum possible transient. The mean frequency of this switching waveform will be 500 Hz (480 Hz on 60 Hz systems) with the fast edges clocked to the front porch time of the demodulated video.

The timing of this fast switch waveform must be locked to the head position and then timed to the following front porch. The most convenient method of achieving this is to use a 1kHz (960 Hz on 60 Hz) AFC locked oscillator, locked to the head position pulse, as seen in Fig. 6.15. The output frequency is then re-timed to the front porch switch time by means of a

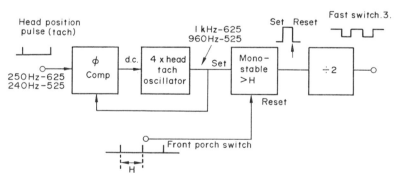

Fig. 6.15. The fast switch generator.

mono-stable which is triggered in both directions. It is set by the AFC oscillator output and re-set by the *FP* switch.

The circuit does not operate as a mono-stable unless a reset pulse is missing. By setting the relax time to an amount slightly greater than 64 μsecs a switcher 'lock-out' can be avoided. Without this safety factor a situation might arise where a front porch pulse, which is derived from the video, cannot occur until a switch is made and a switch cannot be made until a front porch switch occurs. The mono-stable relaxing enables the switch to occur and start the correct sequence.

Generation of front porch switch

The front porch switch must be derived from the tape video and the switching action must take place on the *FM* signal before demodulation. The circuit delay between these two points would be in the order of 3 μsec, the greatest delay being in the integration filter following the demodulator. A pulse therefore must be derived from the leading edge of sync to place the switch about 0·75 μsec on the front porch of a signal in advance by 3 μsec. The timing of this pulse therefore has to be 3·75 μsec in advance of the leading edge of sync and variable to allow for changes in integrating filters when standards are altered. One method of producing this would be to delay the preceding sync pulse by 60·25 μsec (59·75 μsec on 525/60). Such an arrangement would create large errors for small changes in the 60·25 μsec delay or input line time.

A more accurate method, which compensates for slight timing changes, is to introduce a delay into a line frequency AFC oscillator loop Fig. 6.16. The

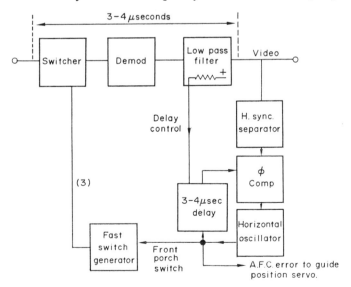

Fig. 6.16. The front porch pulse generator.

111

oscillator phase settles down to a stable condition where the two inputs to the phase comparator are synchronous to within close limits. The signal at the input to the 3 to 4 μsec delay therefore must be in advance of the tape reference input. This is substantially true for all input line times, once the oscillator has locked in. The circuit lends itself to changing the advance in timing and preset resistor can be incorporated in the demodulator integrating filter which will set the timing correctly for the delay of that filter.

The elements of the circuit also provide a convenient measure of timing error caused by vacuum guide positional errors and a d.c. correction voltage for a guide position servo can be derived.

Demodulation

The disadvantage with using more conventional frequency discriminators, such as the Foster Seeley or Ratio detector on VTR *FM* signals is the problem of linearity over such a wide deviation. Such circuits provide excellent performance at centre frequencies of 10·7 MHz, deviations of ±75 KHz and audio modulating frequencies. With deviations of ±1 MHz it is difficult to provide the linearity, and at modulating frequencies comparable to the centre frequency it is difficult to separate the *RF* from the video.

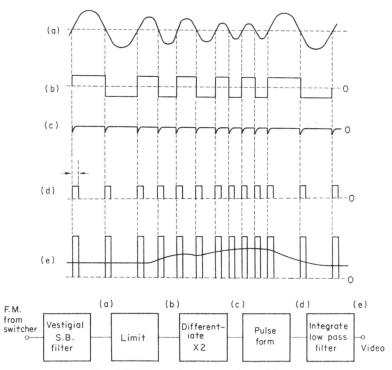

Fig. 6.17. The pulse counter demodulator.

The discriminator which is most suitable and is used almost to the exclusion of all others is the 'pulse counter' type. The technique is to detect the zero cross over points of the modulated signal and determine the pulse repetition rate of the resulting pulse chain. The signal path of the complete demodulator can be seen in Fig. 6.17. Amplitude modulation is removed by limiting and several stages may be necessary to achieve this. At least 50 dB of limiting is required to provide an output square wave signal whose edges are unaffected by input amplitude changes. The edges are detected by differentiating the square wave. Simple differentiation would result in negative and positive spikes. If the negative spikes were removed by clipping the resultant pulse chain would have the fundamental frequency of the *FM* signal.

The pulse repetition frequency is determined by integrating, by means of a filter, to produce a signal whose amplitude is proportional to the input frequency. The response of the filter should be such as to pass all frequencies up to the highest video frequencies and stop all frequencies down to the lowest *FM* centre frequency (i.e: sync tip). For the low-band standards this would place an intolerable design constriction on the low pass filter, because for 625 low-band the sync tip frequency is 5·16 MHz with the highest video frequency being 5·00 MHz. Such a sharp cut-off is obviously impractical. One solution is to frequency double the pulse repetition frequency by inverting the negative spikes and adding them back to the positive spikes. The lowest *PRF* is now twice that of the lowest carrier frequency.

The spikes are sometimes shaped to provide greater energy, but the maximum pulse width is limited to less than half the periodic time of the highest carrier frequency. Care must be taken to ensure that the pulse amplitude of the inverted pulses match those of the non-inverted. Failure to do this would result in a residual carrier component. An adjustment is normally available called 'demodulator balance' which is set for minimum carrier on the bottom of sync. The symmetry of the pulses is also important and is normally determined by the operating point of the limiter. If this is not about the zero axis of the input sine-wave, an unequal mark-space ratio would also cause a resultant carrier at the bottom of sync. An adjustment of 'limiter balance' is also very often provided.

Methods of producing twice frequency pulses

Figure 6.18 shows three methods of producing twice frequency pulses and ensuring equal amplitude pulses. In circuit (b) the differentiated pulses are phase split, using a centre tapped transformer. The pulses are clipped by means of a transistor which is biased to turn off during the most positive excursions of its base signal. The emitter capacitor charges to a positive value holding the transistor off until the next positive excursion. The differential capacitor is adjusted for equal amplitude pulses on the output.

An alternative approach is that shown in (a) and (c) where the square wave is split into two phases prior to differentiation. In (a) the simple differentiation circuits are balanced by altering the capacitive element of one circuit. In (c) differentiation is achieved by means of a short circuit delay cable to provide well defined pulses, and the balance is effected by adjusting differentially negative bias on the push–pull pulses before the diode clipping circuit.

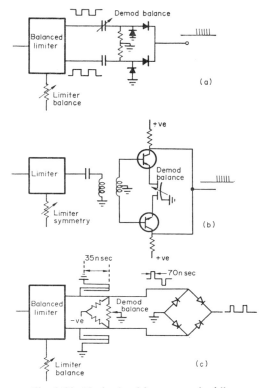

Fig. 6.18. Methods of frequency doubling.

Switch suppression and feedback clamping

The output circuit of the signal system is required to reduce the d.c. level of the video, suppress the unwanted front porch transient and apply deemphasis. Figure 6.19 shows how this may be done. The transient is suppressed by switching on Q1 and applying a ground potential to the video signal during the front porch period. To avoid a transition, either positive or negative, in the signal when this occurs the signal d.c. level is arranged to place the blanking level at zero volts. The feedback clamp ensures this for all input d.c. levels and the d.c. level changes in the input amplifier. The d.c. level of the signal from the integrating filter depends on the average centre frequency of the FM signal, this being higher for high band standards. The back-porch voltage is sampled and held for the line period. This d.c. voltage

114

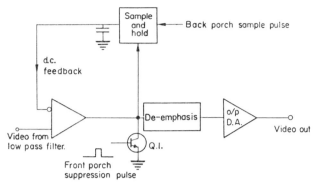

Fig. 6.19. Transient suppression.

is inverted and added to the video signal to provide d.c. negative feedback and restore the d.c. level of the signal.

Drop-out compensation

The reasons for random drop-out are manifold but in general they result from the head and tape parting company and causing a loss in *RF*. The loss in *RF* causes a burst of noise or impaired video signal which at best produces a subjective annoyance and at worst can cause a false sync or elimination of a sync edge or colour burst. One definition of a 'drop-out' is: loss of *RF* level of more than 20 dB for at least 3 μsec. The compensation for drop-out requires two separate functions: the detection of a drop-out and the substitution of an alternative signal.

Figure 6.20 shows a drop-out compensator operating on the *RF* of a playback signal; it is inserted between the switcher and demodulator. The delay line is a quartz one line delay. The principle is that two consecutive lines of a video signal have very similar information and when a drop-out is detected the output of the delay line is switched to the input of the demodulator, this repeating the *RF* from the previous line for the duration of the drop-out. The drop-out is sensed by amplitude detection of the *RF* envelope and the sensitivity of the device is set by the input level. Some form of hysteresis is necessary to avoid marginal signals switching the one line delay in and out and causing a worse impairment of the signal with the switching transients.

Once the signal has fallen below the threshold and has been classified a drop-out, the signal must increase by an amount, equal to the hysteresis, before being redeemed. This can be done by attenuating the input signal during 'drop-out' time. Typically 9 dB of hysteresis is used.

The advantage of connecting the input of the delay to a position after the drop-out switch is that for drop-outs greater than one line the *RF* is re-circulated and the last good line repeated. The advantage of inserting the compensator in the existing *RF* section is mainly economic because the frequency

115

band is quite suitable for quartz delay and it saves separate modulation and demodulation. The disadvantage is that switching transients, as the delayed signal is inserted and removed, are larger than if the switching was done on the video signal. A second disadvantage is that it is difficult to separate the luminance and chrominance information. This is desirable for the correction of PAL colour signals where the chrominance information from one line

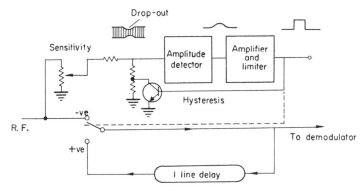

Fig. 6.20. The drop-out compensator.

would not be suitable for the following line, owing to the reversal of the V axis. For correct PAL compensation two lines of delay for the chrominance are required while one line for the luminance is satisfactory. Figure 6.21 shows a compensator inserted after the demodulator. A second modulator/

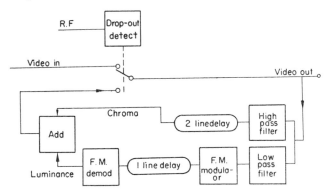

Fig. 6.21. The 'PAL' colour drop-out compensator.

demodulator is required for the luminance channel to obviate the problem of poor LF response in the quartz delay. With switching transients of less than 20 $n$secs on the video signal resulting transients can be imperceptible.

Auto-equalisation

The frequency response on playback is obviously more critical for colour signals than for monochrome. A colour signal however has a reference

116

chrominance amplitude in the form of 10 cycles of subcarrier, on the back porch, of known amplitude. The equalisation on playback could be adjusted to set this burst to its specified level and could also be done automatically. With four heads, obviously a separate adjustment for each would be required, and a head auto-equalisation can be seen in Fig. 6.22. The burst on the output of the demodulator is amplitude detected and its voltage level stored on one of four capacitors, one for each head. If the stored voltage is low, owing to a

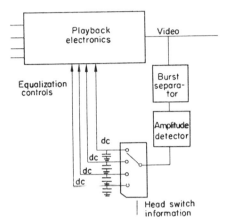

Fig. 6.22. Head by head automatic equalization.

low amplitude burst, it causes that channel equaliser to correct the response until the output burst level is correct. It should be noted that the burst is normally at blanking level and therefore the auto-correction only maintains correct chrominance level at black. If differential gain is present in the system, a chrominance error can still exist at higher luminance levels.

The charge on an individual capacitor is the average value of several head passes, which gives good noise immunity although a sluggish response. One disadvantage is that such a system cannot compensate for response changes as the head scans across its track. These response changes can be caused by thickness variations in tape oxide or a maladjusted vacuum guide causing head penetration errors. Another system is to have a line-by-line adjustment of equalisation with a capacitor store for every line from each of the four heads or 64 stores (68 on 525 line systems). The store indexing is more complex, although most of the computing electronics is already available in the velocity error compensator. The disadvantage is in determining the integration time constant which is a compromise between noise immunity and speed of operation. The amplitude of an individual burst cannot be guaranteed accurate, owing to noise, moire and drop-out. The larger the number of bursts over which the correction voltage is made the more accurate is the result. If 150 bursts are thought to give a good compromise, it would take the capacitor ten head passes on a head by head or 40 msec (41·6 msec on 525/60). On a line by line it would take 150 passes or

117

600 msec to integrate the required amount. A head by head therefore has a faster reaction time for the same noise reduction while a line by line has the ability to effect changes as the head sweeps across the tape although being unable to follow other fast changes such as mistracking.

Like all good engineering solutions the best system is a compromise between the two with a head by head operating as a coarse adjustment followed by a line by line as a vernier.

7 Servo-mechanisms

Most modern electro-mechanical devices involve servo-mechanisms and video tape recorders are no exception.

The two main control systems in a recorder are the head servo for the rotating head-wheel and the capstan servo for the linear transport of the tape. Several other smaller control loops may be used to control the vacuum guide and tape spools on quadruplex machines or the tape tension on helical machines.

The object of the servo is to position an output shaft to the same angle as an input reference. If the input reference is set to a new potential, it is amplified to produce sufficient power in the field winding of a motor. The motor rotates and adjusts the output shaft via a reduction gear. On the output shaft is connected a feedback reference potentiometer, the output of which is fed back to a comparator, in this case a simple resistive matrix, and compared to the input reference. When the potentials of the input and feedback voltages are equal and opposite, drive to the motor ceases.

The elements described form the phase loop of the system and would suffice if the field current could be changed instantaneously and the mechanical system had zero inertia. Because of the winding inductance and the rotational inertia of the system, the output shaft would tend to overshoot its correct position. A correction voltage would cause it to return but if the loop gain is high it could overshoot again and continuously hunt about a mean position. Some form of damping is required to control the velocity or rate of change of the output shaft.

Velocity control methods

A frictional force on the output shaft has the undesirable characteristics of stiction at small error angles and a better method is to apply a force proportional to the velocity of the output.

Velocity control can be achieved in three separate ways and the application of any one can eliminate hunting.

Viscous damping. This can be applied with an eddy current brake applying a retarding force which increases with the velocity of the disc. The power dissipated in the disc must be provided by the motor drive amplifier which can make the technique uneconomic.

Tachometer derived velocity loop. A voltage proportional to the velocity of the shaft can be derived from a tachometer and subtracted from the phase error, causing the input to the drive amplifier to be reduced when the rate of change is fast.

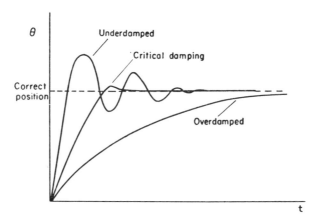

Fig. 7.1. Response with velocity damping.

Derivative of phase error. If the phase error voltage is differentiated, using reactive components, a signal proportional to $\dfrac{d\theta}{dt}$ or velocity can be derived without the additional tachometer. This method provides an economical way of providing a well damped servo. If several time constants are present in the system, extra loops with differing time constants may be introduced to compensate. Adjustment of the velocity gain can be made to provide critical damping of a step impulse as shown in Fig. 7.1.

If the velocity gain is too low, the underdamped condition can occur with several oscillations before settling down. A velocity gain that is too high can cause a slow reacting over damped situation. A setting of gain that gives a slight overshoot provides the fastest correction to an input command.

Servo elements

All the elements of any servo can be seen in the previous example: an input reference, a power amplifier, a motor or equivalent electro-mechanical device to provide movement, a feedback reference of output position, a comparator to determine the difference between output required and output

120

achieved and finally velocity feedback to control the rate of change of output position.

Rotational servos. The video head and capstan control sections of a VTR are rotational servos where there is an extra requirement for the output to be in the correct position at the correct time. The control elements are similar to the positional servo as can be seen in Fig. 7.2. The form of the reference is

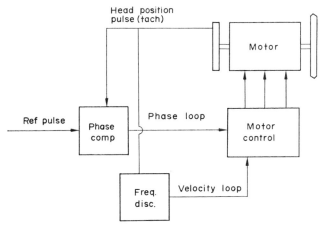

Fig. 7.2. Rotational servo.

more conveniently a timed pulse to which the motor phase and/or frequency is locked. The feedback reference can also be a pulse which is initiated from the motor shaft at a particular phase sometimes referred to as a tachometer. The motor phase can be adjusted until the reference and feedback pulse coincide. A second (velocity) loop is used to control the rate of phase change of the motor and thus avoid hunting.

Phase comparators

The object of the phase comparator is to produce a voltage proportional to the timing difference between two signals. The sample and hold circuit, operating on a trapezoid waveform, is the most common method used but can take several forms. Figure 7.3 shows three types of sample gate. The requirements of any sample gate are that when open it should allow current to flow in or out of the store capacitor with a minimum of impedance to allow the capacitor to rapidly charge up to the instantaneous voltage of the ramp and when closed provide a high impedance to avoid the discharge of the capacitor. Also a high degree of isolation from the sample pulse is required to avoid current flow due to switching. The trapezoid waveform can be derived by using one input pulse to trigger a mono-stable and applying the resultant square wave to a switching transistor. With the transistor in the saturated (ON) condition the ramp capacitor rapidly discharges. When the transistor

121

switches OFF the capacitor charges from a constant current source to form a ramp. The phase difference between the ramp and the sample pulse timing determines the hold capacitor voltage.

A characteristic of phase locked loops is that lock-up can be achieved when the sample pulse frequency is a sub-multiple or multiple of the ramp frequency. In such a condition a sample may only be made on every second

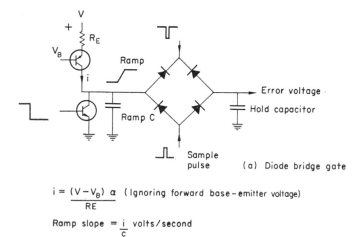

(a) Diode bridge gate

$$i = \frac{(V - V_B)}{RE} \alpha \quad (\text{Ignoring forward base-emitter voltage})$$

$$\text{Ramp slope} = \frac{i}{c} \text{ volts/second}$$

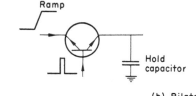

(b) Bilateral gate

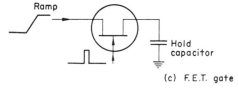

(c) F.E.T. gate

Fig. 7.3. Types of sample gate.

or third ramp. This can be an advantage if rotational speeds that are multiples of the input frequency are required although it can also cause unpredictable results. Another characteristic of phase locked loops is that they work well when the reference and feedback pulses are approximately phased. During the acceleration of the motor the sampling is random, causing a random control voltage and intermittent drive to the motor. A circuit which inhibits lock-up at odd multiples and ensures full power to the motor until the correct

122

velocity is achieved is the forward backward counter which can be included into the phase loop as shown in Fig. 7.4.

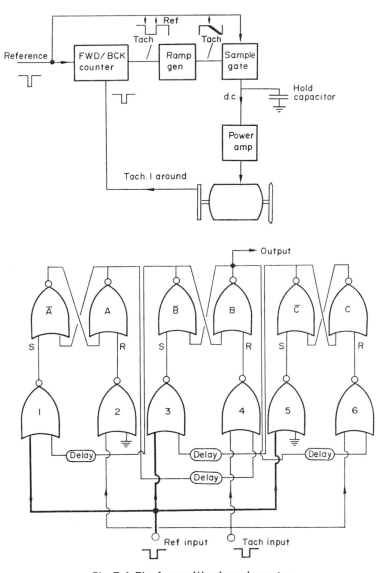

Fig. 7.4. The forward/backward counter.

The forward backward counter

The object of the counter output is to provide a low output if the motor is overspeed, a high output if the motor is underspeed and a square-wave when

123

correct. Once the speed is approximately correct, the analogue sample and hold circuit adjust the final phase of the motor.

Inspection of the circuit shows that it consists of three R-S flip-flops and six trigger gates. A positive pulse on the set input of the flip flop causes the true output to go high. A, B and C are the true outputs. Once set it remains set until a positive re-set pulse causes the true output to go low. $\bar{A}$ is the inverse of A. A high output only occurs on the output of a gate (-ve AND) when both inputs go low.

If the starting condition is assumed where all the counters are re-set and the motor is not rotating, A, B and C are low and only reference pulses are present.

TABLE 6: TRUTH TABLE

A	B	C REF
0	0	0
0	0	1
0	1	1
1	1	1 TACH

The flip-flops can be set by only a +ve pulse. Gates 1 and 3 are inhibited by high outputs.

Only gate 5 will give a high output when the reference input goes low causing C to go high. This now enables gate 3 after a short delay allowing B to go high on the next reference pulse. This in turn allows A to go high on the third reference pulse. Once all set the reference pulses have no further effect until tach pulses are present. Only 4 states for the combination can now exist as shown by the truth table.

If the motor is now allowed to start, the first tach pulse will reset A, gates number 4 and 6 being inhibited. The next reference pulse sets A and the counter will keep transferring from state 111 to 011 (see truth table). The counter cannot progress to state 001 until two tach pulses occur after a single reference pulse, i.e.: the motor is just overspeed. The next reference pulse drops the counter to 011 and the counter switches between 011 and 001.

Examination of the B output reveals an alternating change of state with a transistor from high to low at tach time. This edge is formed into a ramp which is sampled by a reference pulse.

Discriminators

The object of the discriminator is to produce a voltage proportional to the velocity or rate of change of phase of the motor.

The three most common methods of deriving this voltage are shown in Fig. 7.5, i.e:

  a. Derivative of the phase error.
  b. Pulse Integrator.
  c. Comparison with timing reference.

Derivative of phase error. This provides the simplest and most economical method of deriving a velocity error, a simple CR differentiating circuit being sufficient. The only requirement for its use is that the phase comparator has locked on and is sampling correctly on the ramp. This does place a requirement on the phase loop being stable enough without the velocity loop to enable the velocity error to be derived. Such simple methods are therefore only used on systems that are stabilised.

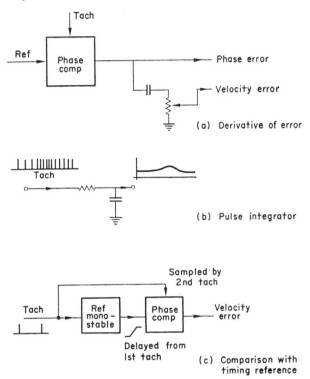

Fig. 7.5. Methods of deriving velocity error.

Pulse integrator. If the tachometer pulses are shaped to provide pulses of equal width, independent of the pulse repetition frequency, the average d.c. level of the pulse chain increases with frequency. The integration of the shaped pulses therefore provides the required measurement of velocity.

Comparison with a timing reference. If the tachometer pulse is used to trigger an accurately timed reference mono-stable, the following tachometer pulse could be phase compared with the delayed edge of the monostable. If the time between tach pulses equals the monostable period, the two inputs to the phase comparator are coincident. If the time between tach pulses is greater, lower in frequency, the tach input to the phase comparator lags the delayed input. The phase comparator output is therefore a measure of tach frequency or motor velocity.

125

Motor control

Several methods of motor control are available in servo design, the most common being:

1. Control of a d.c. supply to an eddy current brake, the motor being supplied with constant power.
2. Frequency control of the a.c. supply to a synchronous motor.
3. Amplitude control of the a.c. supply to a motor running below synchronous speed.
4. Pulse width control of the a.c. supply to a motor running below synchronous speed.
5. Control of the d.c. supply to a d.c. motor.

Of these, methods 1, 2 and 5 are common in CCTV helical machines while methods 2, 3, 4 and 5 can be found in broadcast quadruplex machines.

Eddy current brake. The advantage of this method is that it is inexpensive and some velocity damping is inherent in the system. Its full economic advantage can be gained if the motor is driven directly from the mains; otherwise the system is wasteful of amplifier power. Its control range is also restricted by the amount of power it is possible to dissipate.

Frequency control. A typical system using a three-phase motor can be seen in Fig. 7.6. Two phase systems or single phase systems split to provide two or three phases can also be used.

It is convenient to drive the motor with two state waveforms rather than sine-waves as this allows a high efficiency output stage, where the output drive transistors are either saturated on or off, with the minimum of power dissipation.

The three phase drive voltages are square waves but it is interesting to note that if the windings are star connected the phase currents approximate a sine-wave.

From Fig. 7.6 taking the loop currents:

$$i_a = \frac{V_1 - V_2}{2Z}$$

$$i_b = \frac{V_3 - V_1}{2Z}$$

$$i_c = \frac{V_2 - V_3}{2Z}$$

$$\therefore \qquad i_1 = i_a - i_b$$

$$= \frac{(V_1 - V_2)}{2Z} - \frac{(V_3 - V_1)}{2Z}$$

$$i_1 = \frac{2V_1 - V_2 - V_3}{2Z} \qquad\qquad 1$$

where $Z_1 = Z_2 = Z_3 = Z$ are the winding impedances

$$\text{similarly } i_2 = \frac{2V_2 - V_1 - V_3}{2Z}$$

$$i_3 = \frac{2V_3 - V_1 - V_2}{2Z}$$

i_1, i_2, i_3 therefore are stepped waveforms as shown in Fig. 7.6.

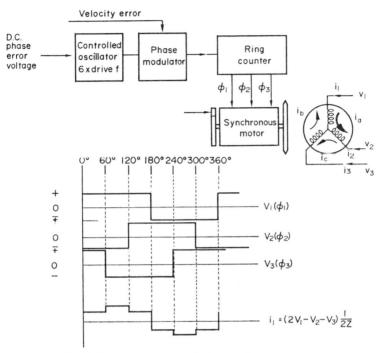

Fig. 7.6. Frequency control of a synchronous motor.

The d.c. error voltage can be used to control the frequency of an oscillator the output of which is divided down by a ring counter to provide the three phase signal. The rate of change of phase can be controlled by means of a phase modulator on the output of the oscillator which is controlled by the velocity error. The oscillator must be at least six times the frequency of the final drive waveforms as an examination of the three phase drive waveforms shows that each phase changes, 1-2-3, with a positive change every 120° and a negative change 180° later. A change therefore occurs every 60° with only one phase changing at any time. The sequence is also such that at any instant two phases are high with one low or two phases are low with one high. A circuit able to provide the three output waveforms for an input pulse at each transition is shown in Fig. 7.7 and is called a ring counter.

127

Ring counter

Assume the three counters are in the correct state for the start (0°) of the voltage waveforms shown in Fig. 7.6. Then the truth table from that point would be as follows:

TABLE 7

Angle	ϕ_1	ϕ_2	ϕ_3	Input pulse
0°	1	0	1	
60°	1	0	0	1
120°	1	1	0	2
180°	0	1	0	3
240°	0	1	1	4
300°	0	0	1	5
360°	1	0	1	6

The trigger pulse is applied to all gates and can either reset or set an R-S flip-flop. At angle 0° gates 6, 4 and 1 are enabled but only 6 is effective, as

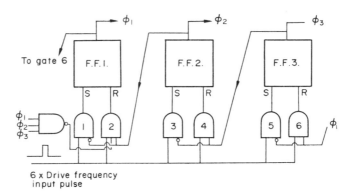

Fig. 7.7. The ring counter.

FF1 is already set and FF2 reset. This allows FF3 to be reset and ϕ_3 to go low on the first input pulse. For the second input pulse only gate 3 is effective and ϕ_2 goes high. The truth table shows that the required waveforms are produced. When the device is initially switched on the outputs can come up in any one of eight possible combinations. If it is any one of the six shown in the truth table, the sequence will progress from that point. The remaining two combinations are 111 and 000 and if all the outputs are low, gates 1, 3 and 5 are enabled allowing all the flip-flops to be set to 111 on the first input pulse. Similarly all flip-flops are reset on the next input pulse. This obviously incorrect sequence can be prohibited by an extra 'AND' function on the input to gate 2. When all outputs are high gate 2 is inhibited causing ϕ_2 to remain high when ϕ_2 and ϕ_3 go low on the next input pulse. The counter is now in the 60° position and will sequence correctly.

128

One disadvantage of a synchronous motor is that the control torque at synchronous speed is very low and better stability would be provided by a control system providing a large torque range at the nominal running speed.

Amplitude and pulse width control of an a.c. supply

In amplitude and pulse width control the frequency of the supply is not critical although the motor is normally arranged to run at approximately

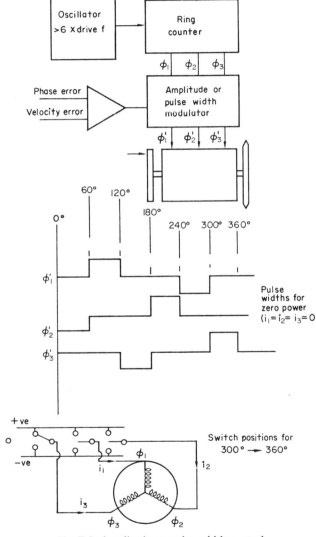

Fig. 7.8. Amplitude or pulse width control.

half its synchronous speed. In this induction mode the motor speed can be controlled by adjusting the power input to the three phase windings. This can be done either by adjusting the amplitude of the input signal or the duty cycle.

The disadvantage of amplitude modulation is that the final output stage cannot be a simple two state device but must be an analogue drive amplifier with all the problems of efficiency and power dissipation.

With pulse width modulation the output can still be digital but with three output conditions of positive, negative or zero, the zero condition being open circuit. It can be readily seen by comparing the waveforms in Fig. 7.6 with those in Fig. 7.8 that if the pulse width is reduced from the 100% duty cycle to 30%, the power input is reduced from 100% to zero. Pulse width control gives excellent stability with efficient drive conditions.

DC control

DC motors provide excellent torque characteristics at all operating speeds and although stable high gain d.c. amplifiers are difficult to design the motor performance in terms of power to weight ratio and resultant stability make the extra circuit complexity worthwhile. The worst characteristic of a d.c. motor is brush noise, particularly if it is used as a head motor. Any commutator sparking radiates high frequency energy which will soon deteriorate the signal/noise ratio of the playback signal.

One solution is the brushless d.c. motor which uses electronic commutation. A simplified concept of the d.c. motor is shown in Fig. 7.9. The stator consists of permanent magnets to provide the field and the motor consists of windings connected via the brushes and commutator to the d.c. supply.

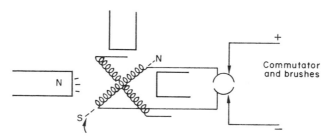

Fig. 7.9. A simplified concept of a D.C. motor.

The polarity of the winding field is such that it is attracted towards the stator field to cause a clockwise rotation. When the fields are aligned the motor would stop were it not for the fact that the polarity to the windings are reversed causing the motor to continue towards the next pole. A d.c. motor cannot operate without this commutation. As far as the windings are concerned they do not see a d.c. voltage but an alternating one.

An electronic equivalent of the commutator can be seen in Fig. 7.10. An indication of the motor position can be determined from the tach wheel and, for a 6-pole motor, six reference pulses are required. The pulses trigger a ring

130

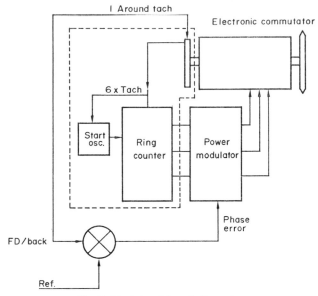

Fig. 7.10. A brushless D.C. motor.

counter, the output of which is very similar to the three phase output already described. There is one important difference and that is that the transitions are precisely locked to the head position at all rotational speeds. The ring counter and tach wheel only provide the same function as the commutator, but without brush noise.

The motor can be designed with a permanent magnet rotor and a wound stator which will exclude the use of slip-rings.

One undesirable characteristic of the electronic commutator described is that the motor can align itself into a fixed position requiring a polarity change to move. This cannot occur until a tach pulse is generated which in turn cannot occur until the motor rotates. To start events a starting oscillator provides an output in the absence of tach pulses and initiates commutating.

A more sophisticated method is to use Hall effect sensors around the motor to detect the field position and switch polarities accordingly.

Practical quadruplex servos

The head wheel and capstan operate in different modes during record and playback. Also during playback one of several different modes can be selected dependant on the accuracy of synchronism and stability required.

Record mode. The first object of the head wheel servo in record is to rotate the headwheel at 250 r.p.s.—five times field frequency, on the 625/50 Hz line standard or 240 r.p.s., four times field frequency, on the 525/60 Hz line standard.

131

The second object is to position the head-wheel so that the vertical sync is recorded in its correct position in the centre of the tape. The phase loop of the servo can achieve this by knowing the relationship between the head position and the tachometer pulse (see Fig. 7.11).

Conveniently the head position pulse can be produced when the head is in the desired position, and if the servo reference is derived from the field sync of the video signal, coincidence between signals would position the video correctly on tape.

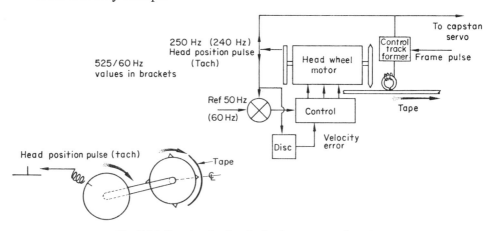

Fig. 7.11. Quadruplex head wheel servo record mode.

A control track signal is recorded to assist the re-scanning of the video tracks on playback and this can be derived from the head position pulse (tach). It is shaped to form a 250 Hz or 240 Hz sine wave giving one complete cycle for every revolution of the head or one cycle per four video tracks. Added to the sine wave is the edit or frame pulse which is positioned on the peak of the sine-wave. The frequency of the edit pulse is 25 Hz on 625 low band or 30 Hz on 525 standards, identifying one field in two and 12·5 Hz on 625 high band standard to identify one field in four for PAL and SECAM signals.

Capstan record mode. The object of the capstan during record is to pull the tape at the correct linear speed in order to obtain the correct track spacing. In some recorders the capstan, being a 60 Hz synchronous motor, is simply driven from a constant frequency a.c. supply.

The linear tape speed is determined by the rotational speed and the diameter of the capstan shaft. A convenient drive signal can be derived by dividing the head position pulse by four.

$$\text{On } 625/50 \text{ Hz} : 250 \text{ Hz} \div 4 = 62 \cdot 5 \text{ Hz}$$
$$\text{On } 525/60 \text{ Hz} : 240 \text{ Hz} \div 4 = 60 \text{ Hz}$$

On the 525/60 Hz standard the capstan diameter is chosen to pull the tape at 15 inches per second. On 652/50 Hz standards the rotational speed is

132

slightly faster and with the same diameter capstan the resultant tape speed is 15⅝ inches/second. This simple arrangement is shown in Fig. 7.13 and does not involve a servo loop.

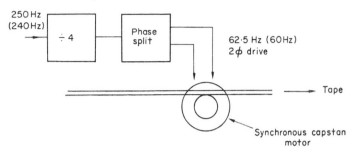

Fig. 7.12. Simple capstan drive for record mode.

If a d.c. motor is used, some form of velocity control is required and this can be seen in Fig. 7.13. The velocity of the capstan shaft can be monitored by means of two optical transparent glass discs on which equally spaced, radial, opaque lines are photographically printed. One disc is held stationary while

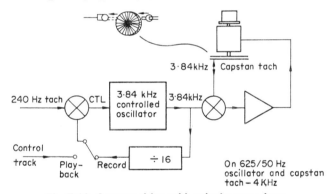

Fig. 7.13. Capstan drive with velocity servo loop.

the other is mounted on the capstan shaft and rotates. A shutter action between the two can be monitored with a light source and photo-cell and the resulting frequency would be a measure of the capstan speed.

It is convenient to make the number of lines on the disc such that when the capstan is running at the correct speed the resulting frequency is a binary multiple of the head position pulse frequency. Example 1: Ampex AVRI.

On 525/60 Hz
The required frequency = 16 × 240 Hz = 3·84 kHz (Fig. 7.13) and the capstan circumference = 6 in (Typical for a non pinch-roller version). Then for a tape speed of 15 i.p.s. the capstan rotates at 2½ times a second.

$$\therefore \text{ Number of radial lines} = \frac{3840}{2·5} = 1536 \text{ lines}$$

133

On 625/50 Hz

$$\text{required frequency} = 16 \times 250 \text{ Hz} = 4 \text{ KHz}$$

$$\therefore \text{Tape speed} = \frac{4000}{1536} \times 6 = 15 \cdot 625 \text{ i.p.s.}$$

Example 2: RCA TR70C

On 525/60 Hz

required frequency $= 240 \times 64 = 15 \cdot 36$ KHz
capstan diameter $= 0 \cdot 62$ in
capstan
   circumference $= 0 \cdot 62 \times \quad = 1 \cdot 95$ in

$$\text{For 15 i.p.s. capstan rotates} \frac{15}{1 \cdot 95} = 7 \cdot 68 \text{ r.p s.}$$

$$\therefore \text{Number of radial lines} = \frac{15\,360}{7 \cdot 68} = 2000 \text{ lines}$$

The head wheel tach pulse is multiplied by an a.p.c. oscillator loop, as shown in Fig. 7.13 to produce the required frequency which in turn is phase compared to the tach frequency to provide the control voltage to the motor.

Drum and capstan simple playback mode (TACH). The simplest playback mode is that shown in Fig. 7.14(a). The control of the head wheel is similar to the record mode although the 50 Hz (60 Hz) reference would be derived from station sync.

The capstan control however has the more complex task of ensuring that the tracks are presented to the video heads in synchronism or in other words for every revolution of the head, four tracks are pulled past the heads. If the phase comparison of the 250 Hz (240 Hz) control track signal to the 250 Hz (240 Hz) head wheel tachometer signal is used to control the capstan, the servoloop will settle down to a condition where the control track is phase and frequency locked to the head. One cycle of control track, denoting four video tracks, is matched to one cycle of head revolution or four head scans. To ensure that the video head is aligned to the video track as it scans, a phasing or tracking control in the form of a delay on the control track signal adjusts the dynamic tape position and is adjusted for maximum *RF* from the video heads on playback. The loop will always settle down to the same phase conditions between the two signals on the input to the phase comparator. A delay in the control track signal will therefore cause an error until the capstan speeds up to advance the control track signal and hence the tape position by the delayed amount. Reference to Fig. 7.13 shows how the same comparator as that used by the a.p.c. loop can be used during playback to control the same oscillator.

The simple playback mode (Tach mode) has the advantage that the only tape signal used is the 250 Hz (240 Hz) control track. It therefore is not vulnerable to tape or video quality. Its two disadvantages are the video

134

timing stability, a function of the head wheel stability, and the lack of phase synchronism with station sync.

Vertical synchronism (or place your bets please). To achieve vertical synchronism on playback the vertical synchronising pulse on the tape must be played back at the same time as the occurrence of the station vertical sync.

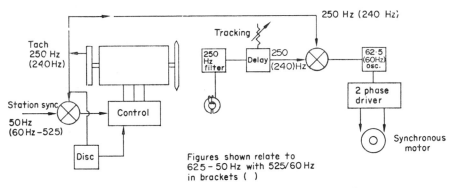

Fig. 7.14(a). Drum and capstan simple playback mode.

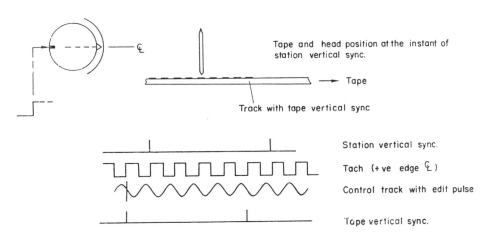

N.B. For 625/50 5 tach cycles per vertical sync. – 250 Hz

For 525/60 4 tach cycles per vertical sync. – 240 Hz

Fig. 7.14(b). A typical 250/240 Hz locked situation out of vertical sync.

In the tach mode a chosen head is aligned to the centre of the tape when station vertical sync occurs (Appendix 4).

The track with the tape video vertical sync however may not be underneath the head at that instant. It is the capstan that adjusts the tape position and Fig. 7.14(b) shows a typical locked situation when the 250 Hz comparator is used.

135

The positive edge of tach coincides with station vertical sync, this being determined by the head wheel servo in playback. If the tape vertical sync is in the centre of the tape (determined by the head wheel servo in record) then this will also coincide with a positive edge of tach.

On the 625/50 Hz standards there are five tach positive edges per vertical sync, therefore there is a one in five chance that the tape and station vertical sync are on the same edge. On the 525/60 Hz standard the chance is 1 in 4. The vertical alignment made may of course be one of opposite fields making the odds for correct field alignment 1 in 10 on 625/50, 1 in 8 on 525/60 and 1 in 20 on PAL and SECAM signals, owing to the four field sequence.

If the exact chroma phasing is taken into account, the 525 NTSC signal has a four field sequence, 625 PAL has an 8 field sequence and SECAM has a 12 field sequence, making the odds 1 in 16, 1 in 40 and 1 in 60 respectively. In practice for a synchronised playback the correct two field alignment is obtained for monochrome and NTSC, and the correct four field alignment for PAL.

The higher order alignments are difficult to define and are only a problem in editing.

Capstan servo vertical mode. To achieve vertical alignment the capstan speed must be controlled to place the correct track under the correct head at the right time.

One method of achieving this is to use a second analogue comparator, to control the capstan oscillator for framing, which compares the station frame pulse with the tape frame pulse. This arrangement can be seen in Fig. 7.15. Once alignment is achieved the control of the oscillator can revert to

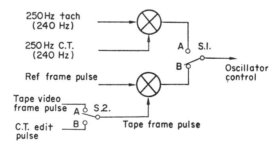

Fig. 7.15. The analogue framing control.

the normal 250/240 Hz comparator which has a better stability, owing to its higher sample rate.

The sample rate of the framing comparator depend on the TV line standard and would be:

30 Hz — 525/60 Hz All standards

25 Hz — 625/50 Hz Low band

12·5 Hz — 625/50 Hz High band.

A second approach, shown in Fig. 7.16, is to speed up or slow down the capstan, whichever is the nearest route, until synchronism is achieved and then revert to normal speed.

The amount of speed change permissible depends on the inertia of the system, but with isolated reels and a low inertia capstan a speed change of ±33% or ±5 inches per second is permissible. The time taken to achieve lock with this second method is very fast although it still depends on the distance the tape must be moved to the nearest frame pulse.

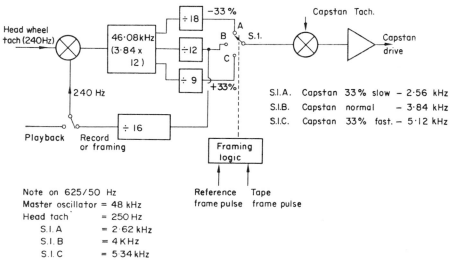

Fig. 7.16. The digital framing control.

On 525/60 Hz

$$\text{one frame occupies } \frac{15}{30} = 0\cdot5 \text{ in}$$

∴ nearest frame pulse is less than 0·25 in
At 5 i.p.s. 0·25 in of travel takes

$$\frac{0\cdot25}{5} = 50 \text{ msec}$$

On 625/50 Hz

$$\text{one monochrome frame occupies } \frac{15\cdot625}{25} = 0\cdot625 \text{ in}$$

one PAL or SECAM frame occupies 1·25 in

At 5·2 i.p.s. (33%)

$$\text{for monochrome } 0\cdot3125 \text{ in of travel takes } \frac{0\cdot3125}{5\cdot2} = 62\cdot5 \text{ msec}$$

for PAL or SECAM 0·625 in of travel takes 125 msec

137

In practice these framing times are about trebled after acceleration, deceleration and decoding time is taken into account.

With a higher inertia system the permissible speed change is less and typically for a pinch roller system a 10% change is used. The time taken to frame is proportionally longer.

Identification of frame pulse

A frame pulse must uniquely identify one field in two (one in four on PAL and SECAM) and therefore a circuit able to identify the odd or even field is required. Figure 7.17 compares the odd and even field synchronising periods for both 525/60 Hz and 625/50 Hz.

The field syncs contain twice line frequency pulses for the equalising and broad sync pulse period. The line sync pulses can easily be separated over this period by a monostable with a period greater than a $\frac{1}{2}$-line period. It should be noted that the line sync is coincident with the first vertical serration in the broads on only one field in two. On 525/60 Hz this coincidence is the start of the even field while for 625/50 Hz the coincidence is on the start of the odd, due to an odd multiple of equalising pulses. An 'AND' gate with one input timed to the first serration of both fields and another input of line sync would produce a pulse output every two fields, i.e. 30 Hz on 525, 25 Hz on 625.

On PAL signals a particular line is different from the corresponding line two fields later owing to the phase alternation of the V signal and an odd number of lines per frame. Similarly on SECAM signals an $R-Y$ chrominance signal on line 1 of field 2 would be a $B-Y$ signal on line 1 of field 4. The signal which identifies the phase of the V signal on PAL or the $R-Y$ line on SECAM is the 7·8 KHz and if this is gated with the two monochrome signals a 12·5 Hz pulse identifying one field in four is produced.

The position of the control track is downstream to the video heads and the field identified may not be the nearest field on tape (Appendix 5). The nearest field on tape is indicated in Fig. 7.17.

Head wheel servo

Vertical mode. If the track with the vertical sync is aligned with the correct head at the correct time and the vertical sync is recorded in the centre of the tape, vertical synchronism will be obtained using the tach comparator. The tolerance on the vertical sync positioning in record is about $\pm\frac{1}{2}$ a line (Appendix 4). To allow for this and for non-standard recordings the head wheel phase is controlled by a second comparator, shown in Fig. 7.18, which compares the vertical sync off tape with a reference station vertical sync. This adjustment need only be $\pm45°$ from the tach mode position if the capstan is phased correctly. The stability of the playback video, which is directly related to the stability of the head wheel, is not improved in this mode because the sample rate is the same as the tach mode. The reliability

138

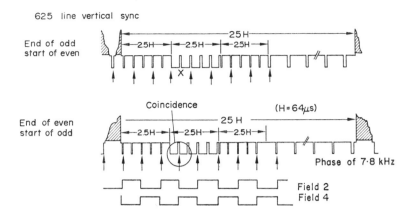

625 line vertical sync

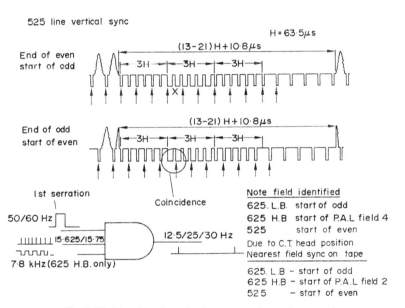

525 line vertical sync

Fig. 7.17. Identification of reference and tape frame pulse.

of the vertical mode is somewhat less owing to the dependence on tape vertical sync which is prone to drop-out.

Horizontal mode. The video stability on playback can be improved and full synchronism with station sync can be achieved with the addition of a third comparator, shown in Fig. 7.18, which compares tape horizontal sync with reference horizontal sync. In this mode the sample rate is over 300 times greater than used in the tach and vertical modes.

For full synchronism or 'automatic lock' the vertical mode must achieve

139

synchronism to within $\pm\frac{1}{2}$ a line before switching to the horizontal comparator. If the stability of the horizontal mode is required but synchronism is not, the vertical framing of the capstan and head wheel can be missed.

Four separate modes of operation are available and can be selected depending on the requirements. Table 8 lists some of the more important requirements.

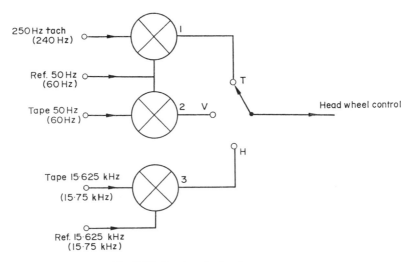

Fig. 7.18. The head-wheel comparators.

TABLE 8

Requirement Mode (stability)	Mono-chrome	Cut without Frame Roll	Fast Lock-up	Mixing	Colour playback with an analogue delay corrector
Tach ($\pm 10\ \mu$sec)	Yes	No	Yes	No	No
Vertical ($\pm 10\ \mu$sec)	Yes	Yes	No*	No	No†
Horizontal non vertical ($\pm 75\ \eta$sec)	Yes	No	Yes	No	Yes
Horizontal and vertical. auto. ($\pm 75\ \eta$sec)	Yes	Yes	No*	Yes	Yes

* Except with isolated reels and low inertia capstan.
† A digital corrector wtih $\pm$ 32 μsec range allows vertical mode to be used.

140

Head wheel comparator

A logic system is required to determine the comparator to be used, which depends on the mode selected and the condition of synchronism. On all modes selected the initial lock-up is achieved on the tach comparator. If a higher mode has been selected and other conditions in the machine are correct, such as the guide being in and tape syncs being available on the output of the

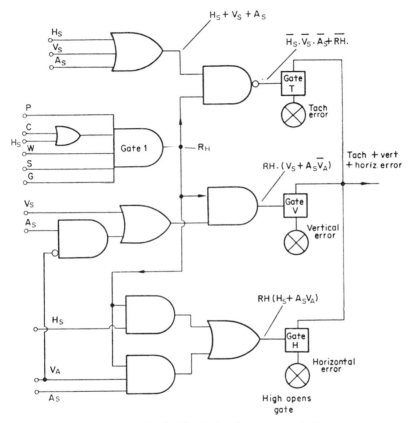

Fig. 7.19. Typical headwheel comparator logic.

signal system, the tach comparator can be switched off and another on. Only one comparator is normally used at any instant. If the vertical or horizontal mode is selected, the vertical or horizontal comparator would be used.

All the conditions can be expressed more clearly with logic equations and illustrated with logic symbols as shown in Fig. 7.19.

$$R_H = P.W.S.G. (C + H_S) \qquad\qquad 1$$

$$T = (H_S + V_S + A_S) R_H$$

$$= \overline{H_S} . \overline{V_S} . \overline{A_S} + R_H \qquad\qquad 2$$

$$V = R_H \cdot (V_S + A_S V_A) \qquad\qquad 3$$

$$H = R_H \cdot (H_S + A_S V_A) \qquad\qquad 4$$

H_S = horizontal synchronism selected

V_S = vertical synchronism selected

A_S = Auto or full synchronism selected

V_H = vertical synchronism achieved

P = VTR in play mode

C = capstan framed

W = head-wheel error stable

S = sync pulses on output of signal system

G = vacuum guide in

R_H = recorder function happy (1)

The pre-conditions to switching off the tach comparator and progressing to a comparator dependent on tape sync are provided by gate 1. The output of gate 1 will only go high when certain states in the recorder exist to make the recorder functions happy (R_H), these being:

Play button pressed and Head wheel stable and vacuum guide in and tape syncs present and capstan framed, except if the horizontal mode has been selected, when it does not matter.

The tach comparator is used if none of the higher modes are selected or if the output of gate 1 is low.

The vertical comparator is used if the recorder functions are happy and vertical mode is selected or until vertical synchronisation has been achieved if auto has been selected.

The horizontal comparator is used if the recorder functions are happy and the horizontal mode has been selected or after vertical synchronism if auto has been selected.

Auto tracking (capstan)

The phase of the tape with respect to the video head is adjusted on playback to a condition where the video head scans exactly down the centre of an existing track. Tolerance variations on control track head position and record phase means that a manual adjustment of control track phase for a maximum amplitude *RF* envelope is required for each tape played back.

An automatic method has been devised which is shown in Fig. 7.20. Adjustment for a peak is difficult because until the output falls a maximum point cannot be sensed. One method is to add a small 10 Hz oscillation to the capstan error which causes the tape to advance and retard in phase. The amplitude of this dither is kept small and produces less than 0·1% flutter on

142

the audio. If the video heads are centred on the track then a reduction in *RF* is caused as the tape is advanced and retarded or in other words a 20 Hz amplitude modulation of the tape *RF*. If the tape's nominal position is advanced, an increasing advance reduces the *RF* while an increase occurs for the retard half cycle. This gives a 10 Hz amplitude modulation reaching a minimum at maximum advance.

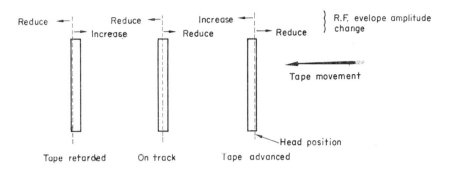

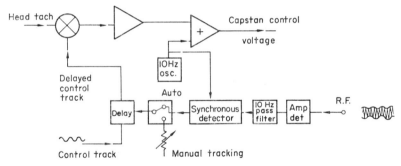

Fig. 7.20. Auto-tracking.

If the tape is retarded, a 10 Hz amplitude modulation would result with a minimum at maximum retard.

By detecting the 10 Hz modulation and phase comparing it with the original dither signal in a synchronous detector, a voltage proportional to the average track position can be derived. This error voltage can be used to adjust the capstan speed either by adjusting the tracking delay, as shown in Fig. 7.20, or, in the absence of a control track, by directly controlling the capstan speed.

Practical helical servos

In helical recorders the principles of operation of the capstan and drum scanner is very similar to those in quadruplex recorders. The techniques however do differ slightly.

143

In helical recorders the head rotation rate is either $\frac{1}{2}$ field rate for two headed machines or field rate for single headed machines.

Drum scanner, record mode. Apart from locking the head rotation to field rate, or a division of field rate, it is important during record to adjust the phase of the head to ensure that the drop out or switching transient occurs either at the bottom of the picture or in field blanking.

The position of the drop-out is known to be at the exit/entrance point of the tape. A tachometer pulse is sensed prior to this point and compared with the vertical sync to produce a control voltage for the motor. For the drop-out to be positioned at the bottom of the picture the vertical sync should occur after the exit point at the start of a new track. For the drop-out to occur in field blanking the vertical sync should be recorded at the end of a track before the exit point. A monostable delay can be adjusted during record as in Fig. 7.21 and 7.22 to position the drop-out accordingly.

Capstan record mode. The object of the capstan in record is to pull the tape at the correct nominal speed to provide the correct track spacing. The accuracy depends upon the requirement for sync 'line-up' and a 1% variation in tape speed would cause about a 0·64 μsec error in sync line up.

Some cheaper recorders drive the capstan motor with local a.c. mains supply thus obviating the requirements for a drive amplifier and control electronics (see Fig. 7.21). This provides an adequate method while the mains is the correct frequency, but changes up to $\pm 4\%$ are not uncommon.

A better system, though more expensive is that shown in Fig. 7.22, where the capstan speed is controlled from a comparison of an input reference to a feedback reference from a capstan tachometer.

On both systems a control track pulse is recorded which is generally derived from the vertical sync of the recorded video. The pulse repetition frequency would be 50 Hz on 625 line systems or 60 Hz on 525 line systems, recording one pulse per video track. On some more complex machines with playback framed to the correct field sequence a 25 Hz or 30 Hz pulse is recorded, giving one pulse per two tracks.

Playback modes

During playback the prime objective is to re-scan the video tracks exactly at a 50 Hz or 60 Hz rate. Basically there are two methods of achieving this:

1. Control of the drum scanner only (Fig. 7.21).
2. Control of both the drum scanner and the capstan (Fig. 7.22).

Drum scanner control. In this arrangement the capstan is driven from the a.c. mains, and the track presentation rate, or field rate, depends on the mains frequency. The rotational rate of the head must now be controlled so that it revolves 360° (180° on two headed machines) for each track or control track pulse. This can be done by comparing the head position pulse with the control track pulse, ensuring a head rotational rate locked to the track rate. The delay used for adjusting the drop-out position in record can now be used in

144

playback as a tracking control to synchronise the track and head for a maximum *RF* off tape.

The technique provides an economical and simple method of control requiring only one controlled motor. Its disadvantage is that the playback video is not locked to any external reference. Owing to changes in capstan

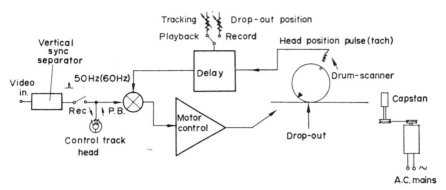

Fig. 7.21. Helical motor control with a non-servo capstan.

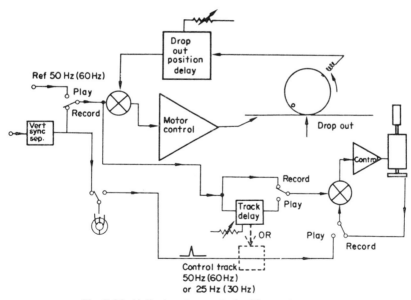

Fig. 7.22. Helical motor control with capstan servo.

diameter and slight tape slippage it is not even locked to mains. Another disadvantage is that the drum input reference is a control track pulse which is prone to phase modulation caused by tape longitudinal speed variations. The phase loop gain of the system must be low to avoid hunting giving a rather loose control of the head position.

145

Control of both drum scanner and capstan. In this system both the drum and the capstan use an external reference which can be either station vertical sync or a.c. mains. The drum scanner is locked to this in an identical manner to record and the reference being stable allows a higher phase gain and stability than with the previous method. This determines the playback field rate.

It is now left to the capstan to synchronize the track rate to the head. This is done by controlling the capstan from a comparison of reference 50 Hz (60 Hz) and control track. Both the track rate and the head rotational rate are now locked to the same reference. Tracking can be adjusted by altering the head phase by delaying the head position pulse or the track phase by delaying either input to the capstan comparator.

Not only is the stability improved by using a capstan servo but vertical synchronism to station sync can be readily achieved. If a greater stability is required with horizontal synchronism, an extra horizontal comparator can be used to control the drum scanner. Because of the extra complexity this is only done on the higher priced helical recorders.

Instability

Unlike quadruplex machines playback instability is not only a function of variations in head speed but is also caused by variations in tape or capstan speed. It is worth determining the rotational speed of the capstan for a recorder which can be anything from 8 Hz to 60 Hz depending on the tape speed and capstan diameter. Knowing this, it is sometimes easier to isolate the causes of instability by knowing its frequency. Typically the causes for fluctuations are as in Table 9.

TABLE 9

Frequency	Probable cause
field rate	Drum scanner imbalance.
$>$ field rate	Drum scanner bearings worn or servo fault.
$<$ field rate $>$ 5 Hz	Capstan eccentric or pulley wheel.
$<$ 5 Hz	Torque variations on take-up or supply spool.

References

1. SADACHIGE, Quadruplex recorder servo systems, new performance criteria *JSMPTE*, Vol. 80, July 1971, 552–557.
2. CLARKE, H. V., *An improved servo system for quadruplex videotape recorders*, Ampex Corporation, Redwood City.
3. ROIZEN, J., Television tape techniques today, *Broadcast Engineering*, Nov. 1963 and April 1964.
4. CRUM, C., *Design considerations for a new generation quadruplex videotape recorder*. Ampex Corporation, Redwood City.

8 Geometrical Errors

In any videotape recorder it is extremely important that the recorded tracks are scanned exactly and that the information from the tape is read at a consistent rate. Any difference in tape path, tape dimensions or head to tape geometry between recording and playback will give rise to tracking or timing errors or both. All errors due to these factors are called geometry errors and are additive to servo stability errors.

There is only one correct tape geometry for a given format and errors on playback can be caused by incorrect geometry in record or playback. During record all controls must be adjusted to produce a tape within the tolerances specified for that format. Alignment tapes are normally provided for this although on most helical machines the controls are preset and the geometry can only be checked.

It is considerably easier to minimise errors by recording and playing back on the same transport because most errors are repeated in playback. However, if it is required to interchange tapes, transports which are similar to within very close tolerances are required. The problem is one of compatibility and it is this requirement that adds to the cost of any VTR. Quadruplex machines are compatible irrespective of manufacturer. Most helical machines are only compatible with similar models from the same manufacturer and some cheaper models do not even claim this. The problems in minimising errors are obviously different for helical and quadruplex machines and it is worth treating them separately.

Adjustments to quadruplex machines

Several of the geometry adjustments to a quadruplex head assembly are preset and the problem of adjustments is a manufacturing one. The tolerances

147

however are extremely small and a check on the parameters affected ensures good interchange.

Azimuth (preset)

The head gap should be perpendicular to the transverse track and, as in audio recorders, a loss in induced e.m.f. results at short wavelengths if an error occurs between record and playback.
The shortest wavelength recorded

$$\lambda = \frac{\text{head/tape speed}}{f\,\text{max}}$$

where $f\,\text{max} = $ highest record frequency (15 MHz on High Band)

$$\lambda s = \frac{1560}{15 \times 10^6} \simeq 100\ \mu\text{in}$$

The tolerance on azimuth would seem intolerable for such short wavelengths were it not for the fact that the gap width is only 0·01 in.

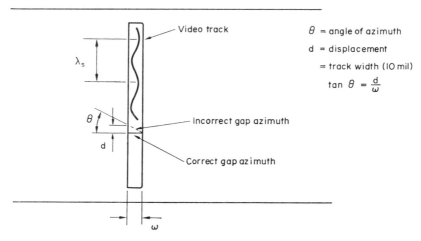

Fig. 8.1. The angle of azimuth.

From Fig. 8.1 it can be seen that if the displacement (d) is small compared with the shortest wavelength (λs) say 1/10, then the loss is negligible.

$$\tan \theta = \frac{d}{\omega} = \frac{10 \times 10^{-6}}{10 \times 10^{-3}} = 10^{-3}$$

$$\theta = 3'$$

or the gap should be at 90° ±1·5′ to the video track for good interchange.
Azimuth problems can readily be detected by comparing the frequency

response of a video head playing back its own recorded track with the response of that same head playing back other recorded tracks. The response should be within 2dB at 15 MHz w.r.t. 8 MHz.

Axial displacement (preset)

The transverse tracks should be equally spaced and this can be achieved only if the longitudinal speed is constant and the heads are accurately positioned axially. Figure 8.2(a) shows the effect of an axial error. The tolerance on track

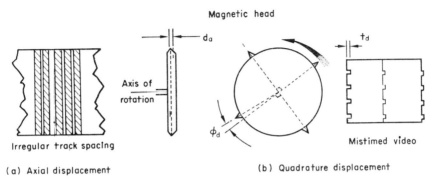

Fig. 8.2. Head displacement.

to track spacing is $\pm0{\cdot}00625$ mm ($\pm2{\cdot}36$ thou), but variations in capstan speed also contribute to this tolerance so that an axial displacement of less than $\pm0{\cdot}001$ in is required. Axial displacement only causes tracking errors which will tend to reduce the *RF* signal level and thus deteriorate the signal/noise ratio for that head or track. Timing errors, which constitute a larger problem, are a function of radial displacement.

Quadrature displacement (preset)

With four heads equally spaced around the periphery of the head wheel, each head should be at 90° to its adjacent heads. If this is not so, as in Fig. 8.2(b), the result is that when the displaced head plays back a recording made on a correctly aligned head the information will be delayed from the rest of the video. The servo action on the head wheel motor would be unable to correct such a rapid change owing to the inertia of the head assembly and the subjective effect on the picture is for sections to be displaced horizontally causing a discontinuity on all verticals in the picture. On the European 625 line/50 Hz field standards the displacement would occur for 15 or 16 lines in five positions per field whilst on the USA 525 line/60 Hz field standard it would be 16 or 17 lines in four positions per field.

149

The timing error for a given displacement can be calculated knowing the angular velocity. On the 625 line/50 Hz the rotational speed of the head

$$N_H = 250 \text{ r.p.s}$$

$$1 \text{ revolution} = \frac{1}{250} = 4 \text{ msec} = 360°$$

For a displacement $\phi d = 1$ min of arc

$$td = \frac{4 \times 10^{-3}}{360 \times 60} = 0·18 \ \mu\text{sec}$$

With a circumference of 6·29 in 1 min of arc represents

$$\frac{6·29}{360 \times 60} = 0·00029 \text{ in}$$

In order to keep this timing error to within 150 ηsec peak–peak the deviation must be better than $\pm 0·5$ min of arc, assuming the worst case of build up of tolerances.

To obtain this accuracy a head assembly is normally adjusted on a standard tape to bring the heads into approximate position. A vernier adjustment can then be made by recording and playing back, adjusting the head positions to achieve a peak–peak error of less than 150 ηsec on all positions of the track selector.

Although the adjustment is a manufacturer's preset, corrections can be made by the user if extreme care is taken. In the author's experience the adjustment should be made only if a spare head assembly is available. The adjustment of a head is normally achieved by means of tapered screws which are mounted either side of each head. By releasing one and tightening the other the head can be made to move radially. It must be appreciated that, owing to the tolerances involved, it is extremely difficult to adjust one head without affecting another.

Guide positional errors (adjustable)

The vacuum guide should have a fixed position between record and playback. It does however have operational controls on its position in order to compensate for variations in recordings.

Being a three dimensional device it can be moved along three axes as shown in Fig. 8.3. The longitudinal position of the guide is normally fixed, inhibiting movement along the z axis while adjustments on the other two axes are permitted. Movement along the x axis increases or decreases the tip penetration into the tape and movement on the y axis affects the guide height with respect to the head wheel. The adjustment of either of these can cause the guide to lose concentricity with the head wheel which in turn causes a timing displacement.

The correct position for the guide is shown in Fig. 8.4(a) where the effective radius of curvature for the guide is concentric with the radius of the head wheel. If a tape is recorded with the guide in the correct setting, but during playback the guide is moved out so that its position, relative to the head, is as shown in Fig. 8.4(b), a timing error will result. At the start of a head scan the video head is in advance of its correct position while at the end of

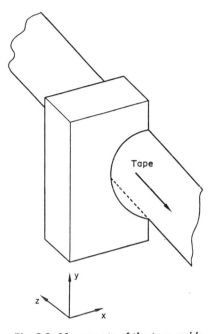

Fig. 8.3. Movements of the tape guide.

its scan the head is late, being correct at the centre. The subjective effect on the displayed picture, sometimes referred to as 'venetian blinding' appears on all verticals.

The displacement error dx

$$dx = x \sin \theta \, . \, . \, . \, . \, . \, (\text{See Appendix 14})$$

and a 0·001 in movement of the guide would give a peak–peak timing error of 0·916 μsec.

The adjustment can be made manually or, by means of a guide servo and timing sensor, automatically. It is interesting to note that there is only one correct setting for the guide position and this is true irrespective of the tip projection from the wheel. No further adjustment is required as the pole tips wear, although it should be checked frequently to allow for temperature changes and guide wear.

The effect of incorrect guide height setting is more complex, but examination of Fig. 8.4(c) shows that if the guide is set too low the effect is that of the

151

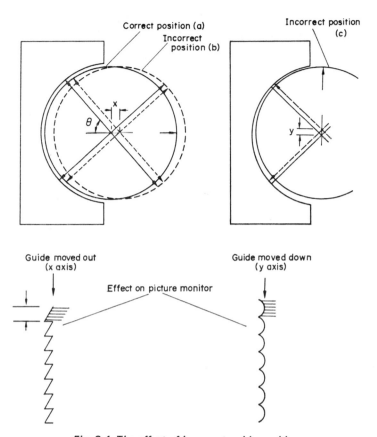

Fig. 8.4. The effect of incorrect guide position.

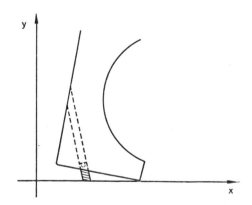

Fig. 8.5. Wrap around or tilt adjustment.

guide being too close at the top and too remote at the bottom. The subjective effect is that of 'scalloping' where the error starts off as if the guide is too far in and ends as if the guide is too far out. A 0·001 in error in guide height would give a peak–peak error of 0·194 μsecs (see Appendix 15), with a displacement error $dy = y \cos \theta$.

This result shows that the height adjustment is not as critical as the tip penetration, but because of its non-linear nature it can be more difficult to correct for electronically.

There is one other guide adjustment and that is the wrap-around or tilt adjustment. This control simply ensures that the guide height and penetration adjustments operate on their correct axes. If the guide is not square on to the relative movement of the guide as in Fig. 8.5, the adjustment of guide penetration will have a component affecting guide height and vice versa.

Velocity errors

The time-base stability required for monochrome signals is considerably less than that for colour. With care and adjustment on every playback, geometrical errors should be contained to within 150 $n$sec which is just tolerable on monochrome although an improvement would be desirable.

For colour systems however a stability of ±3 $n$sec is required and this can be achieved only by correcting these residual errors electronically with variable delays. The exact method of correcting these errors will be covered in the following chapter but basically the error is corrected at the start of each line and it is important that the error does not change significantly between corrections. The important figure therefore is not the absolute timing error of the signal but the rate of change or velocity of the error.

With the advent of colour and the critical nature of the signal, a considerable amount of research investigating other causes of velocity error was made. Most of the causes are manufacturer problems, but they do illustrate areas that affect the interchange of colour videotape recordings. It was shown by Nikolai Laserev in 1969 that, in addition to those errors already mentioned, interchangeability is affected by the following factors.

1. Vacuum guide radius tolerances.
2. Tape transport topology.
3. Erase head temperature change.
4. Tape tension.
5. Ambient temperature and humidity.

Apart from the errors in the guide radius, the errors caused by these factors are in general of a low order. With the demand for multiple generation tapes, however, these errors tend to accumulate.

Guide radius

From our previous arguments it can be appreciated that if the guide radius is increased between record and playback, an angle of 90° on the record

153

radius would be less than 90° on the playback radius. With a constant angular velocity for the head wheel this causes an effective increase in pole tip velocity on playback. The relationship is a linear one, i.e.

$$\text{velocity} = 2\pi r \times N_{\text{H}}$$

$$\therefore \text{velocity} \propto r$$

The tolerance on the guide radius is $\pm$ 250 μin with a nominal radius of 1·03315 in. If the difference in radius between record and playback guides is 500 μin, an error of 500 ηS would result over a 90° rotation of the head (Appendix 16).

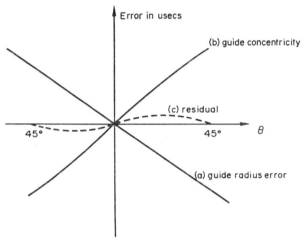

Fig. 8.6. Graph showing residual error after off-setting concentricity to compensate for guide radius error.

This can be compensated for by off-setting concentricity, but as this is a sinusoidal function the error cannot be completely eliminated. Fig. 8.6 shows the relationship between the two errors with the residual error shown in C. The theoretical reduction in timing error is about 23:1 reducing a 500 ηsec peak–peak error to about 22 ηsec.

Tape transport topology

The velocity errors caused by the distortion of the tape is complex and is the result of forming the tape, an elastic medium, into its canoe. Reference to Fig. 3.6 shows that the tape is formed from a flat plane into an arc and back to a flat plane. The tape between the two guides A and B is called a canoe and its shape should be the same in record as it is in playback.

To analyse the distortion on the tape the position of the tape is referred to the 'neutral-plane'. The neutral plane is defined as the path taken by the tape between guides A and B when the video head and vacuum guide is

154

removed. The deformation from the neutral plane when the head assembly is inserted can now be seen in Fig. 8.7.

By means of a simple experiment Laserev showed the importance of spacing the two guides A and B symmetrically about the video head. In this experiment, shown in Fig. 8.8, the tape was simulated by a rubber band clamped at A and B representing the two guides. The head, represented by a frictionless roller

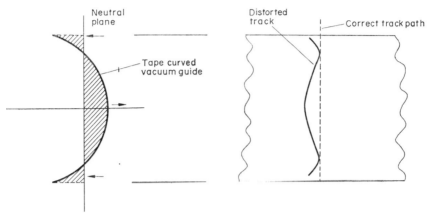

Fig. 8.7. Deformation from the neutral plane causing track distortion when A and B (Fig. 3.6) are asymmetric.

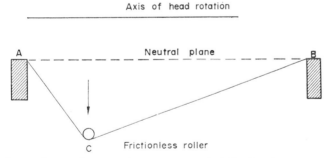

Fig. 8.8. Laserev's experiment to demonstrate track deflection due to tape topology.

C, was moved out to deflect the band from its neutral plane to form ACB. As the component of force along AC is larger than along CB, the band moves toward A until equilibrium is reached. If a mark is made at C and the roller is moved back to the neutral plane, the mark will move toward B. In the case of the tape canoe the recorded track, which is analogous to the mark on the rubber band, will form an M shape where it is deflected in three places.

In practice an assymetry of 1·0 in would cause a deflection of 0·001 in, which in turn would cause a velocity error of 0·5 ηsec per TV line.

The second parameter of importance on canoe shape is the error in parallelism between the neutral plane and the axis of rotation of the head wheel.

155

An error here would cause a *C*-shaped video track. For a similar error of 0·5 *n*sec per TV line the permissible deviation from parallelism would be 0·0035 in/in.

Temperature and humidity

The expansion of the tape relative to the guide is also a cause of timing error and in this respect the action of the erase head increasing in temperature during the recording must be taken into account. In general however an error of 1 *n*sec per TV line should not be exceeded.

The coefficient of hygroscopic expansion for Mylar is 11 μin per inch per cent of relative humidity which would cause about 2·5 *n*sec per TV line per 10% change in relative humidity.

Tape tension

Variations in tape tension due to holdback torque cause errors somewhat less than might be expected and a theoretical value of 1·25 *n*sec per TV line per 5 oz variation is quoted.

Conclusion

In all the cases quoted the timing error per horizontal line is given which means that if a line is corrected at the start of a line and that correction is held, the uncorrected error at the end of the line will be the figure quoted. This is sometimes loosely referred to as the velocity of the error although strictly the velocity is the first derivative of the phase error and can be a complex function with respect to time.

To place the results in perspective it is worth comparing the phase distortion on the colour sub-carrier resulting from each parameter.

$$\text{For 625 PAL } 360° \text{ of subcarrier} = 226 \text{ } n\text{sec}$$
$$\text{For 525 NTSC } 360° \text{ of subcarrier} = 279 \text{ } n\text{sec}$$

therefore 1 ηsec of error causes 1·6° phase error on 625 systems and 1·3° on 525 systems.

For an interchange playback without velocity compensation the resulting phase error should not exceed that shown in Table 10 on modern high-band VTRs.

TABLE 10

Cause of Error	Phase error per TV line	
	525 NTSC	625 PAL
Guide position	20°	24°
Guide radius	10°	12·5°
Transport topology	3°	3·5°
Erase head temperature	1°	1·25°
Tape tension	2°	2·5°
10% humidity	3°	3·5°

Mylar has a very slow rate of moisture absorption and it is therefore only necessary to control humidity when storing tape.

Adjustments to helical machines

The timing stability requirements, for many applications of helical VTRs, are not as critical as for broadcasting. Despite this the problems of head and tape geometry and subsequent compatibility are more exacting, requiring more ingenuity from the designer, a greater allowance for ambient variables and a greater degree of alertness on behalf of the operator.

The magnitude of the problem can be seen from Fig. 4.6, typical helical scan tape formats.

In general, each track carries one television field of information. The length of each track depends on the particular design, but for a single headed machine, with a drum diameter of 5 in, the track length would be over $15\frac{1}{2}$ in. The problem then is to scan the narrow video track, which is of the order of 0·006 in wide, without a deviation of more than 0·001 in over its total length of over $15\frac{1}{2}$ in. An additional problem is to avoid distortion of the tape longitudinally, causing a change in head velocity which would accumulate a large timing error over the scan.

If compatibility is not required, the problem is not a difficult one because any deflections of the tape caused by mis-alignment in the transport are present in record and playback, which avoids mistracking.

With all other parameters being equal the higher bandwidth machines have a more difficult problem, because the higher head to tape speed results in a larger diameter drum and longer video tracks. Advances in high energy tapes, with higher resolution of recorded wavelengths, coupled with the higher efficiency ferrite heads has resulted in designs of helical VTRs with lower diameter drums, making compatibility less of a problem.

Head position

Double headed and single headed machines have very similar problems although two headed machines have the added complexity of aligning the heads with respect to each other.

For a one headed machine the only two important positional parameters are head azimuth, the angle of the gap to the direction of the track, and tip projection, the amount the pole tip projects from the drum into the tape. The tolerance on either of these is not exceptionally difficult for the same reasons given for the quadruplex format. The fact that the gap width is even less relaxes the tolerance even further on azimuth.

For a two headed machine the two extra positional parameters are more critical. Firstly the two heads should rotate in the same plane i.e. no axial displacement. This ensures a minimisation of tracking error and an equal spacing of tracks.

With a guard band of the order of 0·003 in a tracking error of 0·001 in is the maximum permissible due to head axial displacement. This allows for

157

additional tracking errors due to capstan instability. Assuming a worst build up of tolerances this places an error tolerance between the two planes of rotation to be no greater than 0·0005 in.

Secondly the two heads should be positioned at 180° with respect to each other. The tolerance of this adjustment, called dihedral, depends on the permissible time base error. This in turn depends upon the application, but the error should not exceed ±1 μsec.

On a 50 Hz standard

20 msecs = 180°

$$1 \ \mu sec \ = \frac{180 \times 10^{-3}}{20} = \pm16 \ seconds \ \text{of arc}$$

Tape path and interchange

To ensure that the track is recorded in the correct position or that an existing track is scanned correctly, the tape has to be guided around the head with an accuracy of 0·0005 in over its entire length. Techniques differ between manufacturers as to methods of guiding but in general the tape is guided just on entering the drum assembly, on leaving the drum and sometimes intermediate guides are placed around the drum itself.

The difference in height between the entrance guide and the exit guide determines the amount the tape climbs as it wraps around the scanner and thus determines the resultant track angle. The intermediate guides ensure that the tape does not distort from a linear angle. A further requirement for an omega wrap machine is to set the guide arms as close and as parallel to the scanner assembly as possible to ensure a small and well defined drop-out as the head and the tape part company.

Figure 8.9(a) shows the mechanical arrangement used on the Ampex 1 in format, the position of the guide arms in the operating mode. This can be compared with Fig. 4.4 showing the arms in a retracted state. Figure 8.9(b) shows its relationship to the intermediate guide placed at the rear of the drum to intercept the tape half-way. The guides are nominally set to the dimensions shown, leaving the vernier adjustments to be made dynamically on a 'standard interchange alignment tape'. An interchange tape is one manufactured on a very accurately aligned tape deck under very closely controlled temperature and humidity conditions.

The technique of vernier adjustment is to adjust the tape guides during the playback of the interchange tape, until a flat *RF* envelope is obtained with well defined leading and trailing edges. If the video head scans into the guard band, a reduction in *RF* amplitude would result.

The timing position of this reduction of the envelope is an indication of the physical position of the deviation. The ideal envelope is shown in Fig. 8.10(a) with the effect of an incorrect adjustment of the rear guide in Fig. 8.10(b). If the adjustments are even further out then the head will start to

158

read adjacent tracks with a null as it passes through the guard band, giving *RF* envelope shapes as shown in Fig. 8.10(c), (d), (e).

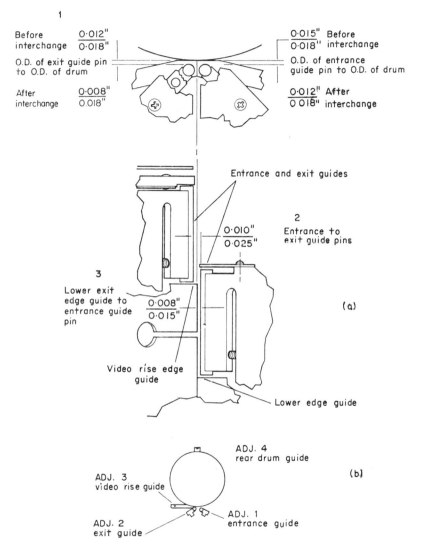

Fig. 8.9. The position of the tape guides on an omega wrap:
(a) *Nominal position of the tape guides.* (b) *Top view of the guide positions.*

Compatibility coefficient

A measurement of how accurately the adjustments have been made can be done by adjusting the tracking control and noting that the *RF* envelope reduces evenly over its length for a given range of the tracking control.

159

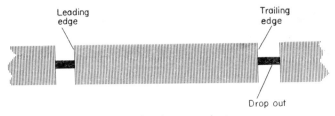

(a)   Ideal interchange envelope

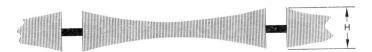

(b)   Interchange envelope when tape
         guide on rear of drum is at its
         lowest position

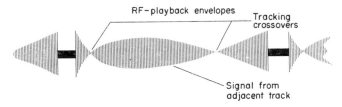

(c)   Envelope with most severe amplitude
         fluctuations near leading edge

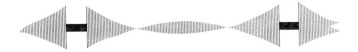

(d)   Envelope improved from that of
         illustration c

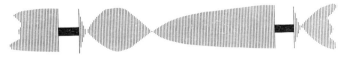

(e)   Envelope with greater guiding error

Fig. 8.10. R.F. envelopes showing various degrees of compatibility.

160

The range over which the tracking control should give a satisfactory picture depends on the format and in particular the video track width and guard band dimensions.

On a 50 Hz standard an adjustment of 20 m sec on the tracking control would move the tape phase from the centre of one track to the centre of the adjacent track. For a format with 0·006 in video track width and 0·003 in guard band, this would result in a 0·009 in movement of the tape with respect to the video head. If a track is being scanned exactly down the centre, an adjustment of tracking control causing a movement of ±0·003 in would only result in scanning in the guard band with a reduction in *RF* level of 6 dB or one-half at the extremes of the adjustment. A satisfactory picture therefore would result for 0·006 in of the total 0·009 in. Further adjustment would cause the scanning of two tracks with a resultant beat or moire between the two *RF* signals, causing a very objectional disturbance on the picture.

The time delay of the tracking control over which a satisfactory picture is obtained is called the 'good time' and for the format discussed should be

$$tg = 20 \times 10^{-3} \times \frac{0 \cdot 006}{0 \cdot 009} = 13 \cdot 3 \text{ msec}$$

the remaining time is called the 'bad time'

$$tb = 20 \times 10^{-3} \times \frac{0 \cdot 003}{0 \cdot 009} = 6 \cdot 67 \text{ msec}$$

If for any reason the video head does not scan the video track exactly in the first place, there would be a reduction of the 'good time'.

An excellent method of expressing compatibility between two machines is to measure the range of tracking delay giving a satisfactory picture on an exchange recording and playback basis and expressing it as a percentage of the known theoretical time for the format used.

Compatibility coefficient

$$C = \frac{tg^1}{tg} \times 100\%$$

tg^1 = measured good time in msec

tg = maximum possible good time

For formats where the guard band dimension is less than the track width and one track represents one field (all known formats to date) tg can be calculated as follows.

For 50 Hz standards.

$$tg = \frac{20 \times 2 \times \text{guard band width}}{\text{centre track spacing}} \text{ msec}$$

For 60Hz standards.

$$tg = \frac{16\cdot67 \times 2 \times \text{guard band width}}{\text{centre track spacing}} \text{ msec}$$

Timing errors

In a similar manner to the quadruplex format, it is important that the same length of tape is around the drum scanner assembly in playback as in record. Failure to do this results in a phase discrepancy during playback in horizontal sync timing between the end of one field and the start of the next, i.e. over the drop-out.

The effect of this is to cause a 'hook', just after the drop-out or head switch time, as the flywheel oscillator in the picture monitor tries to adjust itself to the new sync phase (see Fig. 8.11). Shorter time constants in the line

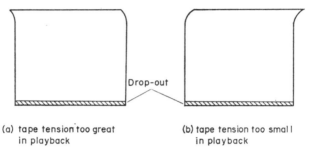

(a) tape tension too great
in playback

(b) tape tension too small
in playback

Fig. 8.11. The subjective effect of 'hooking' with incorrect tape tension.

time base circuits will shorten the recovery time but very often this parameter is not available to the VTR operator. A reduction in the time constant also makes sync circuits more vulnerable to noise.

The effect of the problem can be minimised by arranging the drop-out, or head switch time on two headed machines, to occur at the bottom of the picture just before the vertical synchronising interval. This allows 25 lines of vertical blanking before the active picture period for recovery.

The three main variables to affect tape length are temperature, humidity and tape tension. The first two are normally inconvenient and expensive to control. The third however can be used to compensate for the environmental changes.

Environmental changes

If the tape and the drum scanning assembly expand simultaneously by the same amount, the angle of wrap, for a given length of tape, would be the same before and after expansion. If the angular velocity of the head remains constant, no timing error will result.

162

The most common material for drum scanner assemblies is aluminium and unfortunately this has a different temperature coefficient of expansion from Mylar, the tape material.

Assuming a temperature rise of 30°F between record and play, the net effect can be calculated as follows.

Temperature coefficient of expansion for Mylar
$$= +1.5 \times 10^{-5} \text{ in/in°F}$$

Temperature coefficient of expansion for aluminium
$$= +1.07 \times 10^{-5} \text{ in/in°F}$$

Net temperature coefficient $\qquad = +0.43 \times 10^{-5} \text{ in/in°F}$

For a 30°F change the % change in length
$$lt = 0.43 \times 10^{-5} \times 30 \times 100 = 0.0129\%$$

This small amount however is quite significant.

Each track represents one TV field of 312·5 lines (on 625 line systems)

This expansion therefore represents
$$0.0129 \times 312.5 = 4\% \text{ of a TV line}$$
$$= 2.56 \ \mu\text{sec}$$

This result is independent of the type of wrap, drum diameter or the number of heads.

Changes in relative humidity have a greater effect on timing errors, owing to the wide variation in ambient conditions and the non compensating effect of the drum scanner assembly.

For a 40% change in relative humidity

Humidity coefficient of expansion for Mylar $= 1.1 \times 10^{-5}$ in/in % R.H.

% change in length for 40% change in R.H.
$$= 1.1 \times 10^{-5} \times 40 = 0.044\%$$

% of a 625 standard line

$$= 0.044\% \times 312.5 = 13.7\% \text{ of a TV line}$$

$$= 8.76 \ \mu sec$$

For an increase in temperature and humidity this would result in a total of 11·32 μsec of error.

For one-inch wide, one-mil tape a decrease in tension of $4\frac{1}{4}$ oz would be required to compensate for such an increase. As tape stretch is proportional to tension, a graph of tension change required to compensate for environmental changes is a linear one as can be seen in Fig. 8.12 (a and b).

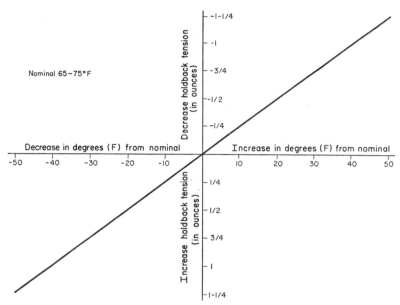

Fig. 8.12. (a) *Graph showing changes in holdback tension required to compensate for temperature changes.*

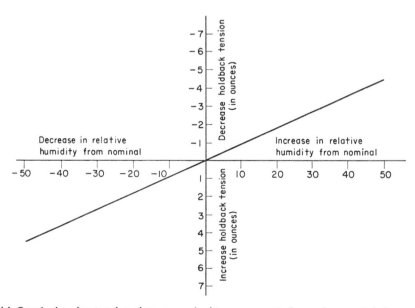

(b) *Graph showing tension change required to compensate for environmental changes.*

164

Tape tension

In most helical recorders a nominal tension of 6 to 8 oz is maintained in record. This can then be varied by ± 5 oz during playback to minimise 'hooking' at the top of the picture.

The tape tension can be controlled by affecting the holdback torque of the supply spool or by affecting the take-up torque. The former is normally a braking action on the supply hub while the latter is a power control on the take-up motor.

The design of the transport must ensure that the tension on the tape is constant over its entire length. Failure to achieve this results in a differential stretch which is very difficult to compensate for.

Theoretically the tension on the tape as it enters the drum scanner can only be the same as the tension on leaving the drum scanner, if the drum has a frictionless surface. In practice this is impossible but surfaces with coefficients of friction as low as 0·02 have been achieved which give a ratio of tensions

$$\frac{To}{Ti} = 1{\cdot}13 \text{ for a } 360° \text{ wrap}$$

where To = Tape tension at output of scanner

Ti = Tape tension at input of scanner

The problem is that this surface must be kept very clean and all stray tape oxide must be removed. A build-up of oxide could easily deteriorate the coefficient of friction to say 0·2 giving a tension ratio of $\dfrac{To}{Ti} = 3{\cdot}5$ (Appendix 17). If the input tension is 5 oz then the output tension would be 17·5 ozs causing gross timing errors due to differential stretch. Meticulous cleaning after every recording or playback results in consistent and controllable results.

A further problem, which is a design one, is to avoid changes in torque as the tape pack increases and decreases in diameter on the spools. This can be done by monitoring the tape tension by means of a sprung tension arm, the deflection of the arm being a measure of the tape tension. By controlling the tension variable to maintain a chosen deflection, any fluctuations in tension can be sensed and corrected for.

This servo action can be seen in Fig. 8.13 which shows the method used on the IVC one-inch format recorders. Here the tension is monitored after the scanner and the tension is controlled by the take-up spool. The pivoted tension arm is loaded against a clock spring so that the correct tension of 8 oz deflects the arm to a central position.

A photocell attached to the tension arm views a lamp and varies its resistance as its position to the lamp changes. This variable resistance forms part of a triac firing circuit and controls the duty cycle of the take-up motor's a.c. supply.

The servo action functions in the following way. If the tape tension increases for reasons such as increased scanner friction, holdback torque or mains variation, the tension arm would be further deflected against the spring. The photocell moving away from the light would increase in resistance and in turn reduce the duty cycle of the triac circuit. This in turn would reduce the power to the take-up motor and cause a reduction in torque and tension, allowing the arm to move back to its central position.

During record this would keep the tension constant over the full range in diameter of the tape pack. During playback however, for reasons previously mentioned, it is required to vary the tension to compensate for environmental changes. This can only be done in the servo loop by changing its reference. In the case of servo described this can conveniently be done by changing the spring tension.

Manual adjustment can be made during playback for minimum 'hooking' by means of a second servo loop.

The second servo loop is a conventional positional servo. The output of the differential amplifier is zero when its two inputs are equal. If the input

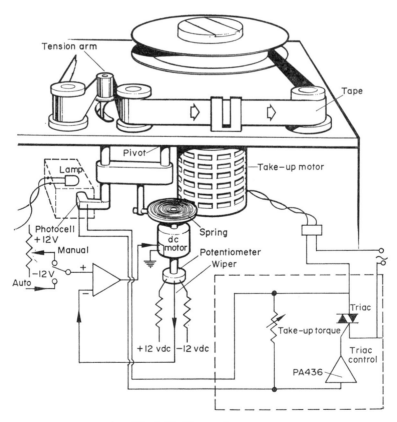

Fig. 8.13. The tension servo.

potentiometer is adjusted to a new potential, the output of the amplifier causes the d.c. motor to rotate until the output from the potentiometer on the motor shaft produces an equal voltage. When the two inputs are equal, drive to the motor ceases. The shaft of the motor will therefore take up an angular position determined by the input potentiometer setting.

Some form of tension servo is required in any helical recorder offering compatibility, but it is normally necessary for the operator to adjust the tension on playback for minimum timing error.

A refinement on the more expensive helical recorders is automatic tension control on playback.

Auto tension

If the tension on playback is to be automatically controlled for minimum timing errors, some form of electronic circuitry is required to detect the timing error and produce a correction voltage. Use can be made of the automatic phase controlled oscillator (a.p.c.) locked to tape horizontal sync pulses. A block diagram of an a.p.c. oscillator can be seen in Fig. 8.14 which shows a complete diagram of an auto-tension error detector.

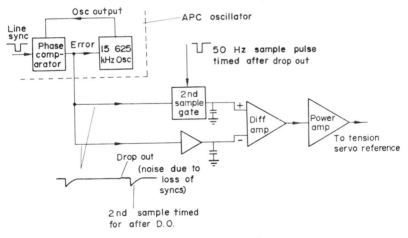

Fig. 8.14. Auto tension error detector.

The oscillator, which is nominally set to the line rate of the playback standard, can be locked in phase and frequency to the playback line sync by controlling the oscillator frequency from a phase comparator. The phase comparator compares the phase between tape sync and the oscillator output and produces an error voltage which increases or decreases the oscillator frequency until coincidence is achieved and the phase error voltage is zero. This phase error voltage is now a measure of playback sync phase.

If the VTR has a horizontal comparator in its servo system, the error can

167

be derived from this. Machines without horizontal servo control require the a.p.c. loop.

The maximum phase change occurs from the end of one track to the start of the next. If the error voltage is examined over this period, a rapid change in voltage should be noticed after the switch. The polarity of the change indicates whether the tension is too large or too small while the magnitude of the change is a measure of the tension error.

A second sample gate comparator is used to sample the error voltage just after the drop out or head switch. The sample pulse can be derived from vertical sync, tach pulse or the drop-out sensor. Its important parameter is its timing which should be timed to occur at the start of a track scan. To determine the change in error the a.p.c. error is integrated and subtracted from the output from the second sample gate in a differential amplifier. This d.c. error is then amplified and used to alter the tape tension. In the servo illustrated in Fig. 8.14 it supplies a d.c. motor which alters the spring tension on the tension arm. On some recorders it supplies the d.c. current in a brake solenoid.

The phase comparators are very similar to those discussed in Chapter 7.

Conclusion

The simplicity of the helical format makes it more vulnerable to geometry errors. Slight environmental changes considerably affect timing errors and slight dimensional changes affect tracking. Solutions to problems have been engineered but not all models incorporate them for economic reasons. It is the user who has to decide his own requirements and the necessity for the refinements. Care in cleaning and checking wear with interchange measurements go a long way in maintaining standards.

References

1. SMPTE R.P. 11, *Tape vacuum guide radius and position for recording standard video records on two-inch magnetic tape.*
2. SMPTE, R.P. 36, *Specification for positioning tape neutral plane and adjacent tape guides for quadruplex video magnetic tape recorders operating on 7·5 i.p.s and 15 i.p.s.*
3. HARRIS, A., Time-base errors and their correction in magnetic television recorders. *JSMPTE*, Vol. 70, July 1961.
4. LASEREV, N., Causes and effects of velocity errors in the interchange of colour video tape recordings. *JSMPTE*, Vol. 78, No. 7, July 1969.
5. JOHNSON, D., *Helical formats*, Ampex Educational Industrial Products.

9 Time Base Error Correction

It has been seen that the unprocessed demodulated video can be mistimed owing to head servo instability, capstan servo instability, and tape path geometry. For monochrome signals the effect of these errors can be minimised by reducing the time constant of the flywheel synchronisation circuit in the picture monitor. If however it is required to mix two video signals, the synchronisation of the signals to within 100 ηsec is necessary. With the sophistication of complex servo functions and automatic geometry compensation, timing errors can be reduced to this order. Without them errors in excess of 100 times that required can accumulate.

A possible method of circumventing the problem and mixing between a studio source and a VTR signal, with gross timing errors, is shown in Fig. 9.1.

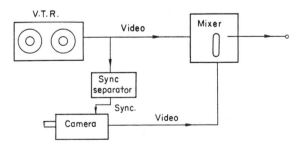

Fig. 9.1. A method for mixing V.T.R. signals with studio source.

In this arrangement the studio camera or telecine is supplied with synchronising pulses derived from the VTR playback signal and not, as is normal, from

169

a stable sync pulse generator. The resultant studio signal then has the same timing error as the VTR signal and the two sources are synchronous to within very close limits. The disadvantage of the system is that the studio relies on the uninterrupted VTR signal for the complete period of time that the studio source is used. Care must be taken to ensure an adequate length of recorded signal before and after the VTR insert. A refinement to the system is to use some form of flywheel sync generator, locked to tape syncs, to provide syncs during periods of missing pulses caused by tape drop out. The main advantage of the arrangement is in its low cost, which makes it very popular in CCTV installations.

The video timing stability has not been improved and a better system is one where the error is electronically corrected.

Nature of timing errors

The important factors *of a timing* error are:

1. Static error.
2. Fluctuating error.
3. Velocity error.

Static error. Static error is the fixed timing error between the average timing of the playback signal and a stable reference. This is normally measured as the time between the average timing of the leading edge of sync on the VTR signal and the leading edge of station-sync. If the magnitude of the error is small a comparison between station colour sub-carrier and tape chrominance information can be made.

Fluctuating error. Fluctuating timing error is a measure of the peak deviations of error from the average timing.

Velocity error. This is the first derivative of the timing error or the rate of change of error. It is an important factor because it gives an indication of the time constant required by flywheel circuits in order to follow the error. For a slow-changing error a relatively long time constant would suffice while for a rapid change a much shorter time constant is required. Another important consideration is that most correction devices do not continuously measure the timing error but sample sequentially at the start of each line. It is important for the error not to change significantly between samples. The velocity of the error therefore must be low.

Methods of monochrome correction

The correction of timing errors can be achieved in a variety of ways and several techniques have been developed, each with their own limitations and cost effectiveness. All systems operate in a similar manner of adjusting the delay of the video signal to cancel out any timing discrepancy between the tape video and a stable reference.

The operation of the corrector can be separated into two distinct functions,

170

that of determining the required delay, and that of applying the delay. The two operations can be connected in an open loop or closed loop configuration. Simplified diagrams of both systems can be seen in Fig. 9.2. In both arrangements the delay is nominally set to the middle of its range. If the tape video is retarded, the appropriate amount of delay is removed while if it is advanced, delay is added

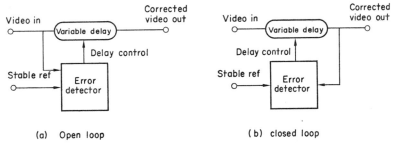

(a) Open loop   (b) closed loop

Fig. 9.2. Methods of correcting timing errors.

In the open loop system the timing of the input video is compared to a stable reference and a correction voltage (or digital signal) derived, the magnitude of this voltage being a function of the timing difference between the two signals. Care must be taken to ensure that the calibration of the detector in terms of volts per μsec error exactly matches that of the delay line in μsec delay per volt of correction. Failure to do this results in under or over correction.

A better system is the closed loop one where the delay is adjusted until the output is correctly timed. Unfortunately most delay arrangements cannot use such a system because only one timing comparison is made per line. If the output is in error then it is too late to do anything about it.

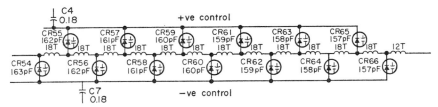

Fig. 9.3. The analogue delay.

Methods of applying delay

The analogue delay. A lumped constant delay as shown in Fig. 9.3 has a delay time

$$td = \sqrt{LC} \text{ seconds per section}$$

A variable delay can be made if the capacitive elements are composed of back biased varactor diodes. By changing the bias a change in capacitance

171

will cause a change in delay. The delay can be continuously variable although large delays require a large number of delay sections. In practice anything up to 90 sections have been used with a nominal delay of 3 μsec and a range of about ± 1 μsec.

The frequency response of the delay line must be satisfactory to 5·5 Mhz and distortions on the video signal kept to a minimum. For these reasons longer delays or ones with a greater range are not practicable.

An added problem to compensating for any high frequency loss is that the frequency response will change as the delay is adjusted. Each section acts as a low pass filter with a cut-off frequency dependent on the value of capacitance. Tracking equalisation is therefore necessary with changes in response depending on the amount of delay. These can either follow or precede the delay line and are controlled by the delay bias voltages. Two control bias voltages are normally used which operate in push–pull. All diodes are back-biased and increase or decrease their capacitance simultaneously. If the delay is reduced (a reduction in the value of capacitance), the bias must be increased. The −ve control goes more −ve and the +ve control more +ve. The use of push–pull control overcomes the problem of transients appearing on the output video. If the required delay needs to be suddenly changed, the control bias will make an abrupt change in value. This change can capacitively couple itself across the diodes and superimpose itself on the video causing a transient at the time of change. With the push–pull arrangement and the careful matching of the diodes a +ve and a −ve transient occurs which cancel each other out.

The amplitude of the video itself will cause the bias of the diodes to alter and in this respect cause an amplitude/phase response or differential phase on the colour signals. This can be minimised by reducing the amplitude of the video to about 125 mV while the control voltages are in excess of 1·0 volt. The problem is further alleviated by the push–pull arrangement of the control bias. The diodes connected to the −ve control will alter in the opposite manner to those connected to the +ve control for all changes in video level. The two effects tend to cancel each other out, but not exactly, owing to the non linearity of the system, i.e.:

The capacitance of a varactor diode

$$C_v \propto \,_N\!\sqrt{\frac{1}{v}} \propto v^{-\frac{1}{N}}$$

where v = bias voltage
and N is between 2 and 3.

The delay of the line $td \propto \sqrt{C_v} \propto C_v^{\frac{1}{2}}$

$$td \propto \left(v^{-\frac{1}{N}}\right)^{+\frac{1}{2}} \propto v^{-\frac{1}{2}N}$$

If $N = 2$

$$td \propto v^{-\frac{1}{4}} \propto \,_4\!\sqrt{\frac{1}{v}}$$

172

The delay of the delay line is proportional to the reciprocal of the fourth root of the voltage. This is not a very linear relationship and it must be ensured that the correction voltage follows this law.

The quantised delay line. A lumped constant delay line could be constructed with fixed components and with output tappings along the line at discrete intervals. The video which is applied at the input, could be delayed by any quantised amount, selecting the appropriate output. The delay is not continuously variable and therefore may not be exactly the correct amount. If the output that is nearest to the correct timing is chosen the maximum error will be half the timing difference between tappings. The number of outputs depends on the required correction range and the tolerance on the residual timing error of the video output. For a range of 2 μsec and a video signal timed to within 20 ηsecs.

$$\text{Number of outputs} = \frac{2 \times 10^{-6}}{40 \times 10^{-9}} = 50 \text{ outputs}.$$

Each output requires a gate and a buffer amplifier with equalisation compensation for a high frequency loss caused by the delay line. The amount of electronics for a quantised delay is considerably greater than for the analogue system, although for the former there is a considerable repetition of circuitry.

The binary quantised delay line. For very long delays the number of outputs required on a simple tapped delay line becomes prohibitive. It is also difficult to design a lumped constant delay line which does not cause group delay problems. The longer the delay the greater the problem. The engineering answer to both these problems is the use of quartz delay lines made in lengths which have a binary relationship to each other (see Fig. 9.4). The appropriate delay can be selected by arranging the relevant delays in series with the video path. By using nine delays from $\frac{1}{8}$ μsec to 32 μsec any delay from $\frac{1}{8}$ μsec to $63\frac{7}{8}$ μsec can be formed. Fewer switches are needed than in the tapped delay line system, but the logic involved in deciding the switching arrangement is complicated.

Quartz delay lines have a very poor low frequency response, making them unsuitable for video signals without some form of modulation. In practice *FM* modulation is used, which alleviates the problem of gain stability. There are 512 different combinations of delay which must not cause differing phase or frequency response. Because of the extra cost of peripheral logic, modulation and demodulation the binary delay configuration is used only for delays in excess of 32 μsec.

If a timing corrector has a range of 32 μsec, a further economic advantage can be made in the servo system. The horizontal comparator would no longer be required because the horizontal information of the tape signal can never be more than 32 μsec displaced from the reference.

173

Binary delay switching

The problems of delay switching can be seen in Fig. 9.4 where the electronic switches are shown as simple toggle switches. Method (a) would seem an obvious method of connecting the delays where each delay is preceded and followed by a single-throw double-pole switch. The video could either be routed through the delay or by-passed. The method suffers from two very serious disadvantages. Imagine that the 16 μsec delay needs to be switched

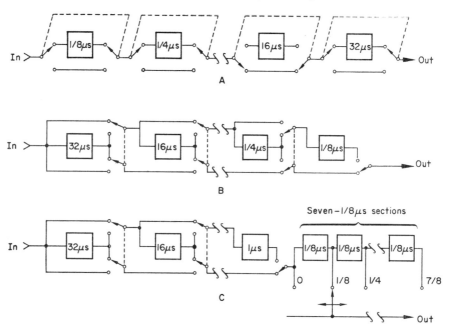

Fig. 9.4. The binary quantized delay line.

in and the delays of lower value switched out. A typical situation where an increase in delay of $\frac{1}{8}$ μsec is required. The presence of the 32 μsec delay means that nothing can happen to the output until 32 μsec *after* the switching action. Secondly the output of the 16 μsec delay will be zero until 16 μsec after an input has been applied. This means that if at the start of a line the delay was changed, nothing would happen for 32 μsec after which 16 μsec of no signal, followed by corrected video.

The problem can be solved, with one restriction, by connecting the delay lines as shown in method (b), where each delay is followed by a double-pole, double-throw switch. The restriction is that the total delay can be adjusted only in increments of the smallest delay, in this case $\frac{1}{8}$ μsec. With the switches in the position shown the delay is 16 μsec. To subtract $\frac{1}{8}$ μsec the output switch ($S\frac{1}{8}$) should move to its upper position, thus producing a delay of:

$$8 + 4 + 2 + 1 + \tfrac{1}{2} + \tfrac{1}{4} + \tfrac{1}{8} = 15\tfrac{5}{8} \ \mu\text{sec}$$

To add ⅛ μsec the 16 μsec and ⅛ μsec delays must be connected in series and this can be done by moving all switches following the 16 μsec delay to their opposite positions. The correctly phased output will not appear until ⅛ μsec after the upper set of switches have been actuated. To maintain continuity the action of the lower set of switches are delayed by ⅛ μsec.

The final question is whether the restrictions of being able to change the delay only in ⅛ μsec increments is any limitation. The delay is normally changed only at the start of each line and the question is whether or not the timing error will change by more than ⅛ μsec in 64 μsec. This equals a velocity of error greater than 1 μsec per 0·512 msec or 1 μsec per 45° revolution of the head on a quadruplex recorder. In general, velocity errors will seldom exceed this. However in the case of a guide penetration error the timing error difference between the last line of a head and the first line of a following head can approach 1 μsec. For this reason the arrangement is modified so that the final binary delay is 1 μsec and the following ⅞ μsec is made up of a tapped delay line with outputs at ⅛ μsec intervals.

Determining the required delay

The analogue error detector. Phase comparators producing an error voltage proportional to the phase difference between two pulses have already been described in the chapter on servo mechanisms. Such circuits are also used in timing correctors where tape horizontal sync is compared in phase to a reference horizontal sync. The error developed however cannot be directly applied to the analogue delay line. Push–pull signals have to be derived and amplified to produce quite a large charging current. Also the error voltage, which is proportional to the timing error, must be modified to produce a fourth power law.

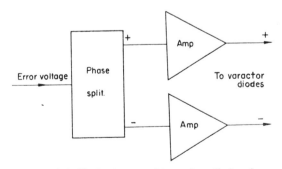

Fig. 9.5. Method to provide push-pull signals.

The arrangement to produce push–pull signals can be seen in Fig. 9.5. The circuits must be accurately matched and be capable of providing a low output impedance to rapidly charge the delay line capacitance. The control input of a 3 μsec delay would typically have an input capacitance of about 0·5 μF and it would be required to charge this in as short a time as possible.

The time required to charge a capacitance is approximately $5 \times CR$, where CR is the time constant of the charging circuit.

For charging time of 1μsec:

$$CR = \frac{1}{5} \mu\text{sec}$$

$$R = \frac{10^{-6}}{5C} \text{ ohms}$$

$$= \frac{1}{2 \cdot 5} = 0 \cdot 4 \text{ ohms}$$

For a 1 volt change in error voltage, the initial charging current would be

$$I = \frac{1}{0 \cdot 4} = 2 \cdot 5 \text{ amps}$$

Fourth power law

An electronic device with the characteristic of a fourth power law ($y = x^4$) is not easy to produce (see Fig. 9.6). A compromise can be reached by approximating to the characteristic with a series of linear functions as in Fig. 9.7. The device operates as a simple divider where:

$$vo = vi \frac{R2}{R1 + R2}$$

$$\frac{vo}{vi} = \frac{R2}{R1 + R2}$$

The value of $R2$ depends on the number of diodes conducting. The bias potential on each diode is set by its position on the ladder network which produces reference potential from zero volts to the peak value of the control voltage. For low values of control voltage all the diodes will be conducting,

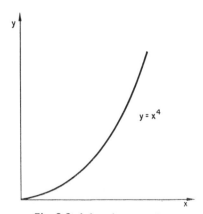

Fig. 9.6. A fourth power law.

causing $R2$ to be low in value. The slope of the transfer characteristic $\dfrac{\delta vo}{\delta vi}$ would be small. As the signal level goes more positive, the diodes turn off as their reference bias is exceeded. $R2$ increases in value causing $\dfrac{\delta vo}{\delta vi}$ to increase. By choosing the values of resistors in series with the diodes and the bias potentials carefully a reasonable approximation to a fourth power law can be made.

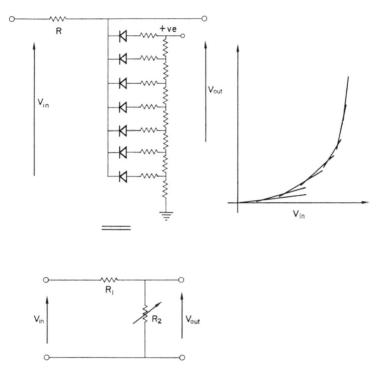

Fig. 9.7. A method of producing a transfer function with a 4th power law.

The stable references

The obvious stable reference for phase comparison is station sync and this can be used where the servo instability error combined with the geometry error does not exceed the range of the delay line corrector. In general, for analogue correction, this necessitates the use of the horizontal comparator in the head-wheel servo for complete correction of the errors. The use of a less stable servo mode however does not preclude the use of the corrector, even though the magnitude of the errors on the input video is well beyond the range of the corrector.

When playing back a signal in a non horizontal locked servo mode the

177

magnitude of the servo error may exceed 10 μsec. The geometry error however seldom exceeds 1 μsec. The inability of the monitor sync circuit to follow fast changes makes the geometry error the most objectionable. A definite advantage therefore is gained by removing those errors with a high velocity, and a corrector working in such a manner is sometimes referred to as being in the 'picture straighten mode'. A complete block diagram of an analogue corrector can be seen in Fig. 9.8.

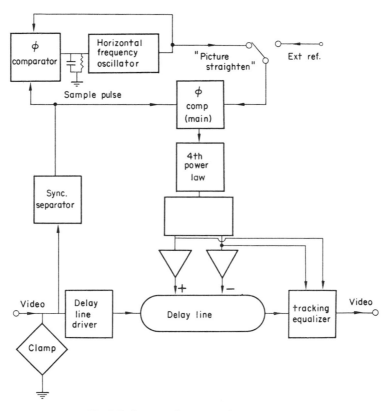

Fig. 9.8. A monochrome analogue corrector.

The object of the reference therefore is to follow the large slow-changing phase errors of the tape signal but not the fast-changing errors. The time constant of the a.p.c. loop can be made such that the oscillator will track the slow errors but integrate the rapid changes. The main phase comparator therefore compares the timing of a tape signal with slow and fast changes in phase with the timing of a reference signal with only slow changes. The error voltage therefore, and the subsequent delay correction, is proportional to the rapid changes in timing error. The corrector working in this mode does not radically improve the timing stability but just removes those errors which are subjectively annoying. For the stable mixing of video signals and all

178

colour applications the corrector must work in the reference mode. The input stability of the signal therefore must not exceed the range of the corrector for full correction of the errors.

The quantised gate

It is possible to produce a closed loop system when all the outputs of a quantised delay are available. The technique is to gate all outputs from the delay and select the appropriate output. The action of detection and selection can be seen in Fig. 9.9. A phase comparison is made for each output, although

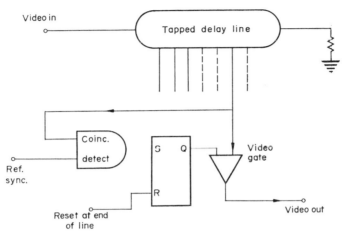

Fig. 9.9 The quantized gate.

only one output circuit is shown, and the coincidence between tape sync and the reference is detected. The coincidence detector is a simple 'AND' function with an output when the two sync inputs are synchronous. This sets a bi-stable latch which opens the gate. The bi-stable remains set maintaining the selected output until the end of the line, when another coincidence comparison is made. The circuit has the advantage of being stable with little requirement for accurately controlled non-linear functions. The cost of the detection of error increases with the number of outputs from the delay line.

Binary error detection

If lumped delay lines with a binary relationship are used, the most convenient form for the error signal to take is a binary number. For nine delays from 32 μsec to $\frac{1}{8}$ μsec a nine bit binary number would be required.

Bit No.	9	8	7	6	5	4	3	2	1
Count	256	128	64	32	16	8	4	2	1
Delay μsec	32	16	8	4	2	1	$\frac{1}{2}$	$\frac{1}{4}$	$\frac{1}{8}$

Binary No. for 19 μsec

$= 152$	0	1	0	0	1	1	0	0	0
Delay $=$		16		$+$	2 + 1				$= 19$ μsec

179

A method of producing this number is to count the number of clock pulses, which are timed at $\frac{1}{8}$ μsec intervals, between a tape signal pulse and a reference pulse. This count would represent the number of $\frac{1}{8}$ μsec delays required to make the two signals coincident. For example assume that the difference between the two signals was 19 μsec.

The total count of $\frac{1}{8}$ μsec pulses $= 19 \times 8 = 152$

$$\text{in binary} = 010011000$$

A 0 denotes the removal of a delay while a 1 denotes the insertion. For the binary number calculated the total delay would be $16 + 2 + 1 = 19$ μsec. The time measurement made can only be in terms of an integral number of

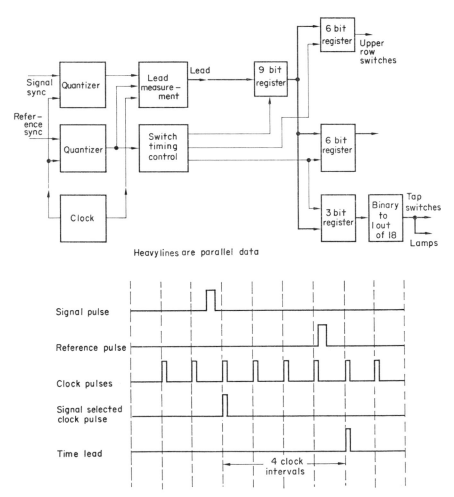

Fig. 9.10. A binary error detector.

clock pulses. In this respect the measurement is 'quantised'. The action of quantisation can be seen in Fig. 9.10 where both the signal and the reference pulses are modified in timing to the nearest following clock pulse time. The difference between the two quantised pulses must now be a whole number of clock pulses which makes the digital processing easier. The nine bit word can be temporarily stored in a register before the two final operations.

First, the final section of the delay is not binary but a $\frac{7}{8}$ μsec long, $\frac{1}{8}$ μsec tapped, delay line and the last three bits of the word is converted to a 'one out of eight' form. Secondly the upper row of switches and the lower set of switches actuate at differing times so that the six most significant bits of the word are transferred into two separate registers whose outputs operate the *RF* switches when required.

Colour correction

The three main colour standards in use are 525 NTSC, 625 PAL and 625 SECAM. Of these NTSC and PAL systems use phase modulation of a colour subcarrier which make them very sensitive to spurious phase modulation introduced by the VTR. SECAM on the other hand uses a line sequential frequency modulated system which is more tolerant of the VTR timing instability. Stability requirements for the latter are no more stringent than for monochrome systems.

One method of overcoming the problems of recording colour signals is to convert the incoming standard into one that is more tolerant to the distortions incurred. Such systems are used but are to be avoided if the maximum performance specification is required. This limits the use of such systems to CCTV applications. Most broadcast and some CCTV systems improve, yet again, the timing stability from the monochrome corrector and reduce the error to limits small enough to cause imperceptible distortion on the colour signal.

For a PAL signal the error should be limited to $\pm 5°$ and for a NTSC signal an error better than $\pm 4°$ is required. This allows for additional errors in the transmission path and the recording of multiple generation tapes.

The tolerance on timing from the above angular displacements would be better than ± 3 nsec for both systems. The colour corrector, which follows the coarse monochrome corrector, acts as a vernier adjustment of phase bringing the phase of the video to within the tolerance mentioned. Because of the small range required from such a corrector and the small limits of error the most suitable method is the analogue delay. The range of such delay lines need be no larger than $\pm 180°$ of subcarrier because this is the maximum phase error possible between two sine waves. The longest delay required therefore would be for an NTSC signal with 3·58 MHz colour subcarrier, requiring a delay range of ± 140 ηsec.

The error detector is very similar to the open loop analogue detector previously described with the exception of the reference used. In a colour corrector, shown in Fig. 9.11, the 10 cycles of burst on the back porch of the

181

tape signal is compared in phase to the reference station subcarrier. Allowance has to be made in PAL signals for the burst swinging $\pm 45°$ on consecutive lines. This is done by swinging the reference subcarrier in sympathy with the burst. The swing of the tape burst is detected to produce a 7·8 kHz switching

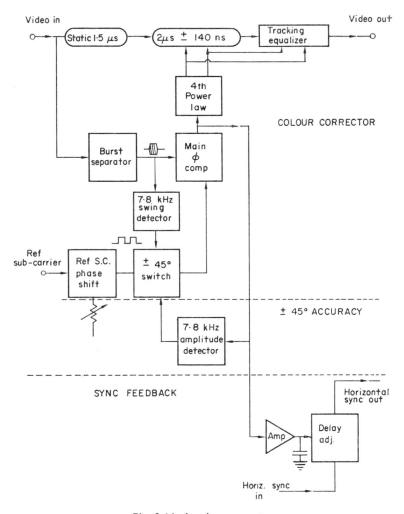

Fig. 9.11. A colour corrector.

signal which is used to switch the phase of the reference subcarrier. An operational adjustment of the reference phase can also be made in order to produce the required output video phase. The video is also delayed by a static delay of about 1·5 μsec to allow for the delay in determining the error voltage and charging the delay line. This was not required in the monochrome corrector as the time available from the leading edge of sync to the start of the active line time is about 10 μsec. For colour correction the time from the last cycle of the burst to the start of the active line is less than 3 μsec. The extra static delay ensures that the variable delay is set correct before the start of the active line period.

A problem is created by the swinging burst in PAL if either the burst swing or the reference swing is not exactly $\pm 45°$. It is quite feasible that the recorded colour signal has a tolerance of $\pm 2°$ from its nominal. If the reference swings $\pm$ 45° while the burst swings $\pm 43°$ then the 2° error would result in a false correction. This could be avoided if the reference is adjusted to $\pm 43°$ to match the recorded signal. This can be done automatically by monitoring the error voltage. Any error between burst and reference due to alternate line swing would result in a 7·8 kHz component in the error waveform. The angle of the reference therefore is adjusted until a zero 7·8 kHz component occurs.

Sync feedback

It is important that the delay line operates in the centre of its delay range to enable the corrector to operate on the peak positive and negative excursions of the error. It would be wasteful to use the device to remove static errors. Without the use of sync feedback the corrector would have no method of adjusting its input phase to achieve this. The input phase to the colour corrector is determined by the head servo and the monochrome detector, and by adjusting the timing of the sync reference to either unit the input video phase can be altered.

The delay line is at the centre of its range when the output of the phase comparator is zero volts. A positive or negative excursion would reduce or increase the delay. The sync feedback loop operates in the following way. The sync reference to the servo is delayed by a nominal 3 μsec. The correction voltage is amplified and integrated to produce a voltage proportional to the average error of the incoming signal. If this is not zero volts, the delay of the sync reference to the servo is adjusted from its nominal timing until the input phase to the corrector causes the average error voltage to be zero. The delay line must now be operating about the centre of its range. Figure 9.12 shows two methods of applying sync feedback. In Figure 9.12(a) the colour corrector error volts adjusts the reference to the monochrome corrector which in turn controls its output video phase. It is of course a requirement of the monochrome corrector to operate about its own centre delay and this can be done with a second feedback loop to the head servo reference. The requirement to manually adjust the monochrome timing cannot now be incorporated in the servo reference. To do this would result in a self cancelling effect. If the servo reference were manually delayed, the resulting change in head position would result in a change in video timing to the monochrome corrector, which in turn would be corrected. The change in error volts via sync feedback would adjust the servo reference reducing its delay to offset the manual adjustment.

Adjustment of the monochrome corrector reference is therefore used,

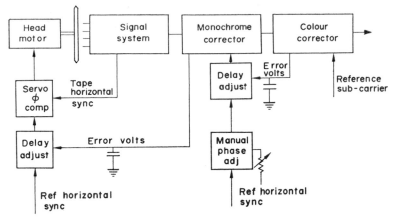

Fig 9.12 (a) *The application of sync feedback.*

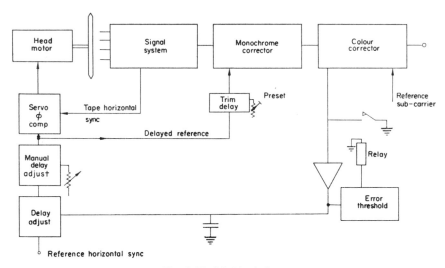

Fig. 9.12. (b) *Single loop.*

which in turn, via sync feedback, affects the servo reference. With two feedback loops care must be taken with the choice of time constants to avoid the
two loops interacting and causing a hunting action. This problem can be
solved and the saving of one adjustable delay can be made, by using the
arrangement shown in Fig. 9.12(b).

The reference for the monochrome corrector and the servo are made the
same by providing two outputs of the manual delay adjustment. A trim
adjustment of the corrector reference is made to bring the monochrome
delay to its centre. Once this is done the input video timing and the corrector
reference will track, keeping the average delay central. If the manual delay
is adjusted, the head wheel, and thus the video, will alter phase by the same

184

amount as the reference to the corrector. The only sync feedback loop is from the colour corrector error to adjust its input timing.

Error dumping

It can be seen in both circuits that the colour corrector has the final decision on the output phase. This obviously is a requirement for the mixing of colour signals. As there is no specification for sync/subcarrier phasing the monochrome phasing can be in error by an amount equivalent to $\pm 180°$ of subcarrier. Adjustment of horizontal phase therefore can only be made in quantised steps of $360°$ of subcarrier, if the desired chroma phase is maintained. This is automatic in both sync feedback circuits. If a manual adjustment of line sync is made, it is cancelled with the feedback, maintaining correct chroma phasing. This is correct until the sync feedback exceeds $180°$ of subcarrier, i.e.: 226 nsec PAL 270 nsec NTSC. When this happens the monochrome phasing is not to within the nearest cycle of subcarrier. An error dumping circuit is used to sense when the control volts to the sync delay circuit exceeds a given threshold, equivalent to a delay of $\pm 180°$ of subcarrier. When this occurs the error volts are forced to ground potential returning the sync delay to its nominal value. The colour corrector then rephases to its nearest cycle of subcarrier and the relay is de-energised to allow sync feedback to continue. This action is referred to as 'dumping'.

Sync/subcarrier lock

For NTSC signals the sync pulses and the subcarrier have a locked frequency relationship. It is sometimes said that the subcarrier is 'an odd multiple of half-line frequency'. This is required to interleave the chrominance and luminance spectra and thus avoid interaction between the two.

More precisely for 525 NTSC

$$f_{sc} = \frac{455 \times fl}{2} = 3·57945 \text{ MHz}$$

fl = line frequency = 15·734264 kHz.

For 625 PAL the relationship is more complex.

$$f_{sc} = fl(284 - \tfrac{1}{4}) - \tfrac{1}{2}ff$$

$$ff = 50 \text{ Hz}$$

$$fl = 15·625 \text{ kHz.}$$

This locked relationship is extremely important if the correctors described are to function correctly. It is imperative that the same frequency relationship between subcarrier and sync exists on the recorded composite signal as between station sync and subcarrier during playback. If this is not so then the monochrome corrector would present the colour corrector with a signal in

185

which the tape chrominance and reference subcarrier are continuously changing in phase with respect to each other. The effect is for the signal to be corrected by the colour corrector until the drift between sync and subcarrier accumulates to 180°, when the circuit dumps and skips one cycle.

The effect of an off-locked subcarrier on a live picture is not very noticeable and it is an easy matter to record such a signal. Playback can be achieved only by arranging exactly the same off-locked relationship, which is extremely difficult. Lock detectors therefore are a useful addition to any colour VTR installation.

Velocity error correction (quadruplex)

The monochrome and colour correctors sample the error and apply correction at the start of each line. This correction is then held throughout the line until the next sample, 64 μsec later. If the error changes between samples, correction is not made until the following sync pulse and colour burst. A problem exists in the correction of errors with a large velocity. Servo errors are random and although the disturbances can be large the head motor does not move from or to its correct position at a very fast rate. This is due to the inertia of the head assembly and partly the intentional damping in the servo electronics.

Head to tape geometry, however, causes relatively large velocity errors. This can be seen in Fig. 9.13 which shows a typical error due to the maladjustment of the guide height. If the peak error of the waveform is 400 $n$sec and the error goes from a minimum value to a positive value in half a head sweep (eight lines), the average change per line is

$$\frac{400 \times 10^{-9}}{8} = 50 \ n\text{sec}$$

This will be larger for some lines where the rate of change is greater. For a given corrected line the error may be corrected to within 3 $n$sec, but at the end of the line, 64 μsec later, the error could be 50 ηsec. The subjective effect is colour banding which increases toward the right hand side of the displayed picture. If standard, 75% colour bars are played back, the yellow bar which is on the left hand side of the screen is substantially unaffected, but the blue bar which is on the right hand side of the screen has errors in excess of $\pm 45°$ as can normally be seen in a vector display. The difficulty in correcting for these errors is that a tape reference timing does not exist. Three solutions have been engineered to minimise the problem:

1. Pilot tone.
2. Memory store.
3. Line delay.

Pilot tone (*velocity compensation*). If during the recording process a pilot tone is added to the *FM* signal, the stability or phase of this tone in subsequent playback is a measure of the timing error of the played back video. The frequency of the pilot tone has to be high enough to enable several samples

186

throughout a line but low enough to avoid interference with the *FM* signal. A division of colour subcarrier is convenient and divisions from 4 to 9 are used.

For PAL $4·43 \div 7 = 0·673$ MHz. This pilot tone frequency gives about

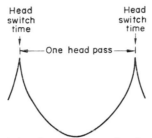

Detail A. Actual time-base error waveform (error caused by misadjustment of vacuum guide height)

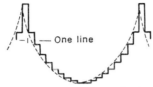

Detail B. Corrector error waveform showing line-by-line correction

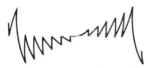

Detail C. Velocity error component remaining (A-B)

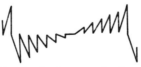

Detail D. Simulated velocity error signal generated by velocity compensator

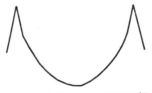

Detail E. Output of velocity compensator (D+B)

Fig. 9.13. The derivation of linear interpolation.

45 cycles per 64 μsec enabling 45 samples per line. On playback this tape reference can then be phase compared to a stable $4·43 \div 7$ to produce a correction signal.

For NTSC $3.58 \div 5 = 0.716$ MHz. This pilot tone also gives about 45 cycles per 63.5 μsec line.

The main disadvantage of this system is that special recordings are required and that the pilot tone, whatever its frequency, adds some extra beat components or moire to the video. For these reasons the memory system is preferred.

Memory store. The object of the memory system is to correct for the velocity errors due to geometry changes only, which constitute the larger proportion of velocity error.

The magnitude of the problem can be seen in Fig. 9.13(b) which shows a comparison of actual error in μsec against the delay in μsec of the delay line. The divergence between the two is a measure of the uncorrected timing error. A sample is made every 64 μsec and the correction held constant between samples. The corrector error voltage therefore is a stepped function with 16 discrete levels, one for each line, which is used to correct the smooth cosine curve. An improvement can be made if the error voltage is interpolated between the discrete levels, changing linearly between samples. This would not follow the curve exactly but would be a good approximation.

The interpolation voltage that needs to be added to the corrector error voltage would be a series of sawtooth ramps whose amplitude and polarity would be determined by the difference in error between the line playing back and the next line. The fundamental problem is to determine what the error is on the following line, this being impossible until that sample is made, by which time it is too late. The solution is found by using a memory, one for each line, which remembers the error between line 1 and 2, line 2 and 3 . . . line 15 and 16, the previous times the head played back. Geometry errors are repetitive, which implies that if the last time the head played back, the error between the two successive lines was $x\mu$sec then, unless the guide moves between scans, the same error will occur on future scans. The error thus stored can now be read one line earlier to determine the sawtooth ramp magnitude and direction. One store is required per line or 16 stores per head; with four heads the total number of stores is 64.

The velocity error compensator is basically a small memory and a computing device which modifies the stepped corrector error to approximate the smooth error function. The interpolated error is then applied to the delay line as a correction voltage in the conventional manner.

A block diagram of a velocity error compensator showing how the stepped error is interpolated is shown in Fig. 9.14. The corrector error is amplified and passed through a subtractor clamp, the object of which is to produce a voltage equal to the difference between the error on two lines. This can be done by applying a positive pulse to $Q5$ at the end of each line and grounding the error signal. The capacitor passes only changes in error and the input to the write gate is a series of pulses whose amplitude represent the differences in error. The store is selected by applying a ground to one side of the selected capacitor. When the write gate is opened the capacitor charges towards the voltage determined by the error pulse amplitude with a time constant CR.

188

With typical values of $R = 100\Omega$
$$C = 1\,\mu F.$$

$$\text{Time constant} = 1 \times 100 \times 10^{-6} = 100\,\mu sec.$$

The time to charge exponentially, in a simple charging circuit, to an aiming potential is $5 \times CR$. Therefore with chosen values, charge time is $500\,\mu sec$. This long charging time is deliberate because the charge accumulated in the store is integrated over many head passes. If the pulse width, $P4$, is $6\,\mu sec$, it would take $\dfrac{500}{6} = 83$ write cycles to load the store, or 83 revolutions of the head which is about one-third of a second. The advantage of doing this is to reduce the effect of false sample errors due to tape dropout and noise, the false sample contributing only one part in 83 of the stored voltage. The only penalty is the speed of operation which takes fractions of a second to settle down after the guide has been moved.

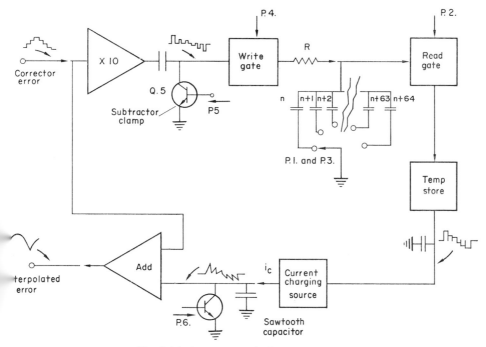

Fig. 9.14. A memory velocity compensator.

The read action is non-destructive, i.e.: the input impedance to the read gate is very high ($>1M\Omega$). For any given line the first operation of the store is to read the accumulated error, which is the estimate for the charge expected at the end of the line. This needs to be done first because the formation of the ramp, which represents the linear interpolation, must start at the beginning of the line. The charge on the selected store is read and stored on a second

189

capacitor which acts as a temporary store. Once this capacitor is charged to the same potential as the read store the read gate can be closed, allowing the write function to operate during the remaining line time.

If the capacitor selected for write is n, during that line $n + 1$ is read. The sequence therefore is Read $n + 1$, Write n, Read $n + 2$. Write $n + 1$ . . . etc. The pulse timings showing the sequence are shown in Fig. 9.15. The voltage on the temporary store acts as a reference potential to a constant current

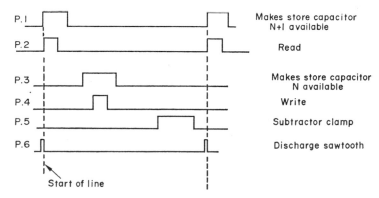

Fig. 9.15. Pulse timing diagram.

charging source for a sawtooth generator, the current (i_c) being proportional to the input voltage. At the end of each line $P6$ turns on $Q6$ and discharges the capacitor. Charging continues at a new rate determined by a new voltage on the temporary store.

The sawtooth ramp, whose peak amplitude should equal the amplitude difference on each step, is now added to the stepped error forming a better approximation to the smooth error curve. Figure 9.13(e).

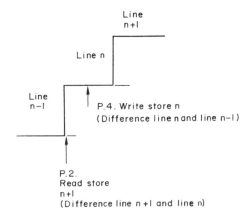

Fig. 9.16. Store read and write sequence.

Two further modifications to the sequence are now necessary and apply to the start and end of a head sweep. For line number one of any head sweep the difference in error from the previous line is of little use because the previous line was from a different head and interpolation between the two errors is meaningless. The write for line 1 therefore, is inhibited. This can most conveniently be done by turning $Q5$ on for all of line 1. This missing error is of no consequence until the end of the head sweep because during line 1 the difference between line 2 and 1 is read, during line 2—line 3 is read . . . etc. during line 15—line 16 is read, during line 16—line 17 read, during line 17 . . . line 18 read. Unfortunately on 625/50 Hz signals line 17 is non-existent and on 525/60 Hz signals line 18 is non existent, this being the line missed

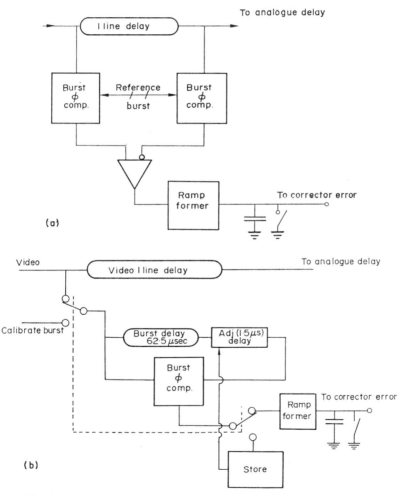

(a)

(b)

Fig. 9.17. (a) *Determination of velocity error using a line delay.* (b) *A self calibrating system.*

by switching to line 1 of the following head. A compromise is reached during the last line (16 or 17) by re-reading store 16 on 625 and 17 on 525. For the last lines of a head sweep on a 625/50 Hz signal the sequence is:

Read 15, write 14, read 16, write 15, read 16, inhibit write 1, i.e.: store 16 read twice. The main advantage of the memory store method is that it can work on all recordings, with no special record process. Moreover, the video is not subjected to any further processing or delay which might add noise or distortion. Its disadvantage is that it can handle only repetitive errors. To remove non-repetitive errors a line delay system is needed.

Line delay. It takes a period of one line to determine the error difference between any two lines. If the video can also be delayed by one line a linear interpolation throughout the line is possible. Two methods are shown in Fig. 9.17 of producing an error difference voltage for the ramp former. In Fig. 9.17(a) use is made of a difference amplifier where the difference in two error samples is formed. A second circuit, shown in Fig. 9.17(b), operates on two colour bursts from two separate lines and uses a burst one line delay, the output of which is the burst from the previous line. Response requirements of the burst delay line are not critical but its timing is very critical, requiring an accuracy better than 1° of subcarrier. This accuracy can be achieved by calibrating the delay once every field during the field blanking interval when velocity compensation is not required. By passing in bursts derived from local subcarrier and known zero velocity any phase error can be measured, stored and used to adjust the delay until correct. During the active field time, the phase differences between tape bursts are made to derive the velocity of the error. A high quality one line delay is of course required for the video

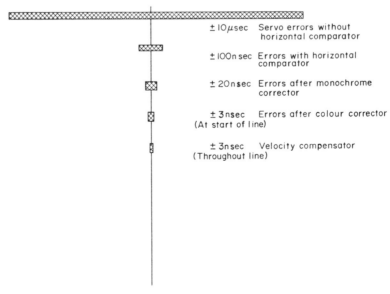

Fig. 9.18. A comparison of timing errors through a V.T.R.

path, which is the main disadvantage of the system. The measurement of velocity, however, is a more accurate one and theoretically most errors are reduced by a factor of 100 by straight line interpolation (see Appendix 18).

Conclusion

The reduction of timing errors is a series of successive attempts to minimise timing errors to within desired limits. Figure 9.18 shows typical orders of magnitude for timing stability through a VTR. This applies to both quadruplex and helical although the use of velocity compensators is normally restricted to quadruplex. Most VTRs use all the methods indicated, but with the use of binary delay switching and their increased range of correction, the horizontal comparator becomes redundant.

References

1. COLEMAN, C. H., *Techniques for multiple generation colour videotapes*. Ampex Corporation, Redwood City, U.S.A.
2. COLEMAN, C. H., *A new technique for time-base stabilization of video recorders*. Ampex Corporation, Redwood City, U.S.A.

10 Colour Correction in CCTV

NTSC colour signals, and PAL signals to a lesser extent, are vulnerable to the phase modulation of the colour sub-carrier caused by time-base instability of the playback signal. It is not possible to completely correct the errors cheaply and some method of reducing the effect of the instability on the chrominance information is required. Numerous methods have been devised each with their own subjective impairment and economic saving. The methods can be grouped into two major categories:

1. Modulation to a more tolerant system.
2. Electronic stabilisation of chrominance errors on playback.

Tolerant systems

SECAM.[1] This is the broadcast colour system of France and the USSR, based on the principle of line sequential transmission of the $R-Y$ and $B-Y$ signals and the use of a line delay or memory in the decoder—'sequential a memoire.'

The chrominance signals are used to frequency-modulate a subcarrier, as shown in Fig. 10.1, which is in turn added to the luminance signal.

The subcarrier frequency is chosen to occupy the upper part of the video spectrum and differs slightly for the two chrominance signals.

On 625

$$F_{R-Y} = 282\,fl = 4\cdot40625 \text{ MHz}$$
$$F_{B-Y} = 272\,fl = 4\cdot250 \text{ MHz}$$

where fl = line frequency = $15\cdot625$ kHz.

194

The deviation of the subcarrier is limited for

the $R-Y$ signal to $+350$ kHz and -500 kHz

and for the $B-Y$ signal to $+500$ kHz and -350 kHz

Even though the frequency deviation is low, SECAM signals are very tolerant towards the phase and frequency modulation experienced in VTR. A 0·15% variation in head speed would cause approximately 6·6 kHz frequency change on a 4·4 MHz carrier. This represents about 0·78% of the

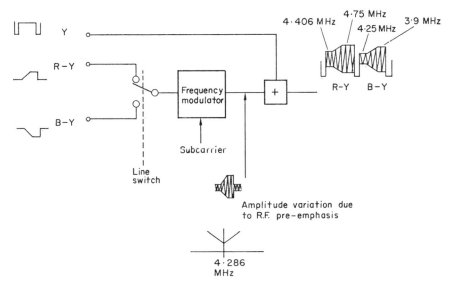

Fig. 10.1. The SECAM coder.

peak–peak deviation of the SECAM signal (850 kHz) or an amplitude variation of 0·78% of the peak value on the demodulated $R-Y$ or $B-Y$ signal.

SECAM signals with different subcarrier frequencies and deviations have been developed for use on 525/60 Hz systems and also with lower subcarrier frequencies for reduced bandwidth recorders. The method becomes expensive if decoding from another standard and recording back again is required. However, if SECAM or RGB signals are available, the system is a good one.

FAM. This method of coding was specifically developed by IRT in Munich,[2] as a low bandwidth system suitable for videotape recording. The system uses a subcarrier of 2·65 MHz which is simultaneously modulated in frequency and amplitude by the $R-Y$ and $B-Y$ signals respectively. The composite signal has a bandwidth of about 3·5 MHz and is developed as shown in Fig. 10.2.

The subcarrier is first frequency-modulated by the $R-Y$ component and the modulator is calibrated for a deviation of ±500 kHz on 100% amplitude colour bars. The amplitude of the frequency-modulated subcarrier is typically

195

0·3 volt and with a *B–Y* signal of 50% amplitude, 100% saturated, the subcarrier is amplitude modulated between 0·07 volts and 0·53 volts, a depth of modulation equal to 0·766. This should not exceed unity as a complete suppression of the carrier would distort the *FM* signal; a value of 0·766 or 76·6% is satisfactory.

For 100% amplitude bars the depth of modulation would be 1·53 which is of course not possible and the amplitudes of the *B–Y* and *R–Y* signals are limited to their 50% values, a limitation which in practice is not too severe. The final chrominance signal therefore has a peak frequency deviation of

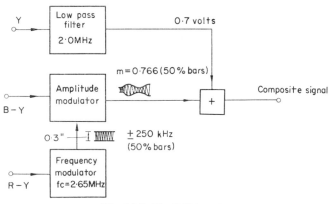

Fig. 10.2. The FAM coder.

±250 kHz (a mod index of 0·25 radians for a 1 MHz *R–Y* signal) and a peak amplitude deviation of about 75%.

If the *R–Y* and *B–Y* signals are bandwidth restricted to about 0·6 MHz, the chrominance signal bandwidth would be 1·7 MHz {2(*fd* + *fm*)} centred on 2·65 MHz, the upper limit being 3·5 MHz.

The FAM system is also tolerant to time base errors with a 0·15% speed change on 2·65 MHz causing a 4 kHz shift which represents 0·8% of 500 kHz.

The signal however requires a very tight tolerance on the amplitude response of the signal path. Any amplitude distortion including a non-unity gain affects not only the luminance signal causing saturation errors but also the *B–Y* amplitude causing hue errors.

Sequential coding. The time sequential system can operate on either the RGB signals, as shown in Fig. 10.3 or on the *Y*, *R–Y* and *B–Y* signals. The three signals are formed into one signal by sequentially operating three input switches and passing only one of the three signals. This composite signal can then be recorded. The three signals can be obtained simultaneously on playback by means of line delay stores and a commutating switch. The system can be either line sequential or field sequential although the former is preferred because of the smaller delays. The most noticeable distortion is caused by the loss of two-thirds of the original information and on a line sequential system this results in a loss of vertical resolution and disturbing beat patterns

196

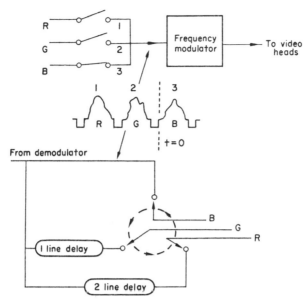

Fig. 10.3. Line sequential coding and decoding.

on vertical movement of the picture. This method of recording is not in common use.

Electronic stabilisation

To understand the various methods used to stabilise the chrominance errors it is first necessary to investigate the effect of time base errors on the decoding of NTSC and PAL colour signals.

The phase of the video chroma represents the hue of the transmitted colour and this is detected by sampling the instantaneous value of the chroma at two points, 90° apart, at which it is equal to the amplitude of the $R-Y$ and $B-Y$ components (see Fig. 10.4).

The chroma phase changes with the relative amplitudes of $R-Y$ and $B-Y$ and the reference subcarrier, normally derived from the colour burst, is regarded as being stable. If the video and hence the chroma is subjected to random timing displacements, this would be mis-interpreted as hue changes in the original scene. The accuracy of phase on playback would have to be within $\pm10°$ or ±6 nsec for a tolerable impairment.

PAL decoding with a one line delay improves performance in the presence of phase errors although errors better than $\pm40°$ or 24 nsec are still required.

If the errors on the video cannot be reduced the only solution is to reduce their effect on the chrominance signals. One such method is to produce a reference subcarrier that has an identical phase error modulation to the chroma, sometimes called a 'sympathetic reference'. If this is used to sample

197

the chroma the phase difference between the two signals is due only to the wanted phase modulation.

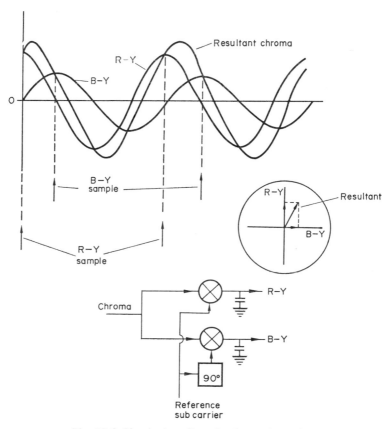

Fig. 10.4. Simple decoding of colour sub-carrier.

Pilot tone

One method of producing a sympathetic reference is to produce a pilot tone which is added to the *FM* signal during record.

On playback this can be separated from the *RF* signal and will contain all the time base variations of the video. It is not possible to make the pilot tone the same frequency as the subcarrier as this would interfere with the *FM* signal and cause severe moire. The pilot tone frequency must be outside the pass-band of the *FM* signal and it is convenient to place it somewhere between 500–700 kHz. The pilot frequency is produced during record by dividing the standard subcarrier by a suitable multiple, as shown in Fig. 10.5, with the exact multiple dependent on the video system response and chosen *FM* standards.

198

On 625/50 Hz PAL.

$$4.43 \div 6 = 738 \text{ kHz}$$
$$\div 7 = 634 \text{ kHz}$$
$$\div 8 = 554 \text{ kHz}$$
$$\div 9 = 493 \text{ kHz}$$

On 525/60 Hz NTSC

$$3.58 \div 5 = 716 \text{ kHz}$$
$$\div 6 = 596 \text{ kHz}$$
$$\div 7 = 511 \text{ kHz}$$
$$\div 8 = 447 \text{ kHz}$$

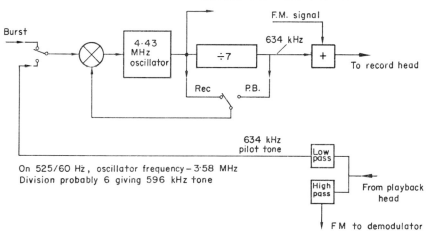

Fig. 10.5. Record and playback of the pilot tone.

On playback the pilot can be separated to lock an a.f.c. oscillator to the correct subcarrier frequency.

In Fig. 10.5 the oscillator is the same as that used during record although this is not always done.

If the time constant of the a.f.c. oscillator is short the subcarrier will have the same timing errors as the chroma and can be used to decode the signal or hetrodyned with it as described later.

Burst locked oscillator

A continuous sympathetic reference can also be derived from an a.f.c. oscillator, with a short time constant, locked to the tape video burst. The only restriction being that the velocity of error is small enough to avoid any significant phase change over a line period. Although this reference does not give a measure of timing as often as the pilot tone, it does have the advantage of not requiring a special record process.

Methods of stabilisation

Decode–encode. The decoding of the chroma signal has already been briefly described. However, if a composite PAL or NTSC signal output is required, re-encoding with a stable local crystal oscillator is necessary. The full corrector is shown in Fig. 10.6. If the decoding of the chroma is on the $B-Y$ and $R-Y$ axis, the two outputs of the decoder would represent the weighted values of the $B-Y$ and $R-Y$ chrominance signal. These two signals are re-coded onto a stable subcarrier and added back to the luminance signal. The output signal

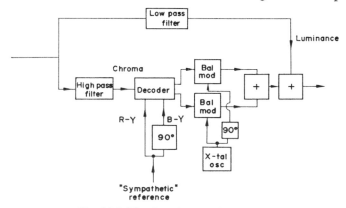

Fig. 10.6. The decode-encode corrector.

of the corrector, therefore, is an unstable video signal with a stable subcarrier frequency. The video would be standard in all respects except for the sync/subcarrier relationship which would not of course be locked.

Two interesting characteristics of the circuit should be noted. First, the decoding need not be on the $R-Y$ and $B-Y$ axis and the nominal phase of the unstable reference is of little consequence. A rotation of the decode axis simply alters the coder axis and rotates the output phase of the coder. If the burst is decoded and coded along with the chroma, the relative phase between burst and chroma is fixed.

The second point, which is an extension of the first, is that the swinging burst and the phase alternation on PAL signals is accommodated by the circuit with no modifications.

This can be seen in Fig. 10.7. It should be noted that both the unstable reference and the crystal oscillator are continuous and are not phase alternated.

Heterodyne. The heterodyne method shown in Fig. 10.8 also requires a sympathetic reference, which follows the tape video instability, and a local stable reference subcarrier. With a combination of heterodyne mixing and filtering a stable chroma signal can be obtained. To facilitate filtering a third frequency, sometimes a multiple of the stable local oscillator, is generated. This would typically be $(2 \cdot 5 - 3 \cdot 5) f_c$ where:

$$f_c = \text{local stable oscillator}$$

If the other components from Fig. 10.8 are:

f_{ch} — stable video chroma

f_{ch}' — unstable video chroma on playback $(f_{\text{ch}} + \Delta f)$

$f_{\text{c}}' =$ tape sympathetic reference $(f_{\text{c}} + \Delta f)$, derived from pilot tone or burst locked oscillator,

the major outputs of each mixer, with the chosen products are as in Table 11.

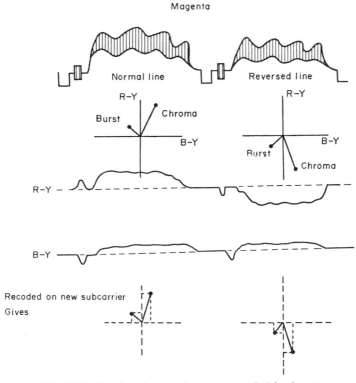

Fig. 10.7. The decode-encode process on P.A.L. signal.

TABLE 11

Mixer	Major products	Filter	Product
A	$nf_{\text{o}} - f_{\text{o}}$ $nf_{\text{o}} + f_{\text{o}}$	High pass	$(nf_{\text{o}} + f_{\text{o}})$
B	$nf_{\text{o}} - f_{\text{o}}'$ $nf_{\text{o}} + f_{\text{o}}'$	High pass	$(nf_{\text{o}} + f_{\text{o}}')$
C	$(nf_{\text{o}} + f_{\text{o}}) - f_{\text{ch}}'$ $(nf_{\text{o}} + f_{\text{o}}) + f_{\text{ch}}'$	High pass	$(nf_{\text{o}} + f_{\text{o}} + f_{\text{ch}}')$
D	$(nf_{\text{o}} + f_{\text{o}} + f_{\text{ch}}') - (nf_{\text{o}} + f_{\text{o}}')$ $(nf_{\text{o}} + f_{\text{o}} + f_{\text{ch}}') + (nf_{\text{o}} + f_{\text{o}}')$	Low pass	$f_{\text{o}} + f_{\text{ch}}' - f_{\text{o}}'$

The final product is

$$nf_c + f_c + f_{ch}' - nf_c - f_c'$$
$$= f_c + f_{ch}' - f_c'$$

but $\quad\quad f_{ch}' = f_{ch} + \Delta f$

and $\quad\quad f_c' = f_c + \Delta f$

$\therefore$ Final product $\quad = f_c + f_{ch} + \Delta f - f_c - \Delta f$
$$= f_{ch}$$

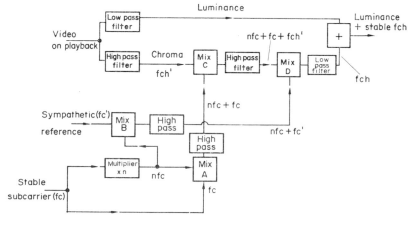

$\cdot$ fc' = fc + Δf
fch' = fch + Δf

Fig. 10.8. Heterodyne correction.

If the local oscillator is from a crystal then f_{ch} would not have an exact locked relationship with tape sync.

Two methods of correction and two methods of obtaining a sympathetic reference have been described. They can be combined to produce one of four possible combinations in any recorder,[5] any one of which is in common use:

Sympathetic reference.	Correction method
Burst locked oscillator	Heterodyne
Pilot-tone	Decode–Encode

Bandwidth reduction

On broadcast NTSC, PAL and SECAM signals the chrominance information is carried on a subcarrier which is positioned in the upper part of the video band.

202

For this reason the recording of these signals necessitates a full bandwidth signal path, an expensive luxury for CCTV applications. It is however quite feasible to re-position the chrominance information on a subcarrier lower down the band prior to recording.[4] A lower frequency subcarrier is obviously subjectively more noticeable although a similar locked relationship between sync and subcarrier to the broadcast standard does help to minimise its subjective effect.

A lower frequency chroma signal can be obtained by beating the higher frequency signal with a stable frequency and taking the difference product. The sync/subcarrier relationship can be preserved by making the stable frequency an exact multiple of horizontal line frequency. The chosen value of the lower subcarrier frequency should be as high as the pass-band of the recorder will permit, allowing for the upper side-band of the chrominance signal.

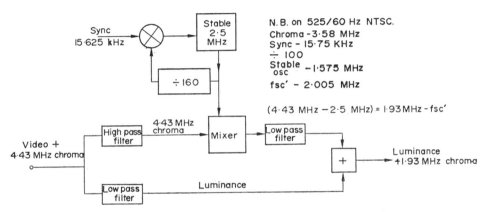

Fig. 10.9. Reduced bandwidth colour signals for 625/50 Hz P.A.L. system.

If the chrominance signal is bandwidth reduced to 0·5 MHz and the composite signal bandwidth is restricted to 2·5 MHz, the new subcarrier frequency (f_{sc}') must be about 2·0 MHz. Figure 10.9 shows a system of producing a new subcarrier at 1·93 MHz from a 625/50 Hz system with a 4·43 MHz subcarrier. A 2·5 MHz stable frequency is produced by multiplying the horizontal line sync by 160.

For 625/50 Hz Broadcast signal

$$f_{sc} = (284 - 1/4)f_h + 25\ \text{Hz} = 4\cdot43\ \text{MHz}$$

where f_h = horizontal line frequency = 15·625 kHz

$$f_{sc}' = (284 - 1/4)f_h + 25\ \text{Hz} - 160 f_h$$
$$= (124 - 1/4)f_h + 25\ \text{Hz} = 1\cdot93\ \text{MHz}.$$

For a 525/60 Hz Broadcast signal

A typical stable beat frequency would be 1·575 MHz (100 × f_h)

$$f_{sc} = (228 - 1/2)f_h = 3·58 \text{ MHz}$$
$$f_{sc}' = (128 - 1/2)f_h = 2·005 \text{ MHz}$$

On playback the perceptibility of the subcarrier could be further reduced on NTSC signals by adding to the luminance signal the subcarrier from the previous line. On NTSC this would give a complete cancellation. On PAL two lines of delay would be required. A reduction in vertical resolution results although only on high frequency components. The delay lines used should be exactly one horizontal line and one important limitation is the requirement that the playback video line time must be held to within very close limits. This requirement normally necessitates the use of a capstan servo. The method of colour correction can be any of those described.

Pilot chroma carrier

Another technique allowing a reduction of the video bandwidth is to separate the chroma from the luminance and convert the chroma subcarrier to a frequency below the *FM* passband, say 560 kHz.

Instead of adding this chroma signal with a lower subcarrier back on to the luminance signal it is added to the *FM* signal and recorded with it.

The distortion on the chroma signal is less than might be expected because the *FM* signal acts as a bias frequency. The only problem is that a pilot tone for colour correction cannot be used because the space for it has been used up by the chroma pilot carrier.

A very novel method of regenerating the correct 4·43 MHz on playback by heterodyning the lower frequency chroma with a stable 4·43 MHz and a sync locked oscillator can be used with the added advantage of cancelling out timing errors.

A block-diagram for a PAL recorder is shown in Fig. 10.10 and will be described.

Record mode. During record a stable reference subcarrier, derived from the input video burst, is mixed with the output of an oscillator locked to 36 times the horizontal sync frequency.

MIXER A output:
    4·43 MHz + 0·5625 MHz — High pass — 4·99 MHz
    4·43 MHz − 0·5625 MHz

MIXER B output:
    4·99 MHz + f_{ch}
    4·99 MHz − f_{ch} — Low pass —
    Chroma on a 562·5 kHz carrier (f_{ch}')

This reduced subcarrier chroma signal is added to (not modulated by) the *FM* signal prior to recording.

Playback mode. On playback the *FM* signal and the chrominance signal are easily separated by filtering. The horizontal sync on the demodulated luminance signal and the carrier of the chrominance signal are both phase modulated by the timing instability of the VTR.

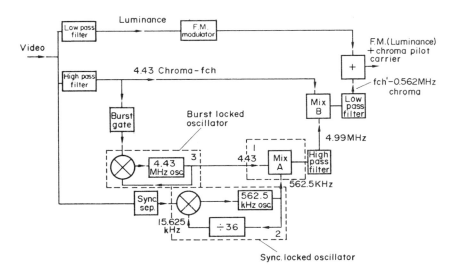

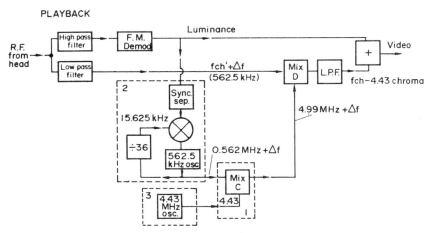

Fig. 10.10. Chroma pilot carrier system.

To remove these errors on the chrominance signal it is processed in the following way. An a.f.c. oscillator with a short time constant is locked to 36 times tape video sync to produce $562 \cdot 5$ kHz $+ \Delta f$, where Δf is the unwanted modulation. This is mixed with a stable $4 \cdot 43$ MHz to produce a $4 \cdot 99$ MHz also with modulation.

MIXER C output:

$$4.43 \text{ MHz} + (0.562 + \Delta f) \text{ MHz} \rightarrow \text{High pass} - 4.99 \text{ MHz} + \Delta f$$
$$4.43 \text{ MHz} - (0.562 + \Delta f) \text{ MHz}$$

The low frequency chrominance information and 4·99 MHz + Δf are now mixed.

MIXER D output:

$$(4.99 + \Delta f) \text{ MHz} + (f_{ch}' + \Delta f) \text{ MHz}$$
$$(4.99 + \Delta f) \text{ MHz} - (f_{ch}' + \Delta f) \text{ MHz} - \text{Low pass} - f_{ch}$$

where f_{ch}' — Low frequency chroma — 0·562 MHz
f_{ch} — High frequency chroma — 4·43 MHz

The Δf component is therefore cancelled on the output chroma.

The block diagram looks quite involved, but it should be noted that several elements of the circuit used in record can also be used in playback. For instance Mixer A in record can be used for Mixer C in playback, the sync locked oscillator is also common and the burst locked oscillator can free run on playback to provide a stable 4·43 MHz. This system is becoming very popular on $\frac{1}{2}$ in and $\frac{3}{4}$ in reel–reel and cassette formats.

Conclusion

Several techniques that are in common use in CCTV recorders have been described and permutations can be made to provide many combinations.

For systems with RGB signal distribution the choice would be restricted to using one of the tolerant colour systems.

Most applications however require to record broadcast signals, probably derived from a receiver or tuner, and this is where the number of combinations escalate.

For example:

The system change methods

1. NTSC	TO	SECAM
2. PAL	TO	SECAM
3. NTSC	TO	FAM
4. PAL	TO	FAM
5. NTSC	TO	LINE SEQUENTIAL RGB
6. PAL	TO	LINE SEQUENTIAL RGB

Time base error compensation methods
7. Decode–encode with burst locked oscillator ⎫
8. Decode–encode with pilot tone ⎬ Full bandwidth
9. Heterodyne with burst locked oscillator ⎭ systems.
10. Heterodyne with pilot tone
11. Reduced bandwidth systems with reduced subcarrier frequency, colour correction same as 7, 8, 9 or 10.

12. Chroma-pilot carrier with heterodyne correction and sync locked oscillator.

13. Chroma-pilot carrier with heterodyne correction and burst locked oscillator.

14. Chroma-pilot carrier with decode–encode correction and burst locked oscillator.

The wide variety of methods used is, to say the least, confusing and adds to the complexity of deriving a common international standard.

In practice methods 7, 8 and 10 are in common use on one-inch formats while method 12 is very common on $\frac{1}{2}$ in and $\frac{3}{4}$ in formats. Recorders using combinations 1, 2, 3 and 4 have been produced and are still in use although they are becoming less popular, while combinations 5, 6, 9, 13, 14 have, to the author's knowledge, existed only in development laboratories.

References

1. COMPAGNIE FRANCAISE DE TELEVISION, *Secam colour T.V. system*, 19 Rue Ernest-Cognacq, 92 Nevallois-Perret.
2. MAYER, N., NOLOCH, G., MOLL, G., FAM, *Rundfunktechnislee Mittellungen*, Vol. 13 (1969) n. 4. 159–169
3. SIMS, H. V., *Principles of PAL Colour Television*, Butterworth.
4. WESSELS, J. H., *A simple colour videotape recording system*, Phillips Research Laboratory.
5. SALTER, M. T. A., *Colour TV Recording on Ampex 1 in format* Ampex G. B. Ltd., Reading, England.
6. BRUCH, DR. W., Selected Papers II P.A.L., Grundlagen-Entwicklung, Hanover, Telefunken A.G.
7. BRUCH, DR. W., Neve methoden der Fanbbildanfzeichnung auf einfachen Magnetoband-genoetan (TRIPAL), *Telefunken-Zeitung*, 40 No. 3, 1967.

11 Cassettes and Cartridges

Audio tape recording started with reel to reel recorders where the tape is rewound on to the feed spool for storage. In the late 60s, it was found that a more convenient method of storing tape was in a cassette with two self contained spools. The minimum of expertise is required to lace-up the tape, a simple plug-in action, and the tape can be left at any point for subsequent playback. Video recorders also started with a reel to reel transport and a similar trend towards cassettes evolved.

However, the broadcaster and the CCTV user have different requirements for the cassette. For CCTV applications ease of use and foolproof operation are the main advantages with the added bonus of tape protection. The broadcaster requires the further facility of playing back several inserts or advertisements without interruption and in any pre-selected order.

Broadcast cassettes

For convenience, the record track format used on broadcast cassettes is the same as reel to reel quadruplex recorders. As the audio and video track spacing are identical, this allows complete interchange between machines.

It is normal, for broadcast requirements, to have two tape transports to enable A–B roll techniques. While transport A is playing back B is searching out the next cassette, lacing up and cueing at the correct start point. At the end of the A sequence, B rolls and A rewinds, changes its cassette and cues up to the correct start point. A typical arrangement can be seen in Fig. 11.1. The cassettes, up to 24, are held in a drum and can be loaded on to either transport A or B automatically. Associated with each transport are pre-amplifiers and head switchers which provide the required level of continuous *RF*.

The rest of the electronics for demodulation and time-base correction need not be duplicated because only one transport will be playing back at any instant. A record facility can be added to the system with the addition of one shared *FM* modulator and two sets of record electronics. The arrangement shown also allows dubbing from one transport to the other.

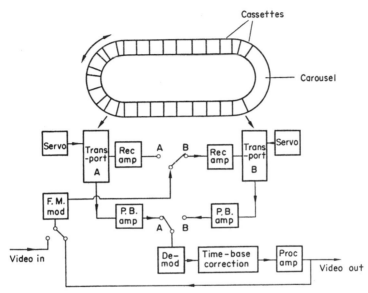

Fig. 11.1. A typical broadcast cassette system.

Tape Format. Although the video and audio track dimensions are the same, additional cue track information is required for the cueing of the parking position of the tape and the remote starting of the following sequence at the end of the tape. Unfortunately, international agreement has not yet been reached and slight differences exist among standards in use. Figure 11.2 shows

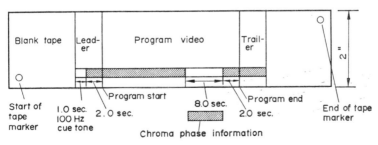

Fig. 11.2. The cassette tape format.

209

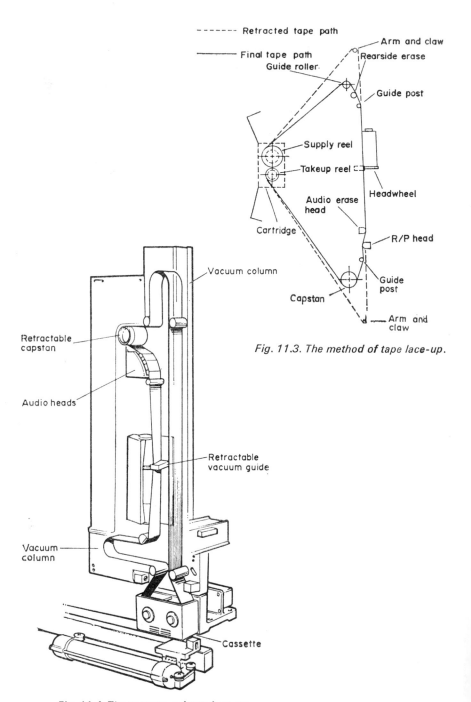

------ Retracted tape path

———— Final tape path

Guide roller.

Arm and claw

Rearside erase

Guide post

Supply reel

Takeup reel

Audio erase head

Headwheel

Cartridge

R/P head

Capstan

Guide post

Arm and claw

Fig. 11.3. The method of tape lace-up.

Vacuum column

Retractable capstan

Audio heads

Retractable vacuum guide

Vacuum column

Cassette

Fig. 11.4. The vacuum column lace-up.

the type of format in common use. The start and stop tones are in the form of bursts of tone on the cue track.

The tones are supplemented by start and end of tape markers, composed of reflective tabs, these can be sensed to avoid complete removal of tape from cassette.

The rest of the cue track is free for digital address codes, programme idents or pre-determined set-up levels for the playback controls. The minimum length of the programme video is two seconds with a maximum cassette capacity of six minutes on the 15 i.p.s. standard. The minimum time for uninterrupted A–B roll sequences is longer than the minimum programme time, as it must be remembered that the duration of a play sequence on A must be greater than the time it takes to stop B tape, rewind, change the cassette, lace the tape, cue up to start point, start and lock-up in sync. This total time depends on the tape transport design, the television line standard and the amount of tape to be rewound on the B transport. A typical timing sequence could be as follows:

Stop and un-lace the tape	1·9 seconds
*Rewind (60 seconds of tape)	2·5 seconds
Change cassette	2·7 seconds
Lace-up	1·3 seconds
Cue	1·3 seconds
Start and lock-up in sync (525/60 Hz)	0·2 seconds
Total	9·9 seconds

* An extra one second is required for each additional minute of tape. Very often the rewind can be inhibited to reduce the cycle time by 2·5 seconds; this can be useful although it requires off-line rewind before the cassette can be used again.

Tape lace-up. The tape path of a cassette recorder is obviously similar to a reel–reel arrangement, because the audio head to video head spacing and the canoe dimensions must be identical to provide interchange. Two methods are in use to extract the tape from the cassette and position it around the guides and head assemblies. Figure 11.3 shows a method where the tape is pulled from the cassette by means of an arm and claw mechanism and slotted into its correct position. A second approach is shown in Fig. 11.4 where, during lace-up, the capstan and vacuum guide are retracted to a position below the baseplate. The tape is then literally sucked out of the cassette by a vacuum to a position around the edges of the transport and across the heads. The capstan and the video tape guide then revert to their normal play positions.

The helical cassette

The helical cassette recorder has one transport and the cassette itself contains enough tape for 60 minutes, 45 minutes or 30 minutes playing time.

Even with the slower tape speeds of helical recorders, it is difficult to contain all the tape on two spools in a compact package. Three methods of containing the tape are in common use:

1. A cassette with two reels in the same plane.
2. A cassette with two reels stacked vertically.
3. A cartridge with a single reel and a leader tape.

Method number 1 is used by the Japanese industry with $\frac{3}{4}$ in (19 mm) wide tape. The resulting cassette with 12 cm diameter reel size becomes 140 × 221 × 32 mm.

Method number 2 is used in Europe and one arrangement is the VCR (video cassette recorder) system which mounts the two spools on top of each other. With a tape width of $\frac{1}{2}$ in, the overall dimensions of the cassette are $5\frac{5}{8}$ in (143·3 mm) × 5 in (127 mm) × $1\frac{5}{8}$ in (41·03 mm), see Fig. 11.5. The angle of rise of the tape as it traverses from the lower spool to the upper spool provides the correct rise when wrapped around the drum scanner.

The method of extracting the tape and wrapping it around the drum can be seen in Fig. 11.6. The drum is mounted on a rotating platform. Also on the platform are two guide pins (P) which are positioned behind the tape when the cassette is plugged in. To lace the tape around the drum, the platform rotates clockwise to take-up the position shown in Fig. 11.6(b). The tape has now a wrap in excess of 180° which is sufficient for a two-headed machine.

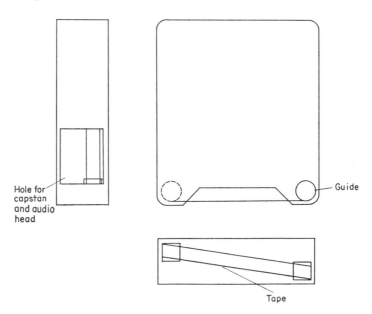

Hole for capstan and audio head

Guide

Tape

Fig. 11.5. The V.C.R. cassette.

The capstan pinch roller and the audio heads also move into the position shown through the cut out in the cassette cover.

End of tape sensors, are required to avoid the tape being run off the spools. These are provided by a highly reflective adhesive tab which can be sensed with a light source and photo-cell.

Self-lacing cartridges (helical). Most of the advantages of a two reel cassette can be obtained with a self-lacing single reel cartridge. The cartridge is

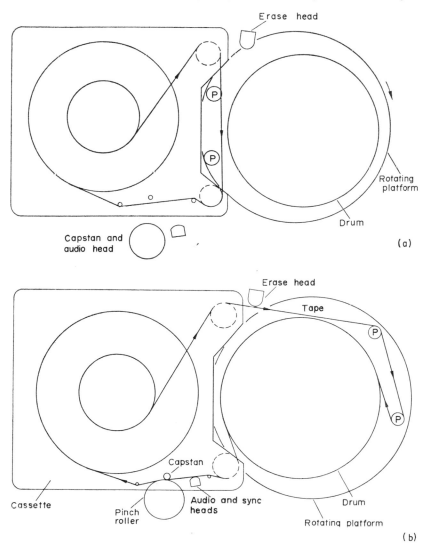

Fig. 11.6. (a) *Cassette loaded ready to lace prior to rotation of drum platform.*
(b) *Cassette loaded and tape laced after clockwise rotation of drum platform.*

similar to a conventional reel of tape except for the leader which is normally made of a thicker and more rigid piece of p.v.c. or similar material. This facilitates a self lacing action which is provided by rollers at strategic positions around the transport. The advantages of a single reel is that the overall volume of the tape package is reduced. The disadvantage is that the tape must be rewound to remove the cartridge, which can be annoying if it is halfway through a programme which one wishes to continue at a later stage.

One method of overcoming this problem is to provide automatic cueing and search facilities. Methods used vary, but one simple procedure is to record on a cue track a continuous tone, say 1 kHz, during the playback of the tape. This tone then over-records an existing tone. If the tape is stopped, a portion of erased track exists because of the spacing between the erase track and record head. This can be increased by leaving the erase on for a short period in rewind. The gap can be detected when spooling the tape.

When the tape is laced up for a second playing, the tape can be spooled in fast forward until an automatic level detector senses the erased section and stops the tape in the correct position. When play is selected the gap is filled with a 1 kHz tone. Whatever method is used, it is important that all previous cues are removed.

Conclusion

Cassettes and cartridges are here to stay. The final standardised arrangements are yet to be decided on, and only after exhaustive experience in the field, of existing and future types, can decisions really be made.

References

1. FOERSTER, G., *Technical aspects of the Phillips VCR System*, 7th ITS, Montreux, 1971.
2. JONGELIE, K., *Magnetic Recording system*, 7th ITS, Montreux, 1971.
3. HEMMINGS, A. J., The philosophy, markets and future of a video cassette system. *RTS Journal*, March/April 1972.
4. Instavideo Recorder system, Ampex *Readout*, Vol. 10, No. 3.
5. ZACCARIN, P., C. B. B. WOOD., *Video player and recorder systems for home use*, EBU Tech. 3093-E.
6. KIHAR, N., Colour cassette system for the NTSC and Japanese colour-television standards, *EBU Technical Review*, No. 125, February 1971.

12 Editing

The requirements of editing videotape range from the removal of slight production errors to the complete assembly of a program from individual shots or sequences. The object of this chapter is to detail the technical requirements of recorders and equipment needed to achieve this. Although there is little information, outside the professional sphere, on artistic techniques it is not the intention to cover them in this chapter. Editing has progressed from the physical cutting of the tape to electronic editing (sequenced switching to the record mode), the semi-automatic programming of electronic editing and finally the fully automatic random access editing.

Physical editing

Videotape, like film, can be cut at the end of a chosen scene and spliced on to the start of a new scene. Also like film it is important to cut synchronously. A disturbance in the servo-mechanisms would result if a cut was made from the end of one frame to the centre of another. In film a physical picture and sprocket holes are available to help the editor. On videotape neither of these are present and a system of determining the frame position has been developed. Iron carbonyl powder, with a particle size from 3 to 5 μm, is suspended in a volatile liquid such as Freon TF and is coated on the control track of the tape. The particles tend to cluster around points of maximum magnetisation and the edit pulse becomes visible as the liquid evaporates. This edit pulse can be used as a reference point although its actual position with respect to the TV frame on tape varies with the control track head position. See Figs. 4.2, 4.6 and 3.4.

215

Quadruplex. The effect of a splice between the guard bands of a quadruplex tape is similar to a straight 'video-cut'. This splice can be made anywhere although subjectively it is preferable to make it during the field blanking. On the 525/60 Hz standard this is in the guard band above the edit pulse while on the 625/50 Hz standard the splice should be made six tracks back (see Fig. 3.4). As far as the synchronisation of playback is concerned the splice can be made anywhere as long as the exit point of the old scene is the same as the entrance point of the new scene. If this is not done then a discontinuity in the video signal and control track signal will occur causing the

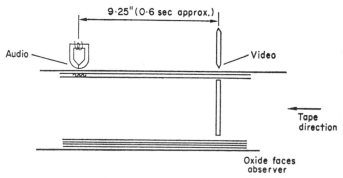

Fig. 12.1. Audio displacement.

machine to mistrack and re-phase during playback. The physical position of the video on the lateral tracks is also important if an error in horizontal timing is to be avoided. The tolerance of ±1·3 mm is in this respect a little wide because it would cause an error of ±31·6 μsec (Appendix 3.1.) If good splices are required a station would keep these errors to within ±0·13 mm (±3·16 μsec).

When the edit pulse has been developed on both the ends of the tape to be joined they are mounted in a splicing fixture which facilitates accurate cutting in the required guard band and the physical butt join of the two pieces with a very thin (0·004–0·0045 in) pressure sensitive adhesive tape.

The audio on a quadruplex tape is recorded 9·25 in downstream from the video. This distance represents about 0·6 sec and creates problems in deciding where to cut. The problem can be seen in Fig. 12.1. Suppose a cut is required at the instant where, on the new scene, a hammer strikes an object. If the cut is made just prior to the audio occurrence, the video cut is 0·6 sec early. If the cut is made just prior to the video occurrence, the audio is lost.

An L shaped cut is impracticable and under such circumstances the audio must be lifted and edited separately on an audio recorder and re-recorded over the splice.

Helical. It is not possible to splice in the guard band of a helical tape although it is quite feasible to cut at right angles to the tape edge. As for quadruplex, the cut must be synchronous and the development of the control track provides the reference.

216

The effect of the splice is different from quadruplex and instead of a cut transition the effect is that of a vertical wipe. It can be seen from Fig. 12.2 that the direction of the wipe depends on the relative head to tape direction. For opposing directions the wipe is up and a down wipe is created if the tape and head move in the same direction. The time of wipe depends on the time taken for the splice to travel around the drum scanner. With a drum circumference of 16 in and a tape speed of 10 i.p.s. the wipe would take 1·6 sec. The technique is useful though obviously limited.

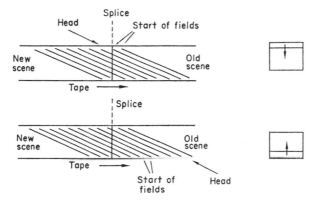

Fig. 12.2. The direction of wipe for a splice on helical format.

General hints. Physical editing requires extreme care and expertise on behalf of the editor and mistakes are normally disastrous. It is expensive because of the time taken in man and machine hours and the fact that it is inadvisable to use the tape again for recording.

Its only advantage is that the final product is still a first generation recording without the deterioration of quality caused by successive dubbing.

The following procedure should be adopted in all cases:

1. Handle the tape with care and avoid touching the surface of the tape.
2. Keep all equipment clean and demagnetised. Airborne dust particles deposited on the surface of the tape will inevitably cause drop-outs.
3. Align the tape accurately to form a butt join without a gap or overlap and ensure that the longitudinal edges are aligned.
4. Apply adequate pressure to the adhesive tape.

Electronic editing

An electronic edit is a controlled switch from the playback of one scene to the record of the next scene in such a manner that synchronism is maintained over the splice point. The new scene can come from another VTR, telecine or live from the studio.

Several functions of the machine need to be controlled during the splice,

217

in particular the capstan servo, erase current, *RF* drive current and head servo. The servos must be controlled to ensure that a rapid phase change does not occur when the record is initiated and a mode change takes place. The timing of the erase turn on and *RF* turn on must be controlled and synchronised to ensure the minimum of overlap and the absence of an unrecorded gap between scenes.

Capstan control during editing. In VTRs with a capstan servo the capstan's mode of operation differs between record and playback. During record the capstan provides the nominal tape speed while in playback it controls the tracking phase with respect to the head. During an electronic edit two methods of control can be used—insert and assemble or add-on—each with their own advantages.

Insert Mode. In this mode the capstan is kept in the playback condition at all times, where it is controlled from a comparison of control track with head tachometer pulse. It is extremely useful where a synchronous ingoing splice and outgoing splice is required, because the new tracks are recorded in exactly the same position as the old tracks. It is therefore possible to insert a new scene in the place of an old one, hence its name.

The disadvantage of the insert mode is that a control track is required over the entire length of programme to be assembled. If a one hour programme is to be made up, a tape with one hour of continuous recording is required as a base for the material. This can be time consuming.

If a series of scenes is to be assembled, it is only required to produce an ingoing splice with a slight overlap at the end of a scene for the next splice. In such a mode it is possible to lay down the control track as one proceeds.

Assemble or add-on mode. In this mode the capstan smoothly transits from a phase control of the tape to a velocity control at the time of splice and the control track head is energised to record a new control track (derived from the head tachometer and frame pulse in the same way as in record) at the same instant. Care must be taken not to cause the capstan to accelerate suddenly by the changing phase of the oscillator. Two methods are in common use as shown in Fig. 12.3.

Method (a) allows the controlled oscillator to be controlled up to the splice point when the error control voltage is grounded and the oscillator is allowed to free run to provide the correct nominal tape speed. For the minimum disturbance the error voltage prior to grounding should be zero volts and the oscillator should be adjusted in normal play for this to be so. At the same instant the control track head should switch to record.

Method (b) does not require prior adjustment of the oscillator and is used on most modern servos. The capstan simply reverts to its normal record mode but to allow this certain precautions are taken. At the point of transition the oscillator is liable to change phase by up to 180°. To minimise the absolute timing error the oscillator frequency is made higher in frequency to the head tachometer rate (ft).

218

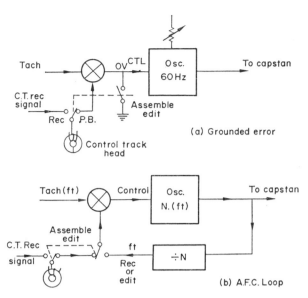

Fig. 12.3. Methods of capstan control in assemble editing.

Figure 7.16 shows that a typical oscillator frequency could be 46·08 kHz with $N = 192$ and ft $= 240$ Hz on the 525/60 Hz standard. The maximum error due to oscillator drift therefore would be half the periodic time of the oscillator frequency.

$$\text{Error} = \frac{1}{2 \times 46·08} \times 10^{-3} = 0·018 \text{ msec.}$$

This compares with an error of 8·33 msec if the oscillator frequency were 60 Hz.

Erase and RF turn-on

The problem of synchronising erase and *RF* drive is created by the physical distance between the erase and video record heads. The problem and solutions are somewhat different on helical and quadruplex and it is worthwhile treating them separately.

Helical editing. The normal erase head gap on a helical recorder is at right angles to the edge of the tape and the tape is erased prior to entering the drum scanner assembly. When an edit is initiated it is impossible for the conventional head to erase between the guard band.

One solution is to provide an extra flying erase head mounted on the same disc as the video head but preceding it by about 30°. The erase frequency, which must be higher than the record signal, and is normally in excess of 15 MHz, is switched on or off a few milliseconds before record drive. The gap width of the erase head encompasses the track and guard band and the

219

plane of the head is mounted slightly off centre to the video head to allow for the tape movement over 30° rotation.

If a flying erase head is not fitted it is still possible to edit with a minor but quite acceptable impairment of the picture quality. The method relies on the fact that the *FM* record signal saturates the tape and almost erases any signal previously recorded.

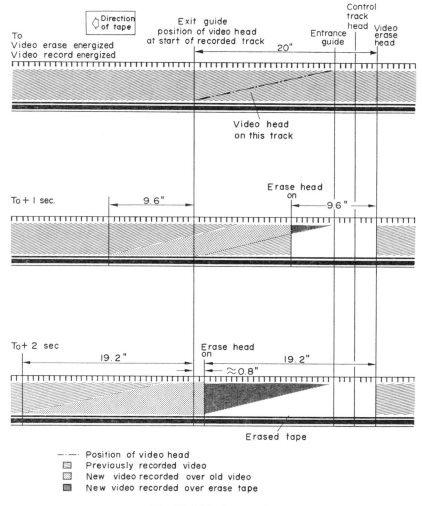

Fig. 12.4. The insert edit.

A short insert (3 seconds) can be made by switching on the *RF* drive and re-recording over existing tracks. Accurate tracking is required to minimise crosstalk from the old signal on to the new but in general a deterioration of signal/noise ratio better than 3 dB can be expected.

220

For longer inserts the normal erase head can be used to erase the major portion of the old scene, but an overlap at each splice point is inevitable, as can be seen on examination of Fig. 12.4. The nominal tape speed is 9·6 i.p.s. and the relative head positions are illustrated.

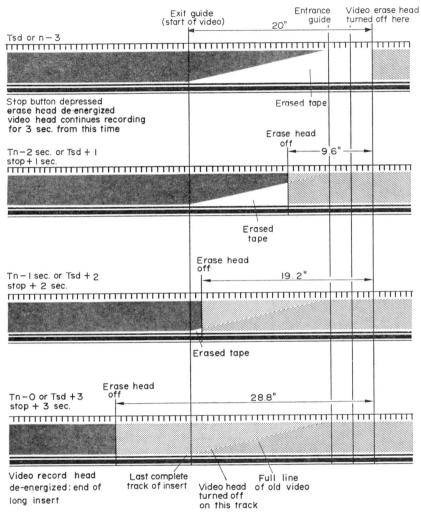

Fig 12.4. The insert edit. (cont.)

At To, the instant the edit is initiated, the *RF* drive to the video head and the erase current are switched on. The recording however is over non-erased tracks.

At To + 1 second, the tape has moved on 9·6 in and the video head is recording over erased tape on the end of their scans.

221

At To + 2 seconds, nearly all the video tracks are being recorded on erased tape.

The subjective effect is that of a cut transition to a new scene with a slightly noisy picture which, over a two-second period starting from the bottom, improves by about 3 dB.

To come out of the splice synchronously the video and the erase cannot simply be turned off because a large erased section would be left. The end of the edit therefore must be pre-meditated by about three seconds and the stop button depressed.

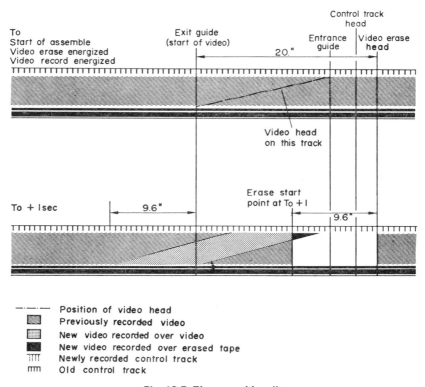

Fig. 12.5. The assemble edit.

If *Tn* = end of insert
Tsd = *Tn* −3 *seconds*—Stop button depressed.

The outgoing sequence can also be seen in Fig. 12.4.

At Tsd or Tn−3 seconds the erase is switched off but recording continues.

At Tn −2 seconds the erased portion is being filled with an overlap at the end of the tracks.

At Tn −1 seconds the erased portion is almost completely filled.

222

At Tn the video head *RF* drive turns off.

The subjective effect of the outgoing splice is a slight deterioration of signal/noise ratio starting from the bottom of the picture progressing to the top followed by a cut transition.

The assemble edit, shown in Fig. 12.5, is very similar to the insert, with two

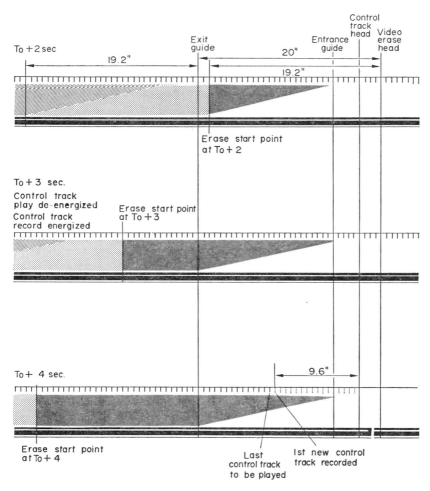

Fig. 12.5. The assemble edit. (cont.)

differences. First, we are only concerned with the ingoing splice. Secondly a new control track has to be recorded. It should be noted that this is delayed until *To* +3 seconds because during the overlap period it is essential to maintain accurate tracking. The only consequence of this delay in recording a new control track is that it must be ensured that at least three seconds of unwanted recording is left at the end of every scene to enable the following assembly edit.

None of the sequence timings are critical and can be provided by simple elapsed timing circuitry.

Quadruplex editing. On the quadruplex format it is quite possible to start the erase between the video tracks. The normal video erase head is angled slightly to enable this. The erase head however precedes the video heads by about 8·86 in. (This varies slightly between manufacturers.)

The technique used, to avoid any overlap or gap, is to switch on the erase in a guard band after vertical sync and delay the *RF* turn on until the erased portion is under the video heads, about 0·58 sec. The time delay could be provided by a simple monostable circuit. However, although the distance between the video and erase heads can be kept to very close limits, the time taken for a point on the tape to move that distance is a function of the tape speed which is dependent on the video standard and field frequency. The track spacing is independent of field frequency (Fig. 3.5) and is only dependent on the relationship between the head and capstan rotational rates.

A more accurate method is to count either frame pulses or tachometer pulses to provide the delay timing. Figure 12.6 shows the relationship in terms of these references. If a frame pulse is being read by the video head the nearest frame pulse upstream to the erase head is 15 frames (150 tach) on 625/50 Hz, or 18 frames (144 tach on 525/60 Hz), from the video head. If a 5 msec delay is subtracted to take-up tolerances it would take a count of 8 tach on 625/50 Hz or 2 tach on 525/60 Hz for the frame pulse to be aligned with the erase head. If the erase is switched on just after this instant it will occur in the guard band after a track with vertical sync. Two more timings are now required which are independent of the line standard. From the initiation of erase the distance to the video head, or *RF* turn on, is 143 tach and this count can be used to switch the *RF* to the video heads, energise the control track record in assemble edits and switch on audio record if required. To prepare the video heads for record the head relays must be switched from the play condition to record just after the head has played back its last track, i.e. one revolution prior to record. A count therefore of 142 is also required.

Figure 12.7 shows a simplified logic diagram for an electronic editor. When the start edit switch is closed the first frame pulse read off tape sets a bi-stable and enables gate *C*. Tach pulses are counted in a series of binary dividers and the required counts, 2, 8, 143 and 142 are derived by matrixing the correct binary outputs. On the count of 2 or 8 the erase is energised via a 5 msec delay to allow for physical tolerances in head spacing. The counter is also re-set. On a count of 142 the video head relays are switched from record after playing back the last track. The head numbering differs between machines but it is assumed that the head position at the time of a tach transition and the reading of a vertical sync is as shown in the diagram with an optional head numbering in brackets.

At a count of 143 the *RF* turn on is energised and the counter and flip flop reset. The editor and VTR remain in this state until the 'stop edit' switch is

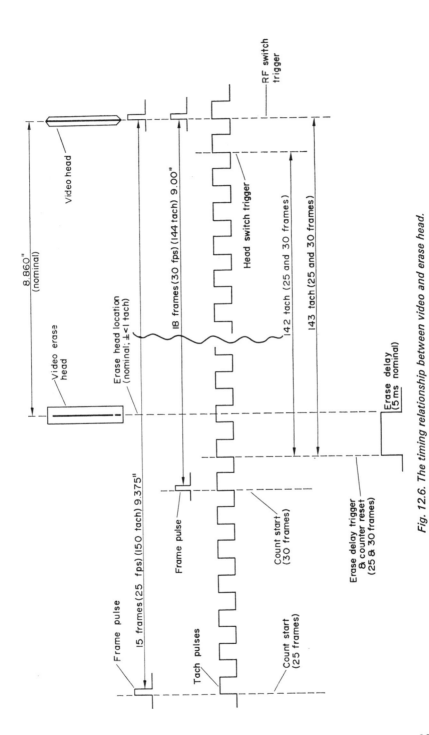

Fig. 12.6. The timing relationship between video and erase head.

225

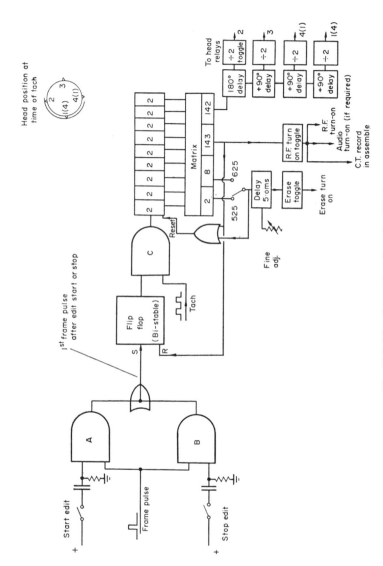

Fig. 12.7. The electronic editor simplified.

226

closed when the same sequence occurs, switching off the erase head relays and *RF* drive. One disadvantage of the arrangement shown is that the stop edit sequence cannot be started until the counter is reset, a time of 0·58 of a second after the start edit. If inserts shorter than 0·58 of a second are required a separate counter must be included for the stop function.

Playback and record phase

It is important that the phase of the video on tape does not change significantly over the splice point. To achieve this two conditions must be satisfied:

Playback phase. The playback phase is normally adjusted for synchronism of the video signal with station sync at some point after the output of the VTR.

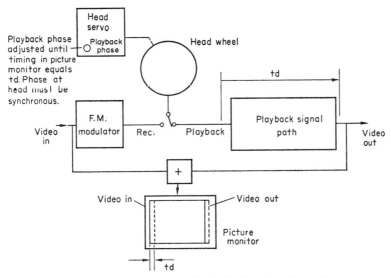

Fig. 12.8. Adjustment of playback phase in edit mode.

Owing to the delay through the signal path this means that the signal is in advance at the video head. For a correctly phased edit the phase of the playback video at the video head itself must be the same as the video to be recorded. One method of achieving this is shown in Fig. 12.8 and is to superimpose the playback and record video pictures and adjust the playback phase for a timing displacement equal to the signal system delay (*td*). Electronic methods are available which achieve the same object.

Record phase. Some VTRs hold the headwheel comparator in the tach mode, with station sync or video as the external reference, during playback before the edit and record after the edit. With such an arrangement adjustment of playback phase is all that is required.

Other VTRs hold the headwheel on the vertical or horizontal comparator

227

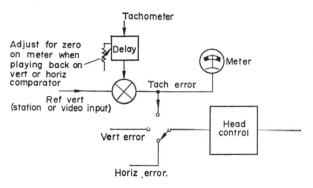

Fig. 12.9. Adjustment of record phase in edit mode.

during playback and switch to the tach comparator during record. With such an arrangement it must be ensured that the head does not change record phase. This can be done by monitoring the tach comparator during playback and adjusting the timing of one of its inputs until its error is zero volts (see Fig. 12.9). At the splice point when the tach comparator is selected the error will be zero, the head wheel undisturbed and the record phase will be the same as the previous sequence.

Editing color sequences

NTSC color signals have a 4 field sequence and PAL an 8 field sequence, if the subcarrier phase with respect to sync is taken into account. This is explained in detail in Chapter 13, Figures 13.4 and 13.8.

On NTSC the subcarrier phase for field 1 is 180° different from field 3 and on PAL the same difference appears between field 1 and 5. The VTR, however, only locks up to a 2 field sequence on 525 and 4 field on 625 high band and therefore there is a 50:50 chance of matching a splice or edit with the wrong sequence. Should this occur, the chroma and burst make a 180° phase shift at the splice point which will be sensed by the colour corrector.

Figure 12.10 shows the relationship between reference subcarrier and burst just after an incorrect edit. If no other gross errors are present this can easily be corrected to a condition shown in Fig. 12.10(b). The sync timing is now out and the subjective effect is for the picture to make a sideways jump equal to half the periodic time of the subcarrier (113 ηsec — 625, 140 ηsec — 525). This is not noticeable if a scene change occurs but is very noticeable on animation editing. A satisfactory solution has not been found for this problem but several techniques all with various defects have been used.

If the VTR locks up to the wrong sequence, then prior to the splice, either the chroma on the new scene can be reversed by placing a 180° phase shift in the subcarrier to the encoder or the VTR lock-up can be inhibited and made to skip to the next frame. The problem with the former is that at the 180° transition the encoded signal is upset and it is important therefore that the signal is not being used elsewhere. The problem with the second solution is

228

that the lock up time is extended and editing to a one-frame accuracy is not possible.

A lock-up to 4 fields on NTSC and 8 fields on PAL by using 15 p.p.s. and 6¾ p.p.s. edit pulses have been suggested, but apart from the limitation of editing to a frame accuracy, the individual fields are difficult to define, especially when it is appreciated that there is no specification for sync to chroma phasing on either NTSC or PAL.

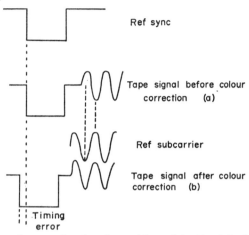

Fig. 12.10. A timing diagram showing the problem of the N.T.S.C. 4 field and P.A.L. 8 field sequence in editing.

A final solution is to separate the luminance and chrominance with a comb filter and adjust the phase of a burst and chroma separately to match that of the incoming signal and then recombine it with the luminance. Several problems of vertical resolution and phase response are created by using comb filters and delay networks and an ideal solution has yet to be found.

Electronic editing, general

All electronic editors that do not use a flying erase head have a significant delay either in their stop cycle or both start and stop cycle. For helical it is about 3 sec and on quadruplex about 0·6 sec second on 15 i.p.s. (1·2 sec on 7·5 i.p.s.). This delay neccesitates a pre-meditated action of events which are difficult to synchronise. Not only can an edit be mis-timed on a master tape but the new scene may be late or early with respect to the master. Very often the errors cannot be detected until after the edit has been made.

Cue tone programming of edits

The requirements for rehearsal facilities with the possibility of changing edit points and the assurance of repeatable results led to the development of cueing edit points. Bursts of cue tone which start and stop the edit sequence

229

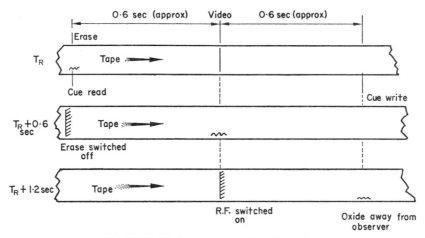

Fig. 12.11. Timing sequence for edit cueing.

are recorded on the cue track. The time delay can be eliminated and indeed made adjustable by reading the cue tone up-stream to where it was recorded.

The cue track record head is positioned 9·75 in downstream from the video head and if a cue read head is positioned near the erase head, say 8·5 in up-stream from the video head, a cue can be read $8·5 + 9·75 = 18·25$ in or about 1·2 sec in advance. With an editor delay of approximately 0·6 sec the advance cue can be delayed a further 0·6 sec to provide an edit at the instant

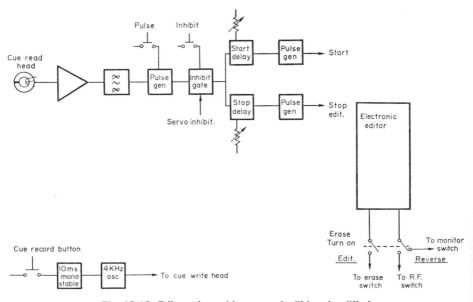

Fig. 12.12. Edit cueing with reverse facilities simplified.

the cue tone reaches the record head position. The timing sequence can be seen in Fig. 12.11. The procedure for rehearsal is to record a cue at the required point of edit, rewind and playback. During playback the cue is read early, delayed by 0·6 sec and allowed to initiate the edit cycle. The erase and *RF* turn on however are disabled and instead a switch from the playback signal to the input signal is made on a monitor at the time of edit. The cue delays can then be advanced by up to 0·6 sec or delayed by any amount until the correct splice is found. The editor can now be switched to edit and the sequence repeated, this time making a permanent edit.

Extra precautions are sometimes built in as can be seen in Fig. 12.12 allowing the cues to be inhibited manually if not required or automatically if the servo is not locked. Provision is also made for manual cueing should a tape cue fail to be read. Extra sophistication is sometimes added to the device to allow different frequency tones for remote start of other machines, the physical shifting of cues, selection of individual cues and automatic animation with a pre-selection of the number of frames.

One of the disadvantages with edit cueing is that although the edit is fixed on the master tape the remote video source may vary slightly. Even if it is started from a fixed cue its start position or run-up time may differ slightly. Finding the edit points on tape is also a time-consuming operation. To overcome these problems time code addressing was developed to allow fully automatic random access editing allowing fast searching of cue points and frame accuracy editing.

Time code addressing

To allow the automatic searching of a particular frame on tape a method of unique addresses for each frame recorded is needed. This can be done by recording a sequential digital code on the cue track with a number unique to that frame. The IEC and the SMPTE have agreed on a code format but before going into details it is worth while investigating the various digital codes available and their advantages.

Recording codes

Many codes have been devised, each with its own application and limitations. The most common ones have been listed in Fig. 12.13.

Obviously the cue track requires a sequential series of binary digits, this can be achieved by storing the composite number in a shift register and reading out the information at clock or bit rate. In the example chosen a 17 BIT binary number 01101000101011111 is used to compare the various codes.

R–Z return to zero. This is the most obvious method of recording a series of 1's and 0's. Each pulse width is one half a bit time and a one is signified by a positive pulse and a zero by a negative pulse. The current falling to zero between pulses. The system is poor as each transition is only half the full

231

possible swing from positive to negative. Also a resolution of twice the number of bits per inch (b.p.i.) is required to resolve the pulses. Thirdly, a redundancy of information exists because two transitions are used to describe each bit.

R–B return to bias. In this system the tape is biased to saturation either with a preceding head or with a *DC* current through the record head. Each pulse saturates the tape in the opposite direction and thus uses the full transition range of the medium. A one is signified by a pulse while a zero is signified by the absence of a pulse. The system is more efficient than *RZ* but still requires a high resolution. It also requires a reference of the bit rate because if a long series of 0's are being played back the number of missing pulses must be determined. On most multi-track computer decks a clock track is recorded on a separate track which gives the bit rate for all other tracks.

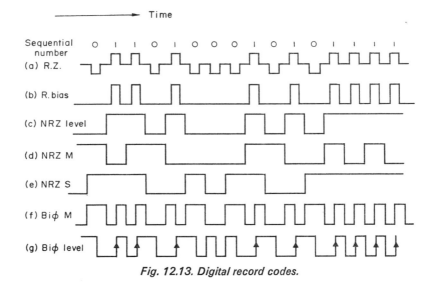

Fig. 12.13. Digital record codes.

N–Z–R non-return to zero (level). This system is even more efficient, using full transitions with no redundant information. With this arrangement a high means one and a low means zero. In terms of transitions a positive transition denotes a change from 0 to 1 and negative from 1 to 0, no transition denotes the same value as the previous bit. One transition per bit is the maximum rate, which is obtained with a recording 101010 etc., a resolution equal to the b.p.i. is therefore required. The system still requires a clock track and also has two major disadvantages:

1. A series of 0's or 1's could result in no transitions giving the signal a very low frequency component. The response of the system must therefore be from *DC* to bit rate. In practice a known phase reversal can be inserted every *n* bits to remove the *DC* component.

232

2. The most serious fault with this system is that if a transition is missed, not only the following bit is read wrongly but all bits until the next transition. In other words for a series 011110, if the first transition from 0 to 1 is missed, all ones will be read wrongly as 0.

N–R–Z mark. This system overcomes objection 2 in the *N–R–Z* level system. In this method a transition is made for every 1 to the opposite state. No transition is made for a 0. The polarity of the signal is immaterial as either a positive or a negative transition represents a 1, an error in reading a transition affects one bit only. The problem of clock rate and *DC* component still exists.

N–R–Z space. This system is the complement of *N–R–Z* mark and it is worthwhile comparing the waveforms of the two systems. In the *N–R–Z* space waveform, a transition indicates a zero and comparison with the *N–R–Z* mark waveforms shows that a transition occurs on the former waveform for the spaces on the latter. One method of producing a clock rate pulse is instead of recording a clock track, to record the complement on a second track. This way a clock rate can be produced with the advantage of a check or parity information. The *N–R–Z* Mark or *N–R–Z* Space are most commonly used systems in multitrack computer systems.

Bi-phase mark or Manchester 1. This system was devised where it is not possible to record a separate clock track and a transition occurs at the start of every bit. An extra transition occurs if the digit is one and no transition for zero. The direction of a transition is immaterial; therefore the phase or polarity of the signal is not important. The decoding of the signal is more complex because the clock edges and the bit information edges have to be separated. Once this is done the signal can be decoded at any speed, which offers many advantages in search processes on audio and video tape recorders.

The complement to this system is the bi-phase space or Manchester I + 180°, where the extra transition represents a 0 instead of a 1. This code is not shown.

At first sight it may seem that the system requires a resolution of twice the bit density, which is true, but it is not quite as bad as it seems when it is realised that the signal is very similar to an FM signal with two discrete frequencies and no low frequency component. Band filtering gives this system excellent noise immunity with the possibility of recovering low level high frequency components.

Bi-phase level or Manchester II + 180°. This is another self clocking code in which a negative transition is made for zero and a positive transition for one. A transition is only made at clock time if it is required to give the correct phase transition for the following bit. In other words a series of '10101010 etc.' would not require an intermediate transition while a series of 1's or 0's would. It can be seen that a clock component is still present whatever the number and the signal is very similar to Manchester I but with the transitions meaning different things.

SMPTE address code

The code adopted as a standard is the Manchester I or Bi-phase mark. This offers the following advantages over other codes:

1. It is self clocking which allows decoding over a wide range of speeds.
2. Inversion of the signal is immaterial, which is useful for transmission on telephone lines.
3. There is no *DC* component.

Manchester I Coder. The basis of a Manchester coder is illustrated in Fig. 12.14. A transition is required every clock time and an extra transition if the bit value is 1. Clock pulses (*C2*) are gated with the sequential binary number (*A1*) to provide the extra transition. $C_1 + C_2 A_1$ triggers a divide by 2 circuit to provide the Manchester code.

Manchester I Decoder. The problem of decoding is to separate the information pulses from the clock pulses and to be able to do this over a range of playback speeds from 1·5 i.p.s. to 150 i.p.s., a range of 1:100. To do this the code is amplified, phase split and differentiated, as shown in Fig. 12.15, to produce a positive pulse for every transition of the code, the equivalent to $C_1 + C_2 A_1$ in the coder. The pulse chain is then masked to separate the clock pulses from the information pulses.

To understand the masking action it must first be accepted that the clock pulses are separated. The clock pulses are used to reset a ramp generator

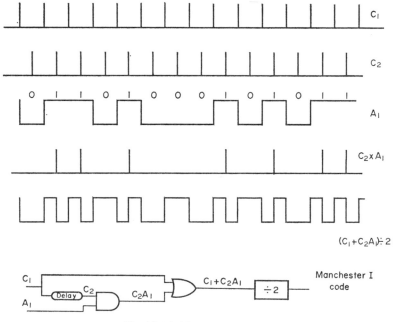

Fig. 12.14. Manchester I coder.

234

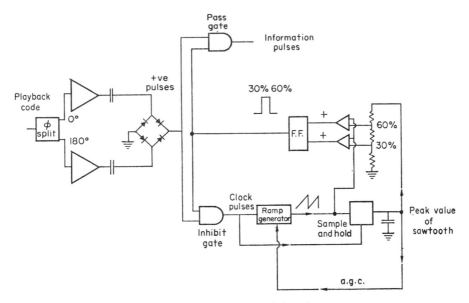

Fig. 12.15. Manchester I decoder.

which consists of a constant current source charging a capacitor. The mask reference is formed by sampling the peak value of the sawtooth and holding the voltage on a store capacitor. The masking pulse is developed by taking two proportions of the held voltage, 60% and 30%, and comparing this with the following ramp in two differential amplifiers. An output from each amplifier is formed when the ramp exceeds the 30% and 60% of the held voltage. These outputs are used to trigger a flip-flop, the output of which is used to open a pass gate, for the information pulse and inhibit the clock gate. The complete timing diagram can be seen in Fig. 12.16. The circuit can work at any speed as the gate pulse is always generated between clock pulses. At very high tape speed however the ramps become very small and an a.g.c. circuit with a long time constant is used to increase the amplitude of the ramps should they become low. The only time the circuit becomes inaccurate is during rapid acceleration or deceleration. The circuit can initially lock-up incorrectly but as shown in Fig. 12.16 these incorrect sequences pull into step in the presence of a modulated signal.

Format of SMPTE code

The code is sequenced in real time as this interfaces well with the human and addresses a frame with the time of a twenty four hour day in hours, minutes, seconds and frame. It is also coded as a binary coded decimal (b.c.d.) to make maintenance and fault finding easier. The maximum number of bits required for each decimal is as follows:

235

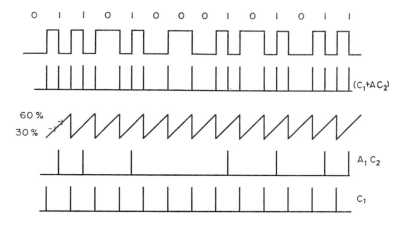

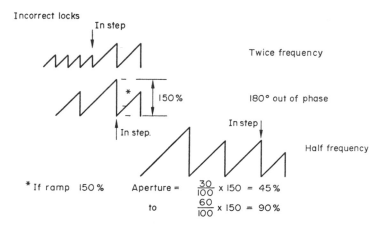

Fig. 12.16. Manchester I decoding.

Maximum Nos:

Hours		Minutes		Seconds		Frames	
Tens	*Units*	*Tens*	*Units*	*Tens*	*Units*	*Tens*	*Units*
2	9	5	9	5	9	2	9
XX10	1001	X101	1001	X101	1001	XX10	1001

If four bits were required for each decimal the total would be 32 bits, however a saving of six bits can be made dure to the fact that the tens of hours and frames column never exceeds five. These six bits are reserved for other functions which will be explained later.

The longitudinal space available for the code is equal to the length of one frame, which is 0·5 in on the 525/60 Hz standard. Packing densities of

236

800 bits per inch are quite common but on a track with uncertain head to tape contact like the cue track it was decided to restrict it to 160 b.p.i. This allows 80 bits per frame which are split up as follows:

> 28 bits—Time address code.
> 6 bits—Assigned for definite information or fixed 0.
> 32 bits—Spare for user option (binary groups).
> 16 bits—Sync word.

Total   80

The bits are assigned as shown in Fig. 12.17 and described as follows

0–3	Units of frames
4–7	First binary group
8–9	Tens of frames
10	Unassigned address bit (0 until assigned by the IEC)
11	Fixed zero
12–15	Second binary group
16–19	Units of seconds
20–23	Third binary group
24–26	Tens of seconds
27	Unassigned address bit (0 until assigned by the IEC)
28–31	Fourth binary group
32–35	Units of minutes
36–39	Fifth binary group
40–42	Tens of minutes
43	Unassigned address bit (0 until assigned by the IEC)
44–47	Sixth binary group
48–51	Units of hours
52–55	Seventh binary group
56–57	Tens of hours
58	Unassigned address bit (0 until assigned by IEC)
59	Fixed zero
60–63	Eighth binary group
64–79	Synchronising word
	64–65 Fixed zero
	66–77 Fixed one
	78 Fixed zero
	79 Fixed one

There is no restriction on the use of the 32 user bits and they can be filled with any binary number. They will most probably be used for tape identity, programme and scene idents, VTR control settings or other production information.

The address bits are arranged as follows:

Units frames
Bits 0–3   4 bit BCD arranged 1–2–4–8   Count 0–9
Tens frames
Bits 8–9   2 bit BCD arranged 1–2   Count 0–2
Units seconds
Bits 16–19   4 bit BCD arranged 1–2–4–8   Count 0–9
Tens seconds
Bits 24–26   3 bit BCD arranged 1–2–4   Count 0–5

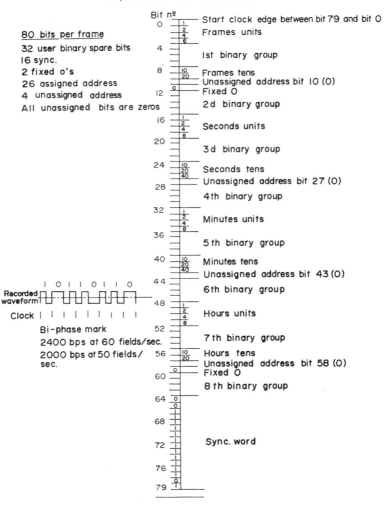

Fig. 12.17. Proposed time and address code.

Units minutes Bits 32–35	4 bit BCD arranged 1–2–4–3	Count 0–9
Tens minutes Bits 40–42	3 bit BCD arranged 1–2–4	Count 0–5
Units hours Bits 48–51	4 bit BCD arranged 1–2–4–8	Count 0–9
Tens hours Bits 56–57	2 bit BCD arranged 1–2	Count 0–2

Functions of sync word

The sync word has two main functions:

1. To indicate the start of the frame address
2. To indicate the direction of tape travel, as it is required to read the code in Fast forward and Rewind where the order of information is reversed.

For condition 1 it must be unique and should not be formed in the time code. The sync word contains 12 ones which should not occur elsewhere. The advantage of splitting up the code in groups of four now becomes apparent as assuming the worst case of all the user bits filled with ones the maximum number of sequential ones is 9, between bits 24 to 35 when the seconds tens indicate 5 and the minutes units 7. i.e.:

```
24 . . . . . . . . . . . . . . . . . . . . . . . 35
1011                   1111                   1110
 5                                             7
```

Similarly, nine sequential ones can occur between bits 40 and 51.

For condition 2 the sync word starts and ends with two identity bits to indicate direction. Once the sync word is detected, 12 consecutive ones, a zero is detected and the state of the following bit indicates the direction of the tape, 1 for forward, 0 for reverse.

The sync is detected by a ÷10 circuit which is reset every time a 0 occurs, the output only going to a high state when at least 10 consecutive ones occur.

The first zero after at least 10 ones sets a flip flop which opens two gates. If the following bit is one a second flip flop is set indicating forward, and if it is zero it is reset indicating reverse motion. The first flip flop is reset until the next sync pulse.

Bit number 10 (the "drop frame flag")

The field rate of a 525/60 Hz colour signal is more precisely 59·94 fields per second or 0·1% lower in frequency than the nominal 60 Hz. Therefore the straight forward counting of frames at 60 fields per second will yield a 0·1% error to real time.

Over one hour, 3600 seconds, this would accumulate to 3·6 seconds. To keep in step with real time a frame can be skipped every 100 frames. To skip a frame may be confusing at a later stage if an address which does not exist

239

is selected for an edit point. To allow the time code to be different to real time is also confusing, requiring added complexity in computing the programme length.

It is left to the user which method is used and the SMPTE have defined the following uses of bit number 10:

Mode zero. In this mode no numbers are omitted from the chain of addresses and when used, bit number 10 is assigned a 'zero'.

Mode 1. In this mode the first two frame numbers (1 and 2) at the start of each minute, exept minutes 0, 10, 20, 30, 40, 50, are omitted from the count. When this mode is used bit No. 10 is assigned a 'one'.

In mode zero the 3·6 seconds of error over one hour equals 108 frames. In mode one, two frames per minute amounts to:

$$60 \times 2 = 120 \text{ frames per hour}$$
$$\text{minus 6 exceptions}$$
$$6 \times 2 = 12 \text{ frames}$$
$$\text{Total omissions} = 108 \text{ frames.}$$

In mode one therefore the code matches real time to within two frames.

Bit number 11 (standard binary groups)

There is no restriction on the way the binary groups are used but at some time in the future the SMPTE and the IEC will standardise on their particular use. When used in this anticipated manner, bit number 11 will be assigned a 'one'.

Bit numbers 27, 43, 58, 59

The uses of these bits are yet to be decided and until a definite decision is made they are assigned a zero.

One possible use is to identify the tape recording standard. Another use might be to identify the PAL four frames or NTSC 2 frame sequence, although this is not absolutely necessary, and would only be required for check purposes, as the information could be contained in the address number itself. If it is arranged that frame 1 of the day is made frame 1 of the TV signal (however it is specified), on a 525/60 Hz NTSC signal, all addresses with an odd number of frames is frame one and an even number of frames indicates frame 2. On 625/50 HzPAL signals it is more complex as the seconds and the frame number must be added and divided by four. A remainder of 1 denotes frame 1, remainder of 2 denotes frame 2 ... etc. and no remainder frame 4. This could be detected either by simple logic or by mental arithmetic from the address number only.

240

Automatic editing

Once a time address has been placed on tape, the control of tape transports is a matter of arithmetic computation. Several edit modes can be used but the two most common methods are:

1. The assembly of a programme on machine B fitted with an electronic editor from a master tape of random scenes on machine A.

2. The assembly of a programme on machine C from two playback machines A and B. The latter can be quicker and allows mixing, keying and wiping between scenes where the former is restricted to the cut transition.

The calculations required for both systems are very similar as two machines must search for their cue points, stop, start together and lock in synchronism. Then at an appropriate time an edit or cut or mix must be made. Figure 12.18 shows a typical arrangement where it is required that two machines are locked together for a cut to be made.

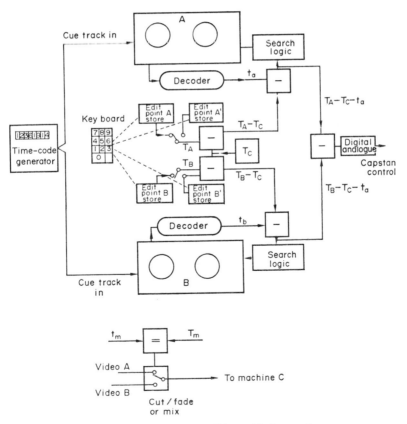

Fig. 12.18. Automatic editing with time codes.

241

If

> ta = dynamic code read from transport A.
> tb = dynamic code read from transport B.
> TA = time code of required transition on tape A (manually set on keyboard).
> TB = time code of required transition on tape B.
> Tc = The cue point advance for lock-up of machines.

Step 1. Each transport cues up to correct position by spooling until for transport A:

$$TA - Tc - ta = 0$$

For transport B:

$$TB - Tc - tb = 0$$

Step 2. Start both machines. To maintain synchronism $(TA - Tc - ta) - (TB - Tc - tb)$ should be kept at zero and the capstan servo of one transport is adjusted for this to be so. For instance if the sum is negative, transport B must be slowed down. Once locked the normal capstan servo on each machine should keep sequence. At a time when $TA = ta$ the cut or mix can be made.

If electronic editing is used the cycle time of the editor must be taken into account.

References

1. Video-Tape splicing, 3M's *Video-talk*, Vol. II, No. 3, 1969.
2. BOUNSALL, N., Electronic editing of magnetic television tape recording, *JSMPTE*, 71 95–99, Feb. 1962.
3. ROIZEN, J., Electronic marking and control for rapid location of vertical blanking area, *JSMPTE*, 67, 732–733 Nov. 1958.
4. MACHEIN, K. R., Factors affecting the splicing of video tape, *JSMPTE*, 67, 730–731, Nov. 1958.
5. BUSBY, E. S., Frame numbering of Television tape recordings, *JSMPTE*, 79, March 1970.
6. BUXTON, A. J., AND HEATHER, J., Automatic Tape Editing, 104th Conference *SMPTE*, Jan. 1969.
7. ANDERSON, C., The problems of splicing and editing colour video magnetic tape *IEEE Transactions*, Vol. BC—15 No. 3, 1969.

13 Magnetic Video Discs and Slow Motion Techniques

Video recorders using a magnetic disc instead of tape offer several applications and special effects attractive to the broadcast industry. Still frame, slow motion, fast motion in forward or reverse are quite feasible. The storage disc used is one where the recording medium is nickel cobalt which is coated with rhodium to provide a hard protective surface. Figure 13.1 shows a typical disc which is 16 in in diameter, weighs about $5\frac{1}{2}$ lb and has a useful recording area on both sides of the disc $4\frac{1}{2}$ in wide from the outer rim.

The number of tracks that can be accomodated on one disc surface depends on the track and guard band width. With a track width of 0·0075 in and a guard band of 0·0025 in the centre-to-centre track spacing is 0·01 in allowing 450 tracks within the 4·5 in of recording area. One field is recorded per track which means that the total disc capacity, using both surfaces is 900 fields. On 625/60 Hz:

$$\text{total time per disc} = \frac{900}{50} = 18 \text{ seconds.}$$

On 525/60 Hz

$$\text{total time per disc} = \frac{900}{60} = 15 \text{ seconds.}$$

Most practical systems use one or two discs.

The tracks, unlike an audio record, are concentric rings and the heads are stepped in when the other head or heads are recording or playing back. The disc rotates once per TV field which gives the following head to disc speeds:

243

On 625/50 Hz

$$\text{Rotational rate of disc} = 50 \text{ r.p.s.}$$
$$\text{Speed(s)} = \pi D 50$$

where D = diameter of track.

For outer track:

$$S = 50 \times 16 \times \pi = 2570 \text{ i.p.s}$$

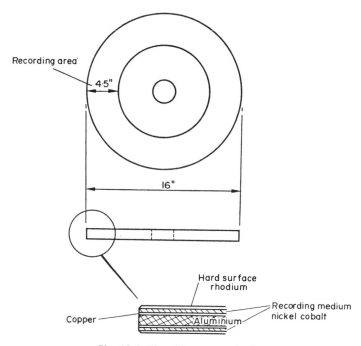

Fig. 13.1. The video magnetic disc.

For inner track

$$S = 50(16 - 9)\,\pi = 1100 \text{ i.p.s}$$

On 525/60 Hz

$$\text{Rotational rate} = 60 \text{ r.p.s.}$$

For outer track

$$S = 60 \times 16 \times \pi = 3080 \text{ i.p.s}$$

For inner track

$$S = 60 \times 7 \times \pi = 1320 \text{ i.p.s}$$

The tracks can be recorded from the outer edge to the inner limit sequentially, recording odd fields on one surface and even fields on the other, moving the head during the field it is not recording.[2] Such an arrangement however requires a rapid flyback when the heads reach the centre with an obvious gap in the recording.

For sporting events where the action is unpredictable it is desirable always to have the discs full with the last η seconds, when η is the capacity of the store. This can be done as shown in Fig. 13.2. On the inward journey the video head records a track and moves in two tracks to record again. When it reaches the centre it has recorded on 225 tracks missing every alternate track. On its outward journey it records on the vacant spaces interlacing the tracks. When the video head reaches the edge the first track is erased and re-recorded over. With such an arrangement each disc surface will always have the last 450 recorded fields of information.

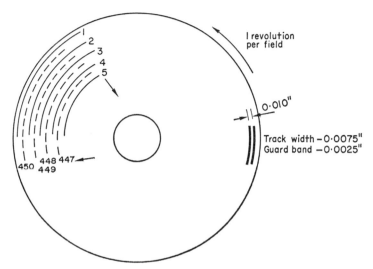

Fig. 13.2. The disc record format (typical).

Record and playback sequence

If a storage capacity greater than 15 or 18 seconds is required, at least two discs must be used, which adds some complexity to the record and playback sequence.[3]

Assuming the video heads on the four disc surfaces are labelled *A*, *B*, *C* and *D* a typical record sequence would be as shown in Table 12.

TABLE 12

HEAD (or channel)	FIELD 1, 5, 9, 13, etc.	FIELD 2, 6, 10, 14, etc.	FIELD 3, 7, 11, 15, etc.	FIELD 4, 8, 12, 16, etc.
A	Record	Step	Step	Erase
B	Erase	Record	Step	Step
C	Step	Erase	Record	Step
D	Step	Step	Erase	Record

245

Note that field 1 is recorded on *A*, 2 on *B*, 3 on *C*, 4 on *D* etc., and after recording a field the head steps in twice, one step being one track, and erases the existing track the revolution prior to recording.

The erase can be performed either by a separate head preceding the video head or by the video head itself on the revolution before recording. The former is preferable as the width of the erase can include the guard band to avoid interference from stray signals during mis-tracking.

A forward playback sequence at normal speed is very similar to record with the erase inhibited and the video head replaying instead of recording as shown in Table 13.

TABLE 13

HEAD (or channel)	FIELD 1, 5, 9, etc.	FIELD 2, 6, 10, etc.	FIELD 3, 7, 11, etc.	FIELD 4, 8, 12, etc.
A	Reproduce ↘	Step	Step	
B		Reproduce ↘	Step	Step
C	Step		Reproduce ↘	Step ↗A
D	Step	Step		Reproduce ↗

Reverse motion at normal speed can be obtained by reversing the stepping direction of the heads and by reversing the order of selection of the heads. This can be done simply by exchanging the *A* and *C* commands and reversing the stepping direction as follows:

```
A        C
B  ＞＜   B
C        A
D        D
```

This gives the result shown in Table 14.

TABLE 14

HEAD or DISC	FIELD 1, 5, 9, etc.	FIELD 2, 6, 10, etc.	FIELD 3, 7, 11, etc.	FIELD 4, 8, 12, etc.
A	Step		Reproduce ↘	Step
B		Reproduce ↗	Step	Step
C	Reproduce ↗	Step	Step	↓ C ↗
D	Step	Step		Reproduce ↗

Stop-motion

A still frame or stop motion can be obtained by stopping the heads and repeating a playback frame. This could be done by playing back any sequential odd and even fields from two tracks. The disadvantage of this is that the

246

frozen action shows an integration of movement over 1/25 sec on 625 or 1/30 sec on 525 signals. A better system is to play back one track or field which will give an integration of only 1/50 or 1/60 sec, ignoring lag in the camera tube.

The only problem now is that the field selected is either an odd or an even field and the playback video should consist of a sequential series of odd and even fields. One method of overcoming this problem is to convert an even field to an odd or vice-versa. Figure 13.3 shows the start and end of two sequential fields and a correct signal should progress from A to A' to B to B' to A.

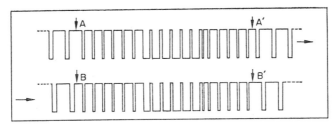

Fig. 13.3. The horizontal sync relationship between fields.

Assume that one track has recorded on it the upper field from A through to B. The following recorded track will of course record from B onwards. If the recorder were just playing back track A, it would be correct for one field up to point B. However it now repeats itself, which is satisfactory up to A' as A to A' is the same as B to B'. At this point the video from track A is incorrect and a half-line delay is required to convert the phase of an odd field to an even and vice-versa. Vertical resolution is impaired but movement rendition is improved compared with the two field playback.

For monochrome signals the insertion of a half-line delay is all that is required to correct the field sequence. For colour, an additional correction is required to maintain chroma phasing. The requirements of chroma correction are different for PAL and NTSC and it is worth treating them separately.

NTSC chroma correction

NTSC colour sub-carrier is chosen to be an odd multiple of half-line frequency in order to minimise the dot pattern and interleave the chrominance and luminance spectra. The effect of this is to cause the subcarrier phase to be 180° different in phase to the subcarrier in the same position on the previous line. Because the system has an odd number of lines over two fields, line one of field 3 is different from line one of field 1. For this reason the 525/60 Hz NTSC signal is sometimes said to have a four-field sequence. This can be seen in Fig. 13.4 where the subcarrier alternates 180° for each line and line one framc 1 is 180° different from line one frame 2. In order to maintain the correct chroma continuity any playback field must be able to be converted to look like any one of the four fields. This can be done by inverting the chroma

247

including burst on certain fields. Table 15 below illustrates the complete correction sequence. The $\frac{1}{2}$ line delay converts dissimilar fields. The chroma invertor is used to convert the chroma of a similar field to a dissimilar frame and also when the $\frac{1}{2}$ line delay is used on a similar frame. This can be seen by referring to Fig. 13.4. *If line 1 (odd field) of frame 2 is converted to line 264 (even field) of frame 2 then a $\frac{1}{2}$ line delay and chroma invertor are required.

Half line delay logic (HL)

It can be arranged that disc surfaces A and C always contain odd fields. This being so the logic required can be easily determined as the $\frac{1}{2}$ line delay is

TABLE 15

Recorded field (disc) \ Required P.B. field	Frame 1		Frame 2	
	Odd	Even	Odd	Even
Odd (A) Frame 1		½ L.D. C.I.	C.I.	½ L.D.
Even (B)	½ L.D.		½ L.D. C.I.	C. I.
Odd (C) Frame 2	C.I.	½ L.D.		½ L.D.* C.I.
Even (D)	½ L.D. C. I.	C.I.	½ L.D.	

Where ½ L.D. = insertion of ½ line delay
And C.I. = chroma signal inverted

not required when the reference sync is odd and playback is either from A or C OR reference is not odd and playback is not from $A + C$.

In Boolean

$$\overline{HL} = Ro\,(A + C) + \overline{Ro}\,(\overline{A} + \overline{C})$$

or

$$HL = \overline{Ro\,(A + C)} \cdot \overline{Ro\,(\overline{A} + \overline{C})}$$

where Ro = Reference odd.

$A + C$ = Playback from disc surface $A + C$.

HL = Half line delay logic.

Chroma invert logic. The chroma invertor logic can be understood by analysing the correction table. It should be noticed that the CI changes state

248

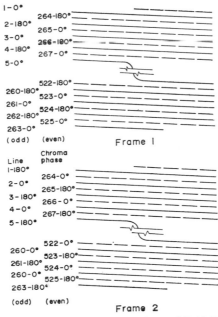

Fig. 13.4. N.T.S.C. subcarrier phase, showing a 4 field (2 frame) sequence.

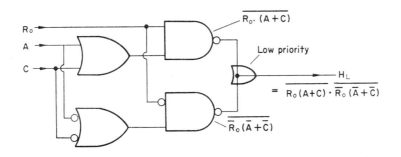

R_0 Reference 30Hz—high for odd field
A   High when playing back on disc A
C   High when playing back on disc C
H_L High when 1/2 line delay is required
C.I.   High when chroma inverter is required

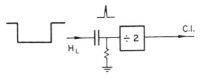

Fig. 13.5. Half line delay and chroma invertor logic for N.T.S.C.

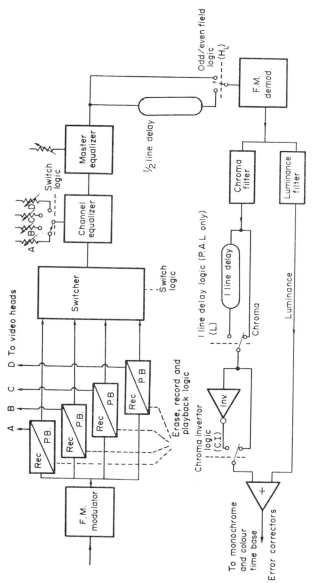

Fig. 13.6. The video disc signal system.

(either removed or inserted) every time the half-line delay is inserted. This can be achieved by using the half-line delay (*HL*) to trigger a binary switch as in Fig. 13.5 every time the half-line delay is inserted.

Video disc signal path

A block diagram of the complete signal path can be seen in Fig. 13.6. It is very similar to a VTR using frequency modulation with similar deviation frequencies. The differences are that the *RF* to the video heads is gated to record the correct fields and an additional erase function may also be required.

In the playback path, the output of the signal system is passed to the half-line delay and chroma invertor correctors before the conventional monochrome and colour time base error correctors.

PAL chroma correction

PAL colour subcarrier has a quarter-line offset which causes the colour subcarrier to phase shift by 90° on successive lines. Because 625 is divisible by four with a remainder one, line one of field 1 is 90° different from line 1 of field 3, 180° different from line 1 of field 5, 270° different from line 1 of field 7, an eight field sequence. A further complication is that on every second line of the PAL signal the *V* component of the chroma signal is reversed giving a four field sequence as shown in Fig. 13.7.

Note that on any line of an odd or even field, say 309 or 621, the *V* component is reversed two fields later. If the complete sequence is plotted over eight fields it would look something like Fig. 13.8.

To convert field 1 to field 3, a half-line delay would not be required but

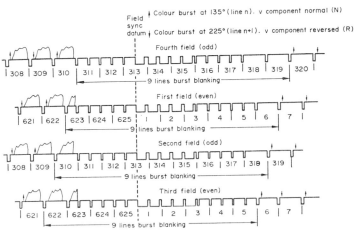

Fig. 13.7. The P.A.L. signal showing the 4 field sequence due to the alternating phase of the V component.

251

Subcarrier

Frame-1

V Component	Chroma phase		
*N	0	314	—Field 1
*R	270	2	—Field 2
R	90	315	
N	0	3	
N	180	316	
R	90	4	
R	270	317	
N	180		

5 to 309 &
318 to 622

R	270	310
N	180	623
N	0	311
R	270	624
R	90	312
N	0	625
N	180	313

*N = Normal, R = Reverse

Subcarrier

Frame-2

V Component	Chroma phase		
R	90	314	—Field 3
N	0	2	—Field 4
N	180	315	
R	90	3	
R	270	316	
N	180	4	
N	0	317	
R	270		

5 to 309 &
318 to 622

N	0	310
R	270	623
R	90	311
N	0	624
N	180	312
R	90	625
R	270	313

Frame-3   Frame-4

Subcarrier

Frame-3

V Component	Chroma phase		
N	180	314	—Field 8
R	90	2	—Field 6
R	270	315	
N	180	3	
N	0	316	
R	270	4	
R	90	317	
N	0		

5 to 309 &
318 to 622

R	90	310
N	0	623
N	180	311
R	90	624
R	270	312
N	180	625
N	0	313

Subcarrier

Frame-4

V Component	Chroma phase		
R	270	314	—Field 7
N	180	2	—Field 8
N	0	315	
R	270	3	
N	90	316	
N	0	4	
R	180	317	
R	90		

5 to 309 &
318 to 622

N	180	310
R	90	623
R	270	311
N	180	624
N	0	312
R	270	625
R	90	313

Fig. 13.8. P.A.L. subcarrier phase and V component position showing an 8 field (4 frame) sequence.

note that the V component is wrong. This can be corrected by delaying the chroma one whole line making line 1 . . . to line 2 etc., The chroma phase is now also wrong by 180° which can be corrected with a chroma invertor. Therefore to convert field 1 to field 3 a one-line delay and chroma inversion is required. If the same analysis is carried out for all fields the following chart can be compiled.

Half-line delay logic. The half line delay logic for PAL is very similar to the NTSC although as shown in the correction the odd fields are now recorded on B and D requiring an inversion of Ro, giving:

$$\overline{H} = Ro\,(A + C) + Ro\,(\overline{A} + C)$$

One-line delay logic. Looking at the Table 16, the requirement for the one-line delay is repeated in each quadrant of the table. The logic therefore can be simplified to produce the diagram in Fig. 13.9. Simple Boolean logic is now required to decide when the 1 line delay is required.

Chroma Invertor. Examination of the correction chart shows that the chroma invertor changes condition every time either the one line delay *or* the half-line

252

TABLE 16

Required playback field → / Recorded field (disc) ↓	Frame 1		Frame 2		Frame 3		Frame 4	
	Even 1	Odd 2	Even 3	Odd 4	Even 5(1)'	Odd 6(2)'	Even 7(3)'	Odd 8(4)'
Frame 1 — 1 Even (A)		1/2 L.D. / I L.D.	I L.D. / C.I.	1/2 L.D.	C.I.	1/2 L.D. / I L.D.	I L.D.	1/2 L.D. / C.I.
2 Odd (B)	1/2 L.D. / C.I.		1/2 L.D. / I L.D.	I L.D. / C.I.	1/2 L.D.	C.I.	1/2 L.D. / I L.D.	I L.D. / C.I.
Frame 2 — 3 Even (C)	I L.D.	1/2 L.D. / C.I.		1/2 L.D. / I L.D.	I L.D. / C.I.	1/2 L.D.	C.I.	1/2 L.D. / I L.D.
4 Odd (D)	1/2 L.D. / I L.D. / C.I.	I L.D.	1/2 L.D. / C.I.		1/2 L.D. / I L.D.	I L.D. / C.I.	1/2 L.D.	C.I.
Frame 3 — 5 (1')Even (A)	C.I.	1/2 L.D. / I L.D.	I L.D.	1/2 L.D. / C.I.		1/2 L.D. / I L.D.	I L.D. / C.I.	1/2 L.D.
6 (2')Odd (B)	1/2 L.D.	C.I.	1/2 L.D. / I L.D.	I L.D. / C.I.	1/2 L.D. / C.I.		1/2 L.D. / I L.D.	I L.D. / C.I.
Frame 4 — 7 (3')Even (C)	I L.D. / C.I.	1/2 L.D.	C.I.	1/2 L.D. / I L.D.	I L.D.	1/2 L.D. / C.I.		1/2 L.D. / I L.D.
8 (4')Odd (D)	1/2 L.D. / I L.D.	I L.D. / C.I.	1/2 L.D.	C.I.	1/2 L.D. / I L.D. / C.I.	I L.D.	1/2 L.D. / C.I.	

delay are removed. This can be provided by the simple circuit shown in Fig. 13.10.

Slow and fast motion

Slow motion can be obtained by playing back each field more than once. By playing back each field twice the effect of half speed is created, repeating each field three times gives one-third speed. Odd fractions, say two-fifths speed, can be created by repeating one field twice, the next three times, an average of $2\frac{1}{2}$ times.

The required correction sequence can be derived from the correction charts

253

by moving across for every station field and down every time a switch to the next disc surface is made. For reverse motion one would move up the chart.

Fast motion is normally created by recording every second or third field and then playing back at the correct speed or thereabouts. The chart can still be used by blanking off the unrecorded fields. If only the odd fields were recorded, a playback at normal speed would require the insertion of a half-line delay on every second field.

Conclusion

A major part of video disc technology is digital logic and only a small section has been covered in a simplified way. Video discs are becoming more and

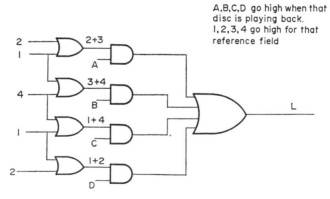

Fig. 13.9. 1 line delay logic (P.A.L. only).

254

more useful as production tools for frame by frame animation assembly of edited sequences, pre-programmed playback sequences at various speeds and in various directions. All this increases the digital computing control logic surrounding a basic machine.

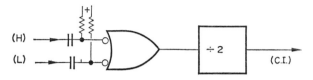

Fig. 13.10. The chroma invertor logic for P.A.L.

Another expanding use of the disc is as a video file with a very fast access time to any track: 450 separate pictures could be stored on one surface of the disc with an indexing system to locate any track within seconds. A buffer track store with a separate head for each user can be placed on the reverse side of the disc. When an individual user wishes to see a particular picture he can call it up to be replayed and recorded on his own track thus releasing the top surface for another user.

References

1. BOICE, C., A new approach to colour slow motion, *Video Recording*, Visual Electronics, Sunnyvale, California.
2. FIX, H., FUNK, H. AND VOLLENWEIDER, E., Slow motion device for monochrome and color television using magnetic disk store. *EBU Review*, Part A No. 112, December 1968.
3. STRATTON, L., Reviewing slow motion disc principles. *Broadcast Engineering*, February 1969.
4. MACLEOD, Magnetic discs for video recording, *JSMPTE*, Vol. 80, April 1971, 295–297.

Appendix

1. Example to show how a back gap in a record head stabilises the reluctance

Mean circumference $-l$

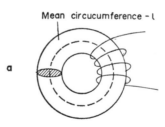

The toroid shown, forms the basis of a magnetic head. Its reluctance (S) can be formulated as:

$$S = \frac{l}{a \times \mu_o \mu_r}$$

where l = mean length of magnetic path.

a = cross sectional area of path.

μ_o = Absolute permeability $(4\pi \times 10^{-7})$.

μ_r = Relative permeability.

typically $l = 0.8$ cm

$a = 0.05$ cm^2

and $\mu_r = 380$.

$$S = \frac{0 \cdot 8 \times 10^{-2}}{380 \times 4\pi \times 10^{-7} \times 5 \times 10^{-6}} = 3 \cdot 33 \times 10^6 \text{ At/Wb}.$$

The permeability can also be expressed in terms of *MMF* and Flux.

$$S = \frac{I \times N}{\Phi}$$

$\hat{\Phi}$ = Flux in Wb

N = Number of turns in winding

I = Current in winding.

If $N = 400$ and $\Phi = 4\mu$Wb.

$$\underline{I = 33mA}$$

If a small gap is cut in the ring 0·004 cm long then reluctance of the air path.

$$= \frac{l}{\mu_0 \times a} = 6 \cdot 04 \times 10^6 \text{ At/Wb}$$

∴ Total reluctance

$$= 3 \cdot 33 + 6 \cdot 04 = 9 \cdot 37 \text{ At/Wb} \times 10^6$$

New current for 4μWb

$$I = \frac{9 \cdot 37 \times 10 \times 4 \times 10^{-6}}{400}$$

$$\underline{= 94mA}$$

With gap included the record drive increases by a factor of 3. However with a large proportion of the reluctance being air the flux for a given current is more stable i.e.: 50% change in μr with no gap gives a 50% change in Φ. With gap, only about 17% change in flux occurs. A similar reduction in flux change occurs for head wear.

2. Loss due to gap effect

From chapter 1 (5).

$$e = K_2 I \omega \cos \frac{2\pi x}{\lambda}$$

As $By \alpha e$

$$By = KI\omega \cos \frac{2\pi x}{\lambda} \qquad 1$$

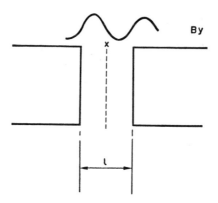

By

If the head has a finite gap length (l) then the average By is the integral of all the flux from $x - l/2$ to $x + l/2$ divided by l.

$$\text{Average } By = \frac{1}{l} \int_{x-l/2}^{x+l/2} By \, dx$$

$$= \frac{1}{l} \int_{x-l/2}^{x+l/2} KI\omega \cos \frac{2\pi x}{\lambda} \, dx$$

$$= KI\omega \cdot \frac{1}{l} \cdot \frac{\lambda}{2\pi} \left[\sin \frac{2\pi(x + l/2)}{\lambda} - \sin \frac{2\pi(x - l/2)}{\lambda} \right]$$

From

$$\sin(A + B) = \sin A \cos B + \cos A \sin B$$

$$\sin(A - B) = \sin A \cos B - \cos A \sin B$$

$$\text{Average } By = KI\omega \cdot \frac{1}{l} \cdot \frac{\lambda}{2\pi} \cdot 2 \cos \frac{2\pi x}{\lambda} \sin \frac{\pi l}{\lambda}.$$

$$= KI\omega \cos \frac{2\pi x}{\lambda} \left(\frac{\sin \pi l/\lambda}{\pi l/\lambda} \right) \qquad\qquad 2$$

This is the same as By modified by a $\dfrac{\sin \alpha}{\alpha}$ term where $\alpha = \dfrac{\pi l}{\lambda}$.

Output falls to zero when

$$\sin \pi l/\lambda = 0$$

i.e. when $l = \lambda$ or 2λ or 3λ, etc.

when gap length equals wavelength on tape.

258

3. Loss due to incorrect azimuth

From Fig. 1.24.

$$a = z \tan \theta$$

where θ = Angle of Azimuth.

z = track width.

If θ is small

$$a = z\theta \qquad\qquad 1$$

Ignoring gap effect the average induction By can be determined by integrating

between $x - \dfrac{z\theta}{2}$ and $x + \dfrac{z\theta}{2}$ and dividing by a.

$$\text{Average } By = KzI\omega \cdot \frac{1}{a} \int\limits_{x-z\theta/2}^{x+z\theta/2} \cos \frac{2\pi x}{\lambda} \, dx$$

with same trig identities as Appendix 2.

$$\text{Average } By = KI\omega \cdot \frac{1}{z\theta} \cdot \frac{\lambda}{2\pi} \left[\sin \left(\frac{2\pi x}{\lambda} - \frac{\pi z\theta}{\lambda} \right) - \sin \left(\frac{2\pi x}{\lambda} + \frac{\pi z\theta}{\lambda} \right) \right]$$

$$By = KI\omega \cdot \frac{1}{z\theta} \cdot \frac{\lambda}{2\pi} \cdot 2 \cos \left(\frac{2\pi x}{\lambda} \right) \sin \frac{\pi z\theta}{\lambda}$$

$$= KI\omega \cos \omega t \left(\frac{\sin \pi z\theta/\lambda}{\pi z\theta/\lambda} \right)$$

The modifying term is now $\dfrac{\sin \beta}{\beta}$ where $\beta = \dfrac{\pi z\theta}{\lambda}$.

Output falls to zero when

$$\sin \pi \frac{z\theta}{\lambda} = 0$$

i.e. when $z\theta = \lambda$ or 2λ or 3λ, etc.

If $z\theta = \lambda$

and $\lambda = \dfrac{s}{f}$

$$fext = \frac{S}{z\theta}$$

4. Alignment of field sync

From Table 3, F = 29·2 ± 1·3 mm

If tach output gives pulse when the head recording the vert sync is in the centre of tape then alignment of tach must be on 3rd serration.*

* Head No 4—Ampex
  Head No 1—R.C.A.

Centre of tape is 25·4 mm (1·00 in) from bottom of tape. Start of field sync precedes this by

$$29·2 - 25·4 = 3·8 \text{ mm.} \quad \text{(E.B.U Spec. Fig. 3.4)}$$

Head to tape speed = 1620 in/sec = 4120 cm/sec

$$\text{Time to travel } 3·8 \text{ mm} = \frac{3·8}{4120} = 92·4 \ \mu\text{sec.}$$

This time from start of field sync corresponds to the 3rd serration.

Tolerance.

$$\pm 1·3 \text{ mm corresponds to } \frac{92·4}{3·8} \times 1·3 = \pm 31·6 \ \mu\text{sec.}$$

$$\simeq \tfrac{1}{2} \text{ line.}$$

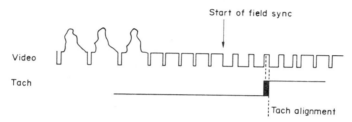

5. Calculation of position of frame pulse due to control track head displacement

Frame pulse is normally generated at first serration of vertical sync, when head is approximately in centre of track.

Control track head position is 45·5 tracks downstream. As one track plus guard bard = 15.625 × 10⁻³., the distance between video head and control track head = 45.5 × 15.6.5 × 10⁻³ = 0.712 in. The nearest field on tape can be calculated as follows:

On 525/60 Hz

$$3 \text{ fields} = 48 \text{ tracks}$$

Control track pulse is 3 fields − 2·5 tracks from the track with field sync.

On 625/50 Hz

$$2 \text{ fields} = 40 \text{ tracks}$$

Control track pulse is 3 fields + 5·5 tracks from the track with field sync.

6. Format dimensions of helical recordings

The following calculations for the format dimensions of helical recordings are made for the four most common formats in use. No standardisation has yet been reached internationally although the $\frac{1}{2}$ in format promulgated by the Electronic Industries Association of Japan (EIAJ) is finding some common use for 60 Hz standards and the Phillips V.C.R. is becoming very popular in Europe on the 50 Hz standards.

Most of the variables in a helical format depend on each other and modify the final conditions. To initially break into the circle two basic requirements are specified:

1. Head speed. This forms the major portion of the head to tape speed, the tape speed adding or subtracting about 1% to the final value. The required head speed is mainly determined by the resolution of the tape and the maximum record frequency:

where $S = \lambda f.$

    S = Head/tape speed
    λ = Minimum wavelength resolved
    f = Maximum record frequency.

For γFe_2O_3 the minimum wavelength is about 0·075 mil (About 2 μm). If the maximum record frequency = 13·3 MHz, the

Head/tape speed $= 0{\cdot}075 \, . \, 13{\cdot}3 \, . \, 10^{-3} \, . \, 10^6$
                 $= 1000$ i.p.s.

For high energy tape, the minimum wavelength is about 0·0375 mil (1·0 μm). This permits a head/tape speed of half that required for γFe_2O_3, to obtain the same frequency response.

If the upper response is lowered to 8·7 MHz,

$$S = 0{\cdot}0375 \, . \, 8{\cdot}7 \text{ MHz} = 325 \text{ i.p.s. } (8{\cdot}25 \text{ m/s})$$

2. Tape speed. The initial required tape speed is a balance between length of playing time and the video signal/noise ratio. A faster tape speed permits a wider video track which in turn gives a higher signal/noise ratio. The second consideration for the tape speed is to maintain horizontal sync line up. The longitudinal movement during one field period should be directly related to the TV line length which in turn is determined by the head to tape speed. In the following calculations the approximate head and tape speed are used as a starting point and subsequently modified.

Ampex 1 in single-headed omega wrap

60 Hz standard (initial requirements)

    Required head speed—1000 i.p.s.
    Required longitudinal speed—9 in i.p.s. (provisional)

Drum diameter

For a single headed machine operating at 60 fields per second. 1 revolution takes 1/60 second.

$$\text{Drum circumference } (C) = \frac{1000}{60} = 16\cdot67 \text{ in}$$

$$\text{Drum diameter} = \frac{16\cdot67}{\pi} = 5\cdot3 \text{ in}$$

Track angle

Space allowed for video tracks $= 0\cdot905$ in

The tape rise must be 0·905 in over the circumference of the drum (16·67 in).

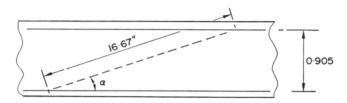

If the tape is stationary then the track angle (α') can be calculated as follows:

$$\sin \alpha' = \frac{0\cdot905}{16\cdot67}$$

$$\alpha' = 3° \, 7'$$

The track angle is modified by the movement of the tape and if the tape moves 9 in in one second then during one field:

$$\text{tape movement} = \frac{9}{60} = 0\cdot15 \text{ in}$$

The effect of this movement depends upon the relative movement between the head and tape. If the tape moves in the opposite direction to the head then the angle is reduced.

The track length would be increased by:

$$\cos 3° \, 7' \, . \, 0\cdot15 \text{ in} \simeq 0\cdot15 \text{ in}$$

True track length:

$$= 16\cdot67 \text{ in} + 0\cdot15 \text{ in} = 16\cdot83 \text{ in}$$

If $\alpha = $ Angle of track when head and tape move

$$\sin \alpha = \frac{0\cdot905}{16\cdot67 + 0\cdot15}$$

$$\alpha = 3° \, 6'$$

Tape movement

For sync line-up the video track movement must be an integral number of lines plus half a line to allow for line sync phase at the start of a new field.

If track length = 16·83 in

$$1 \text{ TV line length on track} = \frac{16·83 \text{ in}}{262·5} = 0·0641 \text{ in}$$

Track movement on consecutive tracks must be:

$$\text{line length } (n + \tfrac{1}{2})$$

where $n = 1, 2, 3 \ldots$, etc.

Tape longitudinal movement during 1 field time:

$$= \frac{(n + \tfrac{1}{2}) \cdot 0·0641}{\cos \alpha}$$

For $n = 2*$

$$\text{longitudinal movement} = 0·1589 \text{ in}$$

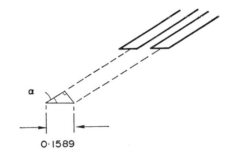

0·1589

The exact tape speed = 60 . 0·1589 in = 9·6238 i.p.s.

The corrected head/tape speed   = 1009 i.p.s.

The centre–centre track spacing:

$$= \sin \alpha \cdot 0·1589 \text{ in} = 0·0087 \text{ in}$$
(6 thou track, 2·7 thou guard band)

50 Hz operation

If the same assembly is used on 50 Hz systems, the following changes occur due to the new head rotational speed of 50 r.p.s.:

New head speed = 16·67 . 50   833 i.p.s.

$$\text{TV line length on track} = \frac{16·83}{312·5} = 0·0539.$$

* $n = 1$ too slow
  $n = 3$ too fast

$$\text{tape speed} = \frac{50\left(n + \frac{1}{2}\right) . 0\cdot0539}{\cos \alpha}$$

If $n = 3$

longitudinal movement $= 0\cdot189$ in
tape speed $\quad\quad\quad = 9\cdot44731$ i.p.s.
Head/tape speed $\quad = 842\cdot4$ i.p.s.

track centre–centre spacing $= \sin \alpha \, 0\cdot189 = 0\cdot0102$ in
(6 thou track width, 4·2 thou guard band)

IVC 1 in single headed alpha wrap

60 Hz standard (initial requirements)

Required head speed $= 717$ i.p.s.
Required tape speed $= 7$ i.p.s.

Drum diameter

1 revolution takes 1/60 second.

$$\text{Drum circumference } (C) = \frac{717}{60} = 11\cdot94 \text{ in}$$

$$\text{Drum diameter} = \frac{11\cdot94}{\pi} = 3\cdot8 \text{ in}$$

Track angle

Space allowed for video tracks $= 1$ in
∴ The tape rise must be 1 in over 11·92 in

Stationary tape

$$\sin \alpha' = \frac{1}{11\cdot92} = 0\cdot0836$$

$$\alpha' = 4° \, 47'$$

Extra tape movement

$$= \tfrac{7}{60} = 0\cdot116 \text{ inches per field}$$

True track length (one field).

$$= 11\cdot94 + 0\cdot116 = 12\cdot056 \text{ in}$$

$$\sin \alpha = \frac{1}{12\cdot056} = 0\cdot0828$$

$$\alpha = 4° \, 45'$$

$\alpha =$ angle of video track when head and tape move in opposite directions.

264

Tape movement

1 TV line length on track $= \dfrac{12 \cdot 056}{262 \cdot 5} = 0 \cdot 046$ in

longitudinal movement for 1 field $= \dfrac{(n + \frac{1}{2}) \, 0 \cdot 0.046}{\cos \alpha}$

for $n = 2 \cdot 0$ $\qquad = 0 \cdot 115$ inches/field.

Exact longitudinal speed $= 60 \cdot 0 \cdot 115 = 6 \cdot 91$ i.p.s.
Exact head to tape speed $= 723 \cdot 9$ i.p.s.
Centre–centre track spacing

$$= \sin 4^\circ \, 45' \, . \, 0 \cdot 115 = 0 \cdot 0095 \text{ in}$$
$$(6 \cdot 5 \text{ mil track width} + 3 \text{ mil guard band})$$

EIAJ Type 1 two headed, $\frac{1}{2}$ in tape

60 Hz standard only

Required head speed—10·9 m/sec (430 i.p.s.)
Required longitudinal speed—200 mm/sec (7·87 i.p.s.) provisional

Drum diameter
For two headed machine, 1 revolution takes $\frac{1}{30}$ of a second.

Drum circumference $(C) = \dfrac{10 \cdot 9}{30} = 36 \cdot 35$ cm

Drum diameter $\qquad = \dfrac{36 \cdot 35}{\pi} = 115 \cdot 82$ mm (4·54 in)

Track Angle
Space allowed for video tracks (excluding overlap) $= 10 \cdot 10$ mm
The tape rise therefore must be 10·10 mm over *half* the circumference of the drum.

Stationary tape:

$$\sin \alpha' = \frac{10 \cdot 10 \times 2}{363 \cdot 5} = 0 \cdot 0556$$

$$\alpha' = 3^\circ \, 11'$$

Extra tape movement:

$$= \frac{200}{60} = 3 \cdot 33 \text{ mm}$$

True track length (1 field) $= 181 \cdot 75 + 3 \cdot 33 = 185 \cdot 1$ mm

$$\sin \alpha \, \frac{10 \cdot 10}{185 \cdot 1} = 0 \cdot 0546$$

$$= 3^\circ \, 7' \, 43''$$

α = angle of video track when head and tape move in opposite directions.

Tape movement

$$1 \text{ T.V. line length or track} = \frac{185 \cdot 1}{262 \cdot 5} = 0 \cdot 705 \text{ mm.}$$

For sync line-up:

$$\text{longitudinal movement for 1 field} = \frac{(n + \frac{1}{2}) \, 0 \cdot 705}{\cos \alpha}$$

For $n = 4 \cdot 0$. $= 3 \cdot 175$ mm/field.

Exact longitudinal speed $= 60 \cdot 3 \cdot 175 = 190$ mm/sec (7·5 i.p.s.)
Exact head to tape speed $= 11 \cdot 09$ m/sec.

Centre–centre track spacing.

$$= \sin 3° \, 7' \, 43'' \, . \, 3 \cdot 175 = 0 \cdot 173 \text{ mm } (0 \cdot 0067 \text{ in})$$

(0·13 mm track width + 0·043 mm guard band)

Phillips VCR Cassette two headed $\frac{1}{2}$ in wide tape

50 Hz Standard (*initial requirements*)

Required Head speed $= 8 \cdot 25$ m/sec.
Required longitudinal speed $= 15$ cm/sec.

Drum diameter

1 revolution takes $\frac{1}{25}$ of a second.
Drum circumference $= 330$ mm
Drum diameter $\quad = 105$ mm

Track angle.

Space allowed for video tracks $= 10 \cdot 6$ mm (excluding overlap)
∴ Tape rise must be 10·6 mm over half the circumference of the drum.

Stationary tape:

$$\sin \alpha' = \frac{10 \cdot 6 \times 2}{330} = 0 \cdot 0642$$

$$\alpha' = 3° \, 41'$$

Extra tape movement:

$$= \frac{150}{50} = 3 \text{ mm per field.}$$

True track length (1 field)

$$= 165 - 3 = 162 \text{ mm}$$

(Note: Head and tape movement in the same direction)

266

Tape movement

$$1 \text{ T.V. line on track} = \frac{162}{312\cdot5} = 0\cdot514 \text{ mm}$$

For sync line-up

$$\text{longitudinal movement for 1 field} = \frac{(n + \frac{1}{2})\, 0\cdot514}{\cos \alpha}$$

For $n = 5\cdot0$

$$= 2\cdot835 \text{ mm/field}$$

Exact longitudinal speed $= 50 \cdot 2\cdot835 = 14\cdot29 \text{ cm/sec}$
Exact head to tape speed $= 8\cdot25 - 0\cdot14 = 8\cdot11 \text{ m/sec}$

Centre–centre spacing:

$$\sin 3^\circ\, 45' \cdot 2\cdot835 = 0\cdot187 \text{ mm}$$
$$(0\cdot130 \text{ mm track width} + 0\cdot057 \text{ mm guard band})$$

IVC/Rank-Cintel 9000 Series

This format is slightly different to other helical wraps. It uses 2 in wide tape and with a two headed drum rotating at 150 r.p.s. it records one sixth of a field per track on the 625/50 field standard. On the 525/60 field standard it rotates at the same rate but records one fifth of a field per track.

The IVC 2 in Format

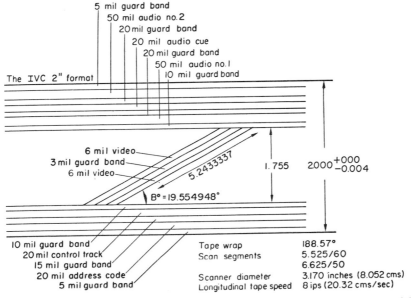

If drum diameter $= 3\cdot17$ in
Circumference $= \pi \times 3\cdot17 = 9\cdot96$ in
Head speed $= 9\cdot96 \times 150 = 1494$ i.p.s.
Tape rise $= 1\cdot755$ in over $188\cdot57°$

If the tape is stationary then the track length $= 9\cdot96 \cdot \dfrac{188\cdot57}{360} = 5\cdot218$ in

$$\sin \alpha' = \frac{1\cdot755}{5\cdot218}$$

$$\alpha' = 19° \; 42' \; (19\cdot70°)$$

Longitudinal tape movement $= 8$ i.p.s.

For one scan movement $= \dfrac{8}{6\cdot0 \,.\, 50} = 0\cdot0267$ in

Increase in track length $= \cos 19° \; 42' \,.\, 0\cdot0267$ in $= 0\cdot025$ in

Track length $= 5\cdot218 + 0\cdot025 = 5\cdot243$ in

$$\sin \alpha = \frac{1\cdot755}{5\cdot243}$$

Track angle with tape movement $\quad \alpha = 19\cdot555°$

Head to tape speed $= 1494 \div \cos 19\cdot555° \,.\, 8 = 1501\cdot5$ i.p.s.

Centre–centre track spacing $= \mathrm{Sin}\, 19\cdot555° \,.\, 0\cdot0267 = 0\cdot009$ in
(6 thou track, 3 thou guard band)

T.V. lines length $= \dfrac{1501\cdot5}{625 \,.\, 25} = 0\cdot0906$ in

T.V. lines per $180°$ scan $\dfrac{625}{2 \,.\, 6} = 52\cdot125$ lines

It can be seen from above that the sync line-up formula must be modified to

$$\text{Longitudinal movement during one scan} = \frac{(n + \tfrac{1}{8}) \times 0\cdot0906}{\cos \alpha}$$

As $n = 0$ produces too slow a tape speed and $n = 1$ too fast a tape speed, this format does not have horizontal sync line-up.

It also is not possible to have still frame or slow-motion.

7. Track angle change resulting from a conical wrap

If the required space for the longitudinal tracks (d) is $0\cdot100$ in and the maximum drum angle of overlap is limited to $65°$, then for drum dimensions calculated in Appendix 6 the length of overlap (l) is:
268

$$l = \frac{16.65 \times 65}{360} \doteq 3 \text{ in}$$

If β equals the angle of the sides of the drum from the perpendicular then the overlap is as shown.

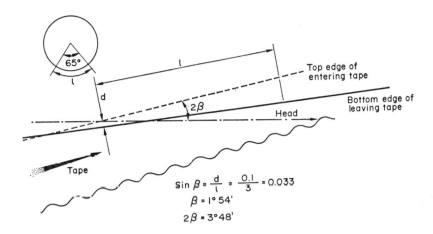

$$\text{Sin } \beta = \frac{d}{l} = \frac{0.1}{3} = 0.033$$
$$\beta = 1° 54'$$
$$2\beta = 3°48'$$

The angle of the track is modified by the change in angle of the tape. In this example it is 3° 48' less on the bottom edge than the top edge.

If the narrowest angle is 3° 6', as calculated in Appendix 6 then the angle must increase to 6° 54'.

8. Modulation index of FM wave

To show that the modulation index of an *FM* wave is $\frac{f_d}{f_m}$ and is equal to the peak phase modulation of the signal.

$$\omega = \omega_c + \omega_d \cos \omega_m t$$

$$\omega = \frac{d\phi}{dt}$$

$$\phi = \int \omega dt$$
$$= \int (\omega_c + \omega_d \cos \omega_m t) dt$$

$$= \omega_c t + \frac{\omega_d}{\omega_m} \sin \omega_m t$$

$\omega_c t$ is an angle increasing with time

$\dfrac{\omega_d}{\omega_m} \sin \omega_m t$ is a sinusoidal modulation of $\omega_c t$ reaching a maximum of

$\pm \dfrac{\omega_d}{\omega_m}$ when $\sin \omega_m t = \pm 1$.

$$\therefore \ \theta = \frac{\omega_d}{\omega_m} = \frac{f_d}{f_m}$$

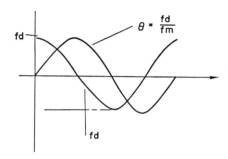

9. Spectrum of sinusoidally frequency modulated signal

$$e = E \sin \phi t$$

$$\phi = \omega_c t + \frac{\omega_d}{\omega_m} \sin \omega_m t$$

$$\frac{\omega_d}{\omega_m} = \theta$$

$$\therefore \ e = E \sin (\omega_c t + \phi \sin \omega_m t)$$

$$e = E[\sin \omega_c t \cos (\theta \sin \omega_m t) + \cos \omega_c t \sin (\theta \sin \omega_m t)]$$

Now

$$\sin (\theta \sin \omega_m t) = 2J_1(\theta) \sin \omega_m t +$$
$$2J_3(\theta) \sin 3\omega_m t +$$
$$2J_5(\theta) \sin \omega_m t + \ldots$$
$$2J_{2n+1}(\theta) \sin (2n + 1)\omega_m t$$

and

$$\cos (\theta \sin \omega_m t) = J_0 \theta + 2J_2(\theta) \cos 2\omega_m t +$$
$$2J_4(\theta) \cos 4\omega_m t + \ldots$$
$$2J_{2n}(\theta) \cos 2n\omega_m t$$

$$\therefore \ e = E \ [J_0 \theta \sin \omega_c t$$

$$+ \ 2J_1(\theta) \cos \omega_c t \sin \omega_m t$$
$$+ \ 2J_2(\theta) \sin \omega_c t \cos 2\omega_m t$$

270

$$+ 2J_3(\theta) \cos \omega_c t \sin 3\omega_m t$$
$$+ \ldots$$
$$+ 2J_{2n}(\theta) \sin \omega_c t \sin 2_n \omega_m t$$
$$+ 2J_{2n+1}(\theta) \cos \omega_c t \sin (2n + 1)\omega_m t].$$

The first term represents the centre frequency, while each of the following terms represents a pair of 'side-bands' symmetrical about the centre frequency and spaced by:

$$\omega_m, 2\omega_m \ldots 2n\omega_m \ldots (2n + 1)\omega_m$$

This can be seen by expanding:

$$e = E[J_0(\theta) \sin \omega_c t]$$
$$+ J_1(\theta)[\sin (\omega_c + \omega_m)t - \sin (\omega_c - \omega_m)t]$$
$$+ J_2(\theta)[\sin (\omega_c + 2\omega_m)t + \sin (\omega_c - 2\omega_m)t] \ldots$$
$$+ J_{2n}(\theta)[\sin (\omega_c + 2_n\omega_m)t + \sin (\omega_c - 2_n\omega_m)t]$$
etc.

10. Calculation of amplitudes of wanted side-bands and unwanted components in a VTR frequency modulated signal, when modulated by colour sub-carrier

625/50 Hz High Band
For 100% amplitude, 100% saturated colour bars.

$$\theta = 0.54 \text{ (chapter 5)}$$

From Bessel functions* wanted 1st order $SB = 0.260$ w.r.t. peak signal.

* Eleven and fifteen place tables of Bessel functions—Enzo Cambi.

For 3rd harmonic:

$$\theta_3 = 1.62$$

From Bessel functions unwanted 3rd lower $SB = 0.075$ w.r.t. 3rd harmonic. For folded SB—3rd lower sideband of the fundamental:

From Bessel functions = 0.0032 w.r.t. peak signal.
Amplitude of wanted $SBs = 0.26$
Amplitude of unwanted SB due to 10% 3rd harmonic = 0.0075
$$(-51 \text{ dB})$$
Amplitude of unwanted folded $SB = 0.0032$ (-58 dB)

525/60 Hz High Band
For 100% Amplitude, 100% saturated colour bars.

$$\theta = 0.935.$$

From Bessel functions wanted 1st order $SB = 0.418$ w.r.t. peak signal
For 3rd harmonic:

$$\theta_3 = 2.8.$$

From Bessel functions unwanted 4th lower $SB. = 0.107$ w.r.t. 3rd harmonic. For folded SB—4th lower sideband of the fundamental:

From Bessel functions $= 0.0019$ w.r.t. peak signal
Amplitude of wanted $SBs = 0.418$
Amplitude of unwanted SB due to 10% 3rd harmonic $= 0.0107$

$$(-52 \text{ dB})$$

Amplitude of unwanted folded $SB = 0.0019$ (-67 dB)

11. Record equivalent circuit of a video head

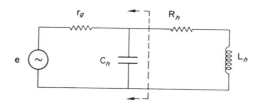

r_g = drive source resistance
C_h = head inter-winding capacity
R_h = head losses. Winding resistance, eddy current, hysteresis.
L_h = head winding inductance.

Thevenin equivalent

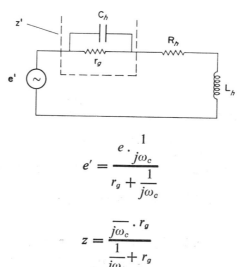

$$e' = \frac{e \cdot \dfrac{1}{j\omega_c}}{r_g + \dfrac{1}{j\omega_c}}$$

$$z = \frac{\overline{\dfrac{1}{j\omega_c}} \cdot r_g}{\dfrac{1}{j\omega_c} + r_g}$$

272

If $r_g \ll \dfrac{1}{j\omega_c}$

$$e' = e$$

$$z = r_g$$

12. The Cosine equalizer

From Fig. 6.12

$$V_{\text{in}} = V \sin \omega t$$

$$V_D = V \sin (\omega t - \theta)$$

$$V_{\text{Ref}} = \frac{V}{2} \sin (\omega t - 2\theta)$$

$$V_0 = V_D - K(V\text{in} + V_{\text{Ref}}) = V \sin (\omega t - \theta) - \frac{K}{2} (V \sin \omega t - V \sin$$

$$(\omega t - 2\phi)$$

$$\phi = \frac{2\pi td}{tp}$$

$td = $ Delay line time $tp = $ periodic time of input frequency $= \dfrac{1}{f}$

This shows that when $K = 0$, $V_0 = V \sin (\omega t - \theta)$, i.e.: equal to V_D in amplitude and phase for all frequencies.

$$\sin (A - B) = \sin A \cos B - \cos A \sin B.$$

$$V_0 = V \sin (\omega t - \theta) - \frac{KV}{2} (\sin \omega t + \sin \omega t \cos 2\theta - \sin 2\theta \cos \omega t)$$

If $\theta = 0$, i.e.: Delay $= 0°$ then $\dfrac{td}{tp} = 0$

$$V_0 = V \sin \omega t - \frac{KV}{2} (\sin \omega t + \sin \omega t \times 1 - 0 \times \cos \omega t).$$

$$V_0 = (V - KV) \sin \omega t.$$

V_0 is less than V, decreases with increase of K, same phase as V_D, adjustment of K causes no phase change.

If $\theta = \dfrac{\pi}{4}$, i.e.: Delay $= 45°$ then $\dfrac{td}{tp} = \frac{1}{8}$

273

$$V_0 = V \sin\left(\omega t - \frac{\pi}{4}\right) - \frac{KV}{2}(\sin \omega t + \sin \omega t \times 0 - 1 \cos \omega t)$$

$$= V \sin\left(\omega t - \frac{\pi}{4}\right) - KV(\sin \omega t - \cos \omega t).$$

$$= \left(V - \frac{\sqrt{2}\,KV}{2}\right) \sin\left(\omega t - \frac{\pi}{4}\right).$$

V_0 is less than V, decreases with increase of K, same phase as V_D, adjustment of K causes no phase change.

If $\theta = \dfrac{2\pi}{4}$, i.e.: Delay $= 90°$ or $\dfrac{td}{tp} = \tfrac{1}{4}$.

$$V_0 = V \sin\left(wt - \frac{\pi}{2}\right) - \frac{KV}{2}(\sin \omega t + \sin \omega t \cos \pi - \sin \pi \cos \omega t)$$

$$V_0 = V \sin\left(wt - \frac{\pi}{2}\right) - \frac{KV}{2}(\sin \omega t + \sin \omega t \times -1 - 0 \cos \omega t).$$

$$= V \sin\left(wt - \frac{\pi}{2}\right) - 0.$$

At Frequency where delay $= 90°$ $V_0 = V_D$.

Amplitude and phase unaffected by K. This frequency called the 'turnover frequency'

$$\theta = \frac{3\pi}{4}, \text{ i.e.: Delay } 135° \text{ or } \frac{td}{tp} = \tfrac{3}{8}.$$

$$V_0 = V \sin\left(wt - \frac{3\pi}{4}\right) - \frac{KV}{2}\left(\sin \omega t + \sin \omega t \cos \frac{3\pi}{2} - \sin \frac{3\pi}{2} \cos \omega t\right)$$

$$= V \sin\left(wt - \frac{3\pi}{4}\right) - \frac{KV}{2}(\sin \omega t + \cos \omega t)$$

$$V_0 = V \sin\left(\omega t - \frac{3\pi}{4}\right) + \frac{\sqrt{2}KV}{2} \sin\left(\omega t + \frac{3\pi}{4}\right)$$

$$= \left(V + \frac{\sqrt{2}KV}{2}\right) \sin\left(\omega t - \frac{3\pi}{4}\right)$$

i.e.: greater than V, increases with increase in K, same phase as V_D, adjustment of K causes no phase change.

If $\theta = \pi$, i.e: Delay $= 180°$ or $\dfrac{td}{tp} = \tfrac{1}{2}$

274

$$V_0 = V \sin(\omega t - \pi) - \frac{KV}{2}(\sin \omega t + \sin \omega t \cos 2\pi - \sin \cos \omega t)$$

$$= V \sin(\omega t - \pi) - KV \sin \omega t$$

$$= (V + KV) \sin(\omega t - \pi).$$

i.e.: greater than V, increases with increase in K, same phase as V_D, adjustment of K causes no phase change.
More generally

$$V_D \quad = V_{\text{in}} \, \backslash \omega t$$

$$V_{\text{REF}} = \frac{V_{\text{in}}}{2} \, \backslash 2\omega t$$

$$V' \quad = K\left(\frac{V_{\text{in}}}{2} + V_{\text{REF}}\right) = \frac{KV_{\text{in}}}{2}(1 + \backslash 2\omega t)$$

Cosine Rule

$$A^2 = B^2 + {}^2 + 2BC \cos\phi$$

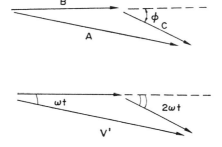

$$\therefore (V^1)^2 = (1 + 1 + 2\cos 2\omega t) \, \overline{\backslash \omega t} \cdot \left(\frac{KV_{\text{in}}}{2}\right)^2$$

$$(V^1)^2 = (2 + 2\cos 2\,\omega t) \, \overline{\backslash \omega t} \cdot \left(\frac{KV_{\text{in}}}{2}\right)^2$$

$$(V^1) = \sqrt{2}\,(1 + \cos 2\,\omega t)^{\frac{1}{2}} \, \overline{\backslash \omega t} \cdot \frac{KV_{\text{in}}}{2} \qquad\qquad 1$$

But $\cos^2 \omega t = \frac{1}{2}(1 + \cos 2\,\omega t)$

$$\therefore \cos \omega t \quad = \frac{1}{\sqrt{2}}(1 + \cos \omega t)^{\frac{1}{2}} \qquad\qquad 2$$

275

Sub 2 into 1

$$V' = 2 \cos \omega t \; \overline{\backslash \omega t} \cdot \frac{KV_{\text{in}}}{2} = KV_{\text{in}} \cos \omega t \; \overline{\backslash \omega t}$$

$$V_0 = V_D - V' = V_{\text{in}} \overline{\backslash \omega t} - KV_{\text{in}} \cos \omega t \; \overline{\backslash \omega t}$$

$$\therefore V_0 = V_{\text{in}} (1 - K \cos \omega t) \overline{\backslash \omega t} \text{ (as shown in Fig. 6.12c)}$$

13. Analysis of an A-stable multivibrator modulator

Equivalent circuit of discharge path of coupling capacitor for Fig. 6.4

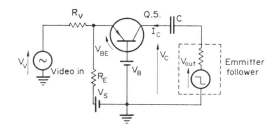

Where

$$R_E = 2R_1 + \frac{R_2}{2}$$

$$R_V = \frac{R_3}{2}$$

Typical values:

$V_B = 6 \cdot 2$ volts
$V_S = 12$ volts
$V_{BE} = 0.4$ volts
$V_{\text{out}} = 4 \cdot 0$ volts (output from E.F.)

$\therefore R_E = 1 \cdot 05 \, K\Omega$
$R_V = 3 \cdot 5 \, K\Omega$

$h_{fe} = 0 \cdot 98$
$C = 50 \, pf$
$R_1 = 400 \, \Omega$
$R_2 = 500 \, \Omega$
$R_3 = 7000 \, \Omega$

When V_c discharges to 0 volts circuit 6.4 (b) will commutate.

$$\text{Frequency of oscillation} = \frac{1}{2t_1} \qquad\qquad 1$$

Where $t_1 = t_2$ and is the time for V_c to discharge from V_{OUT} to 0 volts.

$$I_E = \frac{V_S - (V_B + V_{BE})}{R_E} + \frac{V_V - (V_B + V_{BE})}{R_V} \qquad\qquad 2$$

276

Charge on a capacitor $Q = CV$

$$I_c \times t = CV_{\text{out}}$$

$$t = \frac{CV_{\text{out}}}{I_c}$$

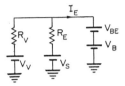

From (1)

$$f = \frac{1}{2t} = \frac{I_c}{2CV_0} = \frac{h_{fe}I_e}{2CV_{\text{out}}} \qquad \qquad \textbf{3}$$

NOTE frequency $\propto I_e$

For example given. If $V_V = 0$ volt

$$I_e = \frac{12 - (6\cdot2 + 0\cdot4)}{1\cdot05 \cdot 10^{-3}} + \frac{0 - (6\cdot2 + 0\cdot4)}{3\cdot5 \times 10^{-3}}$$

$$= 5.15 \ mA - 1\cdot9 \ mA$$

$$= 3\cdot25 \ mA$$

From (3)

$$f = \frac{0\cdot98 \cdot 3\cdot25 \cdot 10^{-3}}{2\cdot50 \cdot 4 \cdot 10^{-12}} \backsimeq 8 \ MHz$$

If $V_V = 1\cdot35$ volts

$$I_e = 5\cdot15mA - \frac{6\cdot6 - 1\cdot35}{3\cdot5 \times 10^{-3}}$$

$$= 3\cdot65mA.$$

$$f \backsimeq 9 \ MHz$$

A deviation of 1 MHz.

14. Calculation of timing error due to guide displacement x

Triangles ABC and A′B′C′ are similar

Angle ABC = Angle A′B′C′ = θ

where θ = Angle of head to centre of Tape.

$$\sin \theta = \frac{A'C'}{B'A'} = \frac{dx}{x}$$

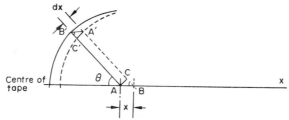

displacement (d_x) $\therefore$

$$d_x = x \sin \theta$$

If $x = 0\cdot001$ in and the nominal Head/Tape speed $= 1570$ in/sec

$$td_x = \frac{x \sin \theta \times 10^6}{1\cdot570} \; \mu\text{secs}.$$

The maximum angle θ will occur for a head playing back 16 lines 8 above the centre line and 8 below

$$\theta = \pm 45° = 90° = 1 \; mS = 15\cdot625 \text{ lines}$$

$$16 \text{ lines} = 90 \times \frac{16}{15\cdot625} = 92° \; 8' = \pm 46° \; 4'$$

The peak–peak error for a $0\cdot001$ in $\times$ axis movement

$$td_x p{-}p = \pm \frac{0\cdot001 \sin 46° \; 4'}{1570} \times 10^6 = \pm 0\cdot459 = 0\cdot916 \; \mu\text{sec}$$

15. Calculation of timing error due to guide displacement y

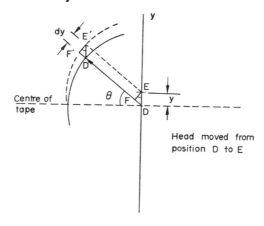

Head moved from
position D to E

278

DEF = D'E'F'

$$\text{Angle DEF} = \text{D'E'F'} = \theta \quad \cos \theta = \frac{\text{E'F'}}{\text{E'D'}} = \frac{dy}{y}$$

$$EF = E'F' = dy = y \cos \theta$$

The error reaches a maximum at $\theta = 0$ and a minimum at maximum values of θ. The peak-peak error

$$tdy \ p\text{-}p = \frac{0.001 \times 10^6}{1570} (1 - \cos 46° \ 4') \ \mu sec$$

$$= 0.194 \ \mu sec$$

Unlike tdx the error is symmetrical about the centre in both sign and amplitude.

16. Calculations of timing error due to guide radius change

Pole tip velocity

$$v = 2\pi r \ Nh.$$

r = guide radius
Nh = Head rotational speed in r.p.s.

If radius is increased to r' then new velocity

$$v' = 2\pi r' \ Nh$$

The difference

$$v - v' = 2\pi Nh \ (r - r')$$

displacement error over 90° rotation = 1 m S

$$d = v - v' \times 10^{-3} \ (\text{distance} = \text{velocity} \times \text{time})$$

Timing error

$$td = \frac{d}{\text{velocity}} = \frac{v - v' \times 10^{-3}}{v}$$

$$\text{From (a)} = \frac{2\pi Nh \ (r - r') \times 10^{-3}}{2\pi r \ Nh} = \frac{(r - r') \times 10^{-3}}{r}$$

For a nominal radius = 1 in
and a difference $r - r' = 500 \ \mu$ in.

$$td = \frac{500 \times 10^{-6} \times 10^{-3}}{1} = 500 \ \eta secs.$$

279

17. The effect of friction between the head drum scanner and the tape on tape tension

The formula for the tension ratio for a wrap on a cylindrical surface

$$\frac{To}{Ti} = e^{\mu\theta}$$

e = 2·7183
μ = coefficient of friction
To = Tension on tape outgoing
Ti = Tension on tape ingoing
θ = Angle of wrap in radians
μ = 0·02 to 0·1 for well designed drum.

For μ = 0·02, 360° wrap

$$\frac{To}{Ti} = e^{.0\cdot02 \times 2\pi} = 1\cdot13$$

If Ti = 5 oz To = 5·65 oz
For μ = 0·1 360° wrap

$$\frac{To}{Ti} = 1\cdot88$$

If Ti = 5 oz To = 9·4 oz
μ = 0·2 *360° wrap*

$$\frac{To}{Ti} = 3\cdot5$$

If Ti = 5 oz To = 17·5 oz
μ = 0·2 *180° wrap*

$$\frac{To}{Ti} = 1\cdot88$$

Ti = 5 oz To = 9·4 oz

The results show the importance of low coefficient of friction and the singular advantage of 180° wrap in terms of tape tension.

18. The reduction of velocity errors using interpolation

The development of an interpolation between error samples to provide velocity compensation can be achieved in several ways. Straight line interpolation is normally used and this obviously is an approximation leaving a residual error when used to correct a sinusoidal component due to guide displacement. See Appendices 14 and 15.

The following equations describe the residual error for the various options.

280

Error without correction

For a 0·001 in error in the x direction the error for any angle:

$$dx = \sin \theta \,.\, 10^{-3}$$

For a 0·001 in error in the y direction the error for any angle:

$$dy = \cos \theta \,.\, 10^{-3}$$

The timing error can be found by dividing by the head to tape speed
Nominally:

$$1620 \text{ i.p.s.} — 625/50 \text{ Hz}$$
$$1560 \text{ i.p.s.} — 525/60 \text{ Hz}$$

Error after line by line correction

The error is corrected at the start of every line
i.e.: every 5·76° rotation of the head on 625/50 Hz or
every 5·49° rotation of the head on 525/60 Hz.

For direction x (625/50 Hz):

$$dx^{\text{I}} = (\sin \theta - \sin . n \,.\, 5\cdot76°) \,.\, 10^{-3}$$

For direction y:

$$dy^{\text{I}} = (\cos \theta - \cos . n \,.\, 5\cdot76°) \,.\, 10^{-3}$$

where $n =$ the number of whole lines from point where $\theta = 0°$.

Error with straight line interpolation between end points

$$\text{Slope} = \frac{f(n + 1)\, 5\cdot76 - f(n)\, 5\cdot76}{5\cdot76}$$

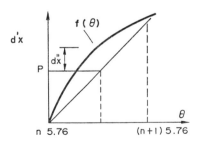

Residual error:

$$\text{Value at } p = \frac{\theta - n\, 5\cdot76}{5\cdot76} (f(n + 1)\, 5\cdot76 - f(n)\, 5\cdot76)$$

281

∴ Residual error:

$$dx^{II} = \sin \theta - \sin . n . 5\cdot76° - \frac{\theta - n . 5\cdot76°}{5\cdot76°} (\sin [n + 1] 5\cdot76°$$

$$- \sin . n . 5\cdot76°)$$

$$dy^{II} = \cos \theta - \cos . n . 5\cdot76° - \frac{\theta - n . 5\cdot76°}{5\cdot76°} (\cos [n + 1] 5\cdot76°$$

$$- \cos . n . 5\cdot76°)$$

Error with straight line interpolation between the last two previous sample points, as on the last line of any head sweep using the error store technique.

$$dx^{III} = \sin \theta - \sin . n . 5\cdot76° - \frac{\theta - n . 5\cdot76°}{5\cdot76°} (\sin . n . 5\cdot76°$$

$$- \sin [n - 1] 5\cdot76°)$$

$$dy^{III} = \cos \theta - \cos. n . 5\cdot76° - \frac{\theta - n . 5\cdot76°}{5\cdot76°} (\cos . n . 5\cdot76°$$

$$\cos [n - 1] 5\cdot76°)$$

If a memory is used to store the line error for every line on one complete revolution then the interpolation is not quite the same as case 3. On one revolution 62·5 lines are recorded. Therefore line 1 of head 1 is $\frac{1}{2}$ a line displaced in head angular position to the same line one revolution later. The error stored is the average over several revolutions making:

$$dx^{IV} = \sin \theta - \sin . n . 5\cdot76 - \frac{\theta - n \, 5\cdot76°}{5\cdot76°} (\sin[n + 1] 5\cdot76 -$$

$$\sin . n . 5\cdot76 + \sin [n + \tfrac{1}{2}] . 5\cdot76° - \sin [n - 1] 5\cdot76°)\tfrac{1}{2}$$

$$dy^{IV} = \cos \theta - \cos . n . 5\cdot76° - \frac{\theta - n \, 5\cdot76}{5\cdot76°} (\cos [n + 1] 5\cdot76 -$$

$$\cos . n . 5\cdot76 + \cos [n + \tfrac{1}{2}] 5\cdot76° - \cos [n - 1] 5\cdot76°)\tfrac{1}{2}.$$

The above equations can be used to calculate the maximum errors for any line (1–8) from = 0° to 52°, for a 0·001 in error in the x or y movement of the guide.

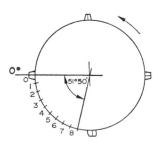

Line Number: n	Maximum Timing Error (Angle) $t^{I}\,dx$ η sec	$t^{I}\,dy$ η sec	$t^{II}\,dx$ η sec	$t^{II}\,dy$ η sec	$t^{III}\,dx$ η sec	$t^{III}\,dy$ η sec	$t^{IV}\,dx$ η sec	$t^{IV}\,dy$ η sec
0	63·8* (5° 45')	3·2 (5° 45')	0·04 (3° 20')	0·8* (2° 52)	0·04 (5° 20')	6·41* (5° 45')	0·04 (5° 45')	1·60* (5° 45)
1	63·2 (11° 31')	9·6 (11° 31')	0·12 (8° 48')	0·79 (8° 38)	0·64 11° 31'	6·39 (11° 31')	0·20 (11° 31')	1·60 (11° 31')
2	61·8 (17° 16')	15·9 (17° 16')	0·20 (14° 29')	0·78 (14° 23)	1·28 (17° 16')	6·27 (17° 16')	0·36 (17° 16')	1·56 (17° 16')
3	60·0 (23° 2')	22·0 (23° 2')	0·28 (20° 13')	0·75 (20° 10')	1·90 (23° 2')	6·13 (23° 2')	0·51 (23° 2')	1·52 (23° 2')
4	57·4 (28° 47')	27·9 (28° 47')	0·35 (25° 58')	0·72 (25° 54')	2·50 (28° 47')	5·89 (28° 47')	0·66 (28° 47')	1·45 (28° 47')
5	54·3 (34° 33')	33·5 (34° 33')	0·42 (31° 44')	0·68 (31° 39')	3·09 (34° 33')	5·62 (34° 33')	0·80 (34° 33')	1·38 (34° 33')
6	50·7 (40° 19')	38·9 (40° 19')	0·49 (37° 29')	0·64 (37° 25')	3·64 (40° 19')	5·29 (40° 19')	0·94 (40° 19')	1·30 (40° 19')
7	46·5 (46° 4')	43·7 (46° 4')	0·55 (43° 14')	0·59 (43° 10')	4·14 (46° 4')	4·88 (46° 4')	1·06 (46° 4')	1·19 (46° 4')
8	41·9 (51° 50')	48·2* (51° 50')	0·61* (49° 0')	0·53 (48° 57')	4·62* (51° 50')	4·45 (51° 50')	1·18* (51° 50')	1·08 (51° 50')

* Maximum error per head sweep.
NOTE: Method II provides the best velocity correction giving a reduction of 100:1 over line-by-line correction. This method, however, requires a 1 line delay for the video. Method IV is most common giving a 50:1 reduction although Method III is used on the last line which may only have a 15.1 reduction.

19. Standards organizations

ANSI: American National Standards Institute, 1430 Broadway, NY USA (formerly USA Standards Institute, USASI, formerly American Standards Association, Inc., ASA). ANSI does not originate standards itself, but rather provides procedures for establishing national standards called "American National Standards" based on a consensus of those substantially concerned with the scope of the corresponding standards. ANSI has approved a number of audio standards sponsored by EIA, IEEE, and SMPTE. Most foreign and international standards are distributed in the USA by the ANSI. Write ANSI for the current free catalog of ISO, IEC, and American National Standards.

ARD: Arbeitsgemeinschaft der Rundfunkanstalten der Bundesrepublik Deutschland (Association for Radio Stations of the

German Federal Republic). The standards are published for ARD by the Institut für Rundfunktechnik, 2000 Hamburg, Mittelweg 113, West Germany.

BS: Standards published by British Standards Institution (BSI), British Standards House, 2 Park Street, London W.1, England. BSI Sales Branch, Newton House, 101 Pentonville Rd., London N.1, England. These standards are available in the USA through ANSI. Write BSI for the following Sectional Lists: SL 10, Acoustics; SL 1, Cinematography; SL 26, Electrical Engineering; and SL 29, Nomenclature.

CCIR: International Radio Consultative Committee, International Telecommunication Union, Place des Nations, Geneva, Switzerland. The texts of CCIR recommendations and reports are published in the documents of the Plenary Assemblies of the International Radio Consultative Committee, every three years. The volume on Broadcasting and Television (Study Group X and others) sells to non-members of CCIR for approximately $6 including packing and postage, and may be ordered directly from the ITU at Geneva. (Not available from ANSI).

DIN: Standards published by Deutscher Normenausschus (DNA) (German Standards Committee). This organisation formulates the Deutsche Industrie Normen (German Industrial Standards, DIN) which are widely used in Europe. Although the titles will be given here in English, the original standards are, of course, all in German. Some of the Standards are also available in English translations, sometimes very literal, indicated by "E/DIN." These standards are sold by Beuth-Vertrieb GmbH, 1 Berlin 30, Burggrafenstrasse 4–7, West Germany. Standards in German, and the "E/DIN" translation, are available in the USA from ANSI. Some of the standards are available in unofficial translations in finished form, indicated "E/U-f," and some in very rough draft form, "E/U-d," from J. G. McKnight, Ampex Corp., Mail Stop 26–01, 401 Broadway, Redwood City, Calif., 94063, USA. Write Beuth-Vertrieb GmbH for the "DIN Normen-verzeichnis für die heimstudio-, rundfunk-, magnetton-, verstärker-, und phono-Technik, einschliesslich elektroakustischer Wandler und Messtechnik" ("DIN Standards List for 'high fidelity', radio, magnetic recording, amplifier, and phonograph engineering, including electroacoustic transducers and measurement techniques") (in German).

EIA: Electronic Industries Association, Engineering Department, 2001 Eye Street, N.W., Washington, D.C. 20006, USA. Some EIA standards have been approved as ANSI standards. Write EIA for the current free catalogue of standards.

EIAJ Electronic Industries Association of Japan, 3–14, Maruouchi, Chiyoda-Kin Tokyo, Japan.

IBTO: International Broadcasting and Television Organization (OIRT

284

in French), Liebknechtova 15, Prague, 5 Czechoslovakia. An international organisation of several East European, Asian and African nations and Cuba.

IEC: International Electrotechnical Commission,1, rue de Varembé, Geneva, Switzerland. Standards listed in the ANSI catalogue and available in the USA through ANSI.

EBU: European Broadcasting Union, Technical Centre, Avenue Albert Lancaster 32, B–1180 Bruxelles.

IEEE: Institute of Electrical and Electronics Engineers, Inc., 345 East 47th St., New York, NY 10017, USA (formerly AIEE and IRE). These standards are available from the IEEE order department. Write IEEE for the current free catalog. Some IEEE standards have been approved as ANSI standards.

ISO: International Organisation for Standardisation, 1, rue de Varembé, Geneva, Switzerland. Standards listed in the ANSI catalog and available in the USA through ANSI.

JIS: Standards published by the Japanese Standards Association (JSA), 1–24 Akasaka 4, Minato-Ku, Tokyo, Japan. The standards are available in the USA through ANSI.

MRIA: Magnetic Recording Industries Association. Merged with EIA in 1965; no standards issued.

NAB: National Association of Broadcasters (also called NARTB at one time), Engineering Department, 1771 N. Street, N.W., Washington, D.C. 20036, USA. Standards for use by the USA broadcasting industry. No catalogue.

PPI: Philips Phonographic Industries, Baarn, The Netherlands. PPI publishes a widely used company standard on cassette recording.

RIAA: Record Industry Association of America, Inc., One East 57th St., New York, N.Y. 10022, USA. Tape and disc record standards. No catalogue.

SMPTE: Society of Motion Picture and Television Engineers, 9 East 41st St., New York, NY 10017, USA. These standards are published in the Journal of the SMPTE in their draft and finally approved forms. The approved standards are available from ANSI only. Write SMPTE for the current free index to SMPTE standards.

USA FED.: United States of America, Federal Specifications. Procurement standard for Federal agencies. Bureau of Ships, Department of the Navy standards can be ordered from Naval Ship Engineering Center, Code 6665.2M, Washington, D.C. 20360, USA. General Services Administration standards can be ordered from the General Services Administration's regional offices in Boston, New York, Washington (D.C.), Atlanta, Chicago, Kansas City (Mo.), Dallas, Denver, San Francisco and Auburn (Wash.), USA.

UTE: Union Technique de l'Electricite, 20, rue Hamelin, Paris (16e), France. Available in the USA through ANSI in French only.

20. Standards

Arrangement is by the subject of the standard:

1. General standards (where one document includes several of the subjects)
2. Glossaries, symbols, etc.
3. Recording and reproducing equipment specifications
4. Measuring and adjusting recording and reproducing equipment (including test tapes)
5. Tape
   5.1 Specifications
   5.2 Testing methods
6. Containers for tape
   6.1 Reels
   6.2 Cartridges
7. Tape records
8. Miscellaneous
9. Video Recording

Within a subject, entries are alphabetical by the standardising organization. EIA standards which are also ANSI standards are, nevertheless, listed under EIA.

1. GENERAL STANDARDS

(Including glossaries, recording and reproducing equipment, measurements, tape, containers and tape records in one standard.)
The following two standards are for recording and reproducing equipment and records for professional program exchange.

IEC Publication 94
Magnetic Tape Recording and Reproducing 24 Systems: Dimensions and Characteristics. Third edition, 1968.
Amendment 1
(Changes which replace the "surface induction" specification of recording characteristics with a "recorded tape flux characteristic") (in preparation.)
Addition 1
Tape cassettes for domestic use: twin-hub, four-track, mono-stereo compatible (in preparation). For the time being, see Philips Phonographic Industries, "Tape Cassette, Twin-Hub Four-Track Mono/Stereo Compatible for Domestic Use" (4th Revision, Oct. 1968). GPG 670. 4/4. (Published in *J. AES* **16**, 430–435, Oct. 1968).
BS 1568: 1960 + Amendment
PD 5962, Dec. 1966
Magnetic Tape Sound Recording and Reproduction (Dimensional Features).

The following two standards are for recording and reproducing equipment and records for use by the USA broadcasting industry.

NAB Standard
Magnetic Tape Recording and Reproducing (Reel-to-Reel) (April 1965).

NAB Standard
Cartridge Tape Recording and Reproducing (Oct. 1964).

2. GLOSSARIES, SYMBOLS, ETC.
(See also Sec. 1, General Standards)

ANSI S1.1-1960*
Acoustical Terminology (Sec. 8: Recording and Reproducing).

ANSI Y32.2-1967
Graphic Symbols for Electrical and Electronics Diagrams

DIN 40 700: Part 7
Graphical Symbols for Magnetic Heads (Sept. 1957). E/U-f

DIN 45 510
Magnetic sound recording: Terminology; 6. German, English, French (Draft, Feb. 1969)

IEC Publication: 50 (08)
International Electrotechnical Vocabulary: Electroacoustics. (Sec. 08-25: Recording and Reproduction).

* Standards known to be under revision are shown by an asterisk.

3. RECORDING AND REPRODUCING EQUIPMENT SPECIFICATIONS
(See also Sec. 1, General Standards)

DIN 45 500
Part 4
"High Fidelity" Home Equipment: Magnetic tape recording and reproducing systems (Oct. 1967)

DIN 45 511:
Tape Recorders:
Part 1
Tape recorder for recording on magnetic tape with 6·3 mm (0·25 in) width, mechanical and electrical specifications (Draft, March 1969) E/U-f and E/DIN of March 1966 issue.
Part 2
Tape recorder for 3- or 4-track recording on magnetic tape with 12·5 mm (0·5 in) width, mechanical and electrical specifications (Draft, March 1969)
Part 3
Tape recorder for 4-track recording on magnetic tape with 25·4 mm (1 in) width, mechanical and electrical specifications (Draft, March 1969)

EIA RS-288 (1963)
Audio Magnetic Playback Characteristics at 7·5 in/s.

JIS C5550-1967

Magnetic Tape Recording and Reproducing Equipment (in English).

USA Fed. Specs. W-R-00168a (GSA-FSS)

Recorder-Reproducer, Sound (Magnetic Tape Type) (March 1968)

USA Fed. Specs. W-R-170a

Recorder-Reproducer, Sound (Portable, Battery Operated) (May 1966).

W-R-170a Interim Amendment—2 (GSA-FSS)

Interim Amendment (March 1968).

USA Fed. Specs. W-R-0001404 (GSA-FSS)

Recorder-Reproducer, Sound (Portable. Battery Operated, Cassette Type) (August 1968)

4. MEASURING AND ADJUSTING RECORDING AND REPRODUCING EQUIPMENT (Including Test Tapes)

(See also Sec. 1, General Standards)

ARD

Basic Specifications for Magnetic Sound Recording Equipment, and General Directions for their Adjustment (June 1965). German only.

DIN 45 513

DIN Test Tapes

Part 1

76 cm/s (30 in/s), 6·3 mm (0·25 in) tape width (Apr. 1968). E/DIN.

Part 2

38 cm/s (15 in/s), 6·3 mm (0·25 in) tape width (Oct. 1967). E/DIN.

Part 3

19 cm/s (7·5 in/s), 6·3 mm (0·25 in) tape width (Oct. 1966). E/DIN, E/U-f.

Part 4

9·5 cm/s (3·75 in/s), 6·3 mm (0·25 in) tape width (Jan. 1968). E/DIN

Part 5

4·75 cm/s (1·88 in/s), 6·3 mm (0·25 in) tape width (Mar. 1966). E/DIN—for 1963 issue only.

Part 6

4·75 cm/s (1·88 in/s), 3·8 mm (150 mil) tape width (draft, Mar. 1967).

DIN 45 520*

Magnetic Tape Equipment: Method for Measuring the Absolute Magnitude and the Frequency Response of the Remanent Magnetic Flux of Magnetic Recording Tape (Sept. 1957) E/U-f.

DIN 45 521

Magnetic Tape Equipment: Measuring the Crosstalk Ratio of Multi-track Equipment (Oct. 1963).

DIN 45 524

Evaluation of the tape speed of magnetic tape transports (draft, March 1969).

288

EIA . . .

EIA Reproducer Test Tape (Open-reel) for tape speeds of 7·5 in/s (19 cm/s) and 3·75 in/s (9·5 cm/s) (in preparation; now Standards Proposal 1030)

IBTO Recommendation . . .

OIRT Reference Tapes for the International Programme Exchange.

JIS C5551-1966

Testing Methods for Magnetic Tape Equipment (in English).

UTE C97-110

Electroacoustics: Magnetic Tape Recorders for Semi-Professional or General Public usage: Characteristics and Methods of Measurement (July 1966).

5. TAPE

(See also Sec. 1, General Standards)

5.1 Specifications

DIN 45 500

Part 9

"High Fidelity" Home Equipment: Magnetic tapes (draft, Sept. 1966).

DIN 45 512

Part 1

Magnetic Tapes: Mechanical properties (Aug. 1968)

EIA RS-355 (1968) (ANSI C83.45-1969)

Standard Dimensions for Unrecorded Magnetic Sound Recording Tape

USA Fed. Spec. W-T-0070/1

Tape, Audio Type, Cellulose Acetate Base (Apr. 1963)

USA Fed. Spec. W-T-0070/2

Tape, Audio Type, Polyester Base (Apr. No charge 1963)

5.2 Testing Methods

DIN 45 512

Part 2

Magnetic tapes: Recording performance characteristics (Draft, Feb. 1969) (Aug. 1968)

DIN 45 519

Measuring Methods for Tapes:

Part 1

Print-through (Oct. 1955). E/U-d

Part 2

Signal to DC-Noise Ratio (Oct. 1955). E/U-d

DIN 45 522

Test Methods for Magnetic Tapes:

Part 1

Measurement of the coefficient of friction (Dec. 1968)

Part 2

Measurement of flexibility (Aug. 1968)

Part 3

Measurement of nominal strength (Aug. 1968)

Part 4

Measurement of longitudinal curvature

EIA RS-339 (1967) (ANSI C83.35-1968)

Recommended Test Method—Layer-to-layer Adhesion of Magnetic Tape

EIA RS-342 (1967) (ANSI C83.36-1968)

Recommended Test Method—Magnetic Tape Electrical Resistance Coating

EIA RS-362 (1969) (ANSI C83.56-1970)

Recommended Test Method—Tensile Property of Magnetic Tape

USA Fed. Spec. W-T-0070

Tapes, Recording, Sound and Instrumentation, Magnetic Oxide Coated, General Specifications for (Apr. 1963)

6. CONTAINERS FOR TAPE

(See also Sec. 1, General Standards)

6.1 Reels

DIN 45 514

Magnetic Tape Equipment: Reels, Cine-Type (Mar. 1961). E/DIN, E/U-f

DIN 45 515

Magnetic Tape Equipment: Hub (Mar. 1955). E/DIN

DIN 45 517

Magnetic Tape Equipment: "Disassembleable" Reel (Identical to EIA and NAB "Type A" reel.)

Part 1

Hub, flange, screw and nut (Oct. 1963).

Part 2

Adaptors (Oct. 1963).

EIA RS-346 (1968) (ANSI C83.38-1968)

Type A Hubs and Reels for Magnetic Tape

EIA RS-347 (1968) (ANSI C83.40-1968)

$\frac{1}{2}$ Inch Type B Plastic Reel for Magnetic Tape

EIA RS-351 (1968) (ANSI C83.39-1968)

Type B Plastic Reel for Magnetic Tape

USA Fed. Spec. W-R-175b

Reels and Hubs for Magnetic Recording Tape, General Specification for (May 1967).

USA Fed. Spec. W-R-175/1b

Reels, standard, plastic, and fibreglass, 5/16-inch center hole (May 1967)

6.2 Cartridges

EIA RS-264 (1962)

Magnetic Recording Tape Cartridge Dimensions

EIA RS-332 (1967) (ANSI C83.45-1969)

Dimensional Standards—Endless Loop Magnetic Tape Cartridges, Types 1, 2 and 3.

EIA . . .

Magnetic Tape Cartridge—Co-Planar Type CP-2 (Compact Cassette), Dimensional Standards (in preparation; now Standards Proposal 1055)

7. TAPE RECORDS

(See also Sec. 1, General Standards)

CCIR Recommendation 261-1

Standards of Sound Recording for the International Exchange of Programs, Single Track Recording on Magnetic Tape (1966). Vol. 5, p. 13–15.

CCIR Recommendation 408-1

Standards of Sound Recording for the International Exchange of Programs, Two-Track Stereophonic Recording on Magnetic Tape (1966). Vol. 5, p. 23-24.

EIA . . .

Endless-loop cartridges with eight-track stereophonic records at 3·75 in/s (in preparation; now Standards Proposal 1065)

EIA . . .

Endless-loop cartridges with four-track stereophonic records at 3·75 in/s (in preparation; now Standards Proposal 1066)

EIA . . .

Compact cassettes with four-track mono/stereo compatible records at 1·88 in/s (in ration: now Standards Proposal 1067)

EIA . . .

Open-reel four-track stereophonic records at 3·75- and 7·5 in/s (in preparation; now Standards Proposal 1068)

EIA RS-224 (1959)

Magnetic Recording Tapes (Rev. of REC 138 and REC 132)

IBTO Recommendation 24

Magnetic Tape Recording for the International Programme Exchange

RIAA Bulletin E-5

Standards for Magnetic Tape Records (Feb. 1969).

RIAA . . .

Standards for Multitrack Magnetic Tape Duplicating Masters (preliminary draft, May 1967).

8. MISCELLANEOUS

DIN 45 523

Remote Control by Signals from Magnetic Tape Recorders (July 1968).

DIN 45 525

Evaluation of the Time Period During Which Batteries May be Used in Magnetic Tape Recorders (draft, May 1968).

EIA REC-133 (1949)

Magnetic Recorder Combined with Home Radio Receivers (reprinted June 1954).

9. VIDEO RECORDING

ANSI Standards

ANSI C98.1-1963:
Dimensions of 2-in video magnetic tape.

ANSI C98.2-1963:
Monochrome video magnetic tape leader.

ANSI C98.3 1963 & 70:
Audio records for 2-in video magnetic tape recordings.

ANSI C98.4 1963 & 70:
Speed of 2-in video magnetic tape.

ANSI C98.5 1965:
Dimensions of 2-in video magnetic tape reels.

ANSI C98.6 1965:
Dimensions of video, audio and tracking control records on 2-in video magnetic tape.

CCIR
Recommended practice 469: Standards for the International Exchange of Television Programmes on Magnetic Tape.

SMPTE Recommended Practices

SMPTE RP 5 1964:
Dimensions of patch splices in 2-in video magnetic tape.

SMPTE RP 6 1966:
Reference carrier frequencies and de-emphasis characteristics for 2-in quadruplex video magnetic tape recording.

SMPTE RP 10 1962:
Signal specifications for a monochrome video alignment tape for 2-in video magnetic tape recording.

SMPTE RP 11 1962:
Tape vacuum guide radius and position for recording standard video records on 2 in magnetic tape.

SMPTE RP 16 1964:
Specifications of tracking control record for 2-in video magnetic tape recordings.

SMPTE RP 36 1971:
Specifications for positioning tape neutral plane and adjacent tape guides for quadruplex videotape recorders operating at 15 i.p.s. and 7·5 i.p.s.

SMPTE RP 43 1971:
Video test tape for quadruplex magnetic tape recorders operating at 15 i.p.s.

SMPTE RP 44 1971:
Video test tape for quadruplex magnetic tape recorders operating at 7·5 i.p.s.

EIA

EIA RS-170
Electrical performance standards—monochrome television studio facilities.

EIAJ
EIAJ Type I Format specification for $\frac{1}{2}$-in videotape recorders.

292

EBU
  TECH 3084 E Standards for television tape-recordings
TECH 3093-E
  Video player and recorder systems for home use.

21. The EIA Standard RS–170

The EIA standard RS — 170 specifies in section 2.6 for a monochrome television signal that: "It shall be standard that the the rate of change of the frequency of recurrence of the leading edges of the horizontal sync pulses be not greater than 0·15 per cent per second."

It is more convenient to consider the instability in terms of the peak timing error and the rate of change of the timing error. The rate of change of error is normally assumed to be sinusoidal.

Therefore:

$$t_e = T_e \sin 2\pi f_d t \qquad\qquad 1$$

where:

t_e = instantaneous value of the timing error.
T_e = peak value of the timing error.
f_d = frequency of the change in timing error.

If the periodic time of the sync pulse waveform is t_o, then the angular error θ_e in radians is:

$$\phi_e = \frac{2\pi t_e}{t_0} = \frac{2\pi T_e}{t_0} \sin 2\pi f_d t \qquad\qquad 2$$

The rate of change of error is:

$$\omega_e = \frac{d\phi_e}{dt}$$

or

$$f_e = \frac{d\phi_e}{dt} \cdot \frac{1}{2\pi}$$

From (2)

$$f_e = 2\pi f_d \frac{T_e}{t_0} \cos 2\pi f_d t \qquad\qquad 3$$

The rate of change of frequency error

$$\delta f_e = \frac{df_e}{dt}$$

293

From (3)

$$\delta f_e = (2\pi f_d)^2 \frac{T_e}{t_0} \sin 2\pi f_d t \qquad\qquad 4$$

Substituting $f_0 = \dfrac{1}{t_0}$

where f_0 = frequency of recurrence of horizontal sync pulses

$$\delta f_e = (2\pi f_d)^2 T_e f_0 \sin 2\pi f_d t$$

taking peak values

$$\left| \frac{\delta f_e}{f_0} \right| = (2\pi f_d)^2 T_e$$

For R.S. 170:

$$\left| \frac{\delta f_e}{f_0} \right| \leqslant 0{\cdot}0015$$

$$\therefore T_e = \frac{0{\cdot}0015}{4 \cdot \pi^2 f_d^2} = \frac{38}{f_d^2} \ \mu \text{ seconds}$$

If this is plotted the following graph is produced.

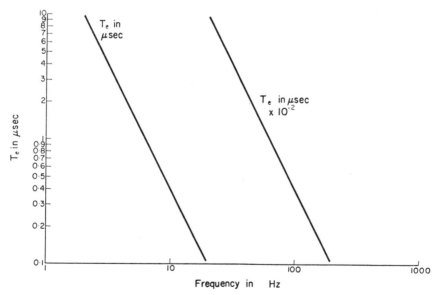

22. Logic symbols

Throughout this book logic symbols to the USA MIL-STD-806B have been used. The basic gates and their functions are illustrated below.

The following table of combinations illustrates the functions of two variables and their equivalents as well as the truth table. H in the truth table illustrates a positive or high potential and L represents a low or negative potential.

And	Or	A t/f	B t/f	X t/f
A, B → X (AND)	A, B → X (NOR)	H t	H t	H t
		H t	L f	L f
		L f	H t	L f
		L f	L f	L f
A (inv), B → X	A, B (inv) → X	H f	H t	L f
		H f	L f	L f
		L t	H t	H t
		L t	L f	L f
A, B (inv) → X	A (inv), B → X	H t	H f	L f
		H t	L t	H t
		L f	H f	L f
		L f	L t	L f
A (inv), B (inv) → X	A, B → X	H f	H f	L f
		H f	L t	L f
		L t	H f	L f
		L t	L t	H t
A (inv), B (inv) → X (inv)	A, B → X	H f	H f	H f
		H f	L t	H f
		L t	H f	H f
		L t	L t	L t
A (inv), B (inv) → X (inv)	A (inv), B → X	H t	H f	H t
		H t	L t	L t
		L f	H f	H t
		L f	L t	H t
A, B → X (inv)	A, B (inv) → X	H f	H t	H f
		H f	L f	H f
		L t	H t	L t
		L t	L t	H t
A, B → X (inv)	A (inv), B (inv) → X	H t	H t	L t
		H t	L f	H f
		L f	H t	H f
		L f	L f	H f

295

Glossary

The terms used in the book comply where possible with those recomended by the Nomenclature Subcommittee of the SMPTE Magnetic Video Tape Recording Engineering Committee. The following glossary denotes terms used in this book in capitals and other frequently used terms in small type.

   * Indicates SMPTE specified terms.

Add-on Edit see ASSEMBLE EDIT.

Amtec A manufacturer's term for a monochrome time base corrector using sync as a reference.

ASSEMBLE EDIT An electronic edit where a new scene or sequence is recorded on the end of an existing recording. A new control track is recorded and only the ingoing splice is synchronous.

a.t.c. A manufacturer's term for a monochrome time base error corrector using sync as a reference.

Audio No 1 Track, see PROGRAMME AUDIO TRACK.

Audio No 2 Track, see CUE TRACK.

Auto-Chroma, see CHROMA AMPLITUDE CORRECTOR.

AUTOMATIC LOCK A V.T.R. playback condition where the playback video is in full synchronism with the station sync.

BANDING* A visible difference in the reproduced characteristics in that portion of a picture associated with one head channel, when compared with adjacent areas associated with other head channels. In quadruplex recorders, these differences occur in horizontal bands of 16 or 17 scanning lines when reproducing a 525/60 Hz signal:

   HUE: Banding in which the visible difference is in the hue
   NOISE: Banding in which the visible difference is in the noise
   SATURATION: Banding in which the visible difference is in the saturation.

BASE FILM* The substrate of tape that supports the magnetic coating

BEARDING An overload condition producing *FM* sidebands outside the pass-band, the loss of which causes black areas to overflow irregularly into white areas after sharp transitions.

296

BINDER* The material used to bond the magnetic particles to each other and to the base film.

BLACK LEVEL FREQUENCY The frequency of the *FM* signal corresponding to the blanking level of the video signal.

Bleeding whites
  BEARDING.

BLOCKING* The tendency of the adjacent layers of tape in a roll to stick together.

CANOE The curved section of tape between the input and output tape guides.

Cartridge, see CASSETTE.

CASSETTE An enclosed tape package containing one or two spools that allows automatic lacing of the tape path when loaded into a cassette player.

CAPSTAN* The driven spindle in a tape machine, sometimes the motor shaft itself, which rotates in contact with the tape and meters the tape across the transport.

Cavec A manufacturer's term for a chroma amplitude and velocity error corrector.

CHROMA AMPLITUDE CORRECTOR A device that automatically adjusts the playback equalisation by referring to the colour burst amplitude.

Colour a.t.c. A manufacturer's term for a colour time base error corrector using colour burst as a reference.

Colortec A manufacturer's term for a colour time base error corrector using colour burst as a reference.

CONTROL TRACK* The area on the tape containing a recording used by a servo mechanism primarily to control the longitudinal motion of the tape during playback in a quadruplex system (see SMPTE RP 16).

CUE TRACK* The area reserved on the tape for audio information relating to production requirements, electronic editing information, or a second programme signal.

DE-EMPHASIS A reduction in the amplitude of the high frequency components of the video signal (equal on opposite to the pre-emphasis) after demodulation.

DOWNSTREAM* The adverb pertaining to locations on the tape longitudinally displaced from a given reference in the direction of a tape motion.

DROP-OUT A drop in playback *RF* level that causes a noticable impairment on the playback video.

Drum, see DRUM-SCANNER—helical; HEAD WHEEL—quadruplex

DRUM-SCANNER The rotational head and cylindrical guiding assembly of a helical VTR.

DUB*
  1. To make a copy of a recording by re-recording.
  2. A copy.

E-E Electronics to electronics, the signal routing of the *RF* signal from the modulator to the demodulator.

Edit Pulse, see FRAME PULSE

Female guide, see VACUUM GUIDE.

FRAME PULSE A pulse superimposed on the control track signal to identify the longitudinal position of a video track containing a vertical sync pulse. Used as an aid to editing and in the synchronisation of some recorders (see SMPTE RP5 and RP 16 and EBU Tech 3084-E).

Freeze Frame see STILL FRAME

GEOMETRY ERRORS Time base and velocity errors caused by changes in guide, head or tape dimensions or position between record and playback.

GUARD BAND The unrecorded section of tape between record tracks.

HEAD CHANNEL* The signal path unique to each magnetic head. In a quadruplex system, the outputs of four channels are combined to provide a continuous *RF* signal.

HEAD CLOGGING* The accumulation of debris on the head, the usual result of which is a loss of signal during playback, degradation, or failure to record in the record mode.

HEAD POSITION PULSE A unique tachometer pulse signifying the position of a rotating head.

HEAD-TO-TAPE-SPEED* The relative speed between tape and head during normal recording or replay.

HEAD WHEEL* A rotating wheel with magnetic heads mounted on its rim.

HIGH BAND*

    1. Pertaining to those frequencies specified in SMPTE RP6 Practice HB (and EBU)

    2. Pertaining to those recordings made in accordance with Practice HB of RP6, or equipment capable of making those recordings.

    3. The carrier frequencies which appear on tape made in accordance with such practices.

HIGH ENERGY TAPE A tape with a higher coercivity and retentivity than ferric oxide. Typically cobalt doped ferric oxide or chromium dioxide.

HORIZONTAL LOCK A VTR playback condition where the horizontal syncs of the video is in synchronism with station horizontal sync.

INSERT EDIT An electronic edit where a new scene or sequence is recorded between two existing scenes. An existing control track is required which is not erased or over recorded. Both the ingoing splice and outgoing splice is synchronous.

Jitter, see TIME-BASE ERROR

Line-lock, see HORIZONTAL LOCK

LONGITUDINAL* Pertaining to dimensions or motions parallel to the tape travel.

LOW-BAND*

    1. Pertaining to those frequencies specified in SMPTE RP6, Practice LBM or LBC (and EBU).

    2. Pertaining to those recordings made in accordance with Practice LBM or LBC of RP6 or equipment capable of making those recordings.

    3. The carrier frequencies which appear on a tape made in accordance with such practices.

MOIRÉ A coherent beat pattern normally produced by the harmonic distortion of the *f.m.* signal. It is most noticable in large areas of large amplitude high frequencies, i.e. colour sub-carrier.

Neutral plane, see TAPE NEUTRAL PLANE

Pix-lock, see AUTOMATIC LOCK

POLE TIPS* Those parts of the video head which protrude radially beyond the rim of the head wheel and form the magnetic path to and from the tape.

PRE-EMPHASIS An increase in amplitude of the high frequency components of the video signal prior to frequency modulation.

PRINT THROUGH* The unintentional transfer of a recorded signal from one layer of magnetic tape on to adjacent layers.

PROGRAMME AUDIO TRACK* The area reserved on the tape for the main audio signal, usually associated with the accompanying video recording.

Pulse interval modulation. A form of frequency modulation.

QUADRUPLEX* An adjective describing a standardized method of video magnetic tape recording which uses four magnetic heads mounted around the rim of a head wheel. The head wheel rotates in a plane perpendicular to the direction of the tape motion.

*RECORD** The magnetic pattern on the tape corresponding to a signal.

RECORD CURRENT OPTIMIZER (RCO) A device that facilitates the optimum setting of the video head current by using the following head to play back a preceding recorded track.

*REFERENCE EDGE** On a videotape containing quadruplex recorded information, that longitudinal tape edge nearest the control track.

RF The modulated video signal.

*RF DUB**

1. To dub by rerecording the *RF* signal recovered from a tape being copied.
2. A copy made by this process.

Scanner, see DRUM SCANNER

SERVO CAPSTAN A servomechanism which controls the rotational velocity and phase of a capstan.

SERVO HEAD WHEEL** A servomechanism which controls the rotational velocity and phase of the head wheel.

Shoe, see VACUUM GUIDE

Shuttle, see SPOOLING

*SPLICE (mechanical)** A butt-joint between two pieces of tape held together by means of a strip of adhesive foil.

SPLICING TAPE The adhesive foil used to secure the butt join mechanical splice.

SPOOLING The movement of tape from one reel to the other without being in record or playback.

*SUPPLY REEL** A reel from which the tape is unwound during record, reproduce or fast-forward modes.

Switch-lock, see VERTICAL LOCK

STILL FRAME The repetitive playback of one picture.

SYNC TIP FREQUENCY The frequency of the *FM* signal corresponding to the bottom of sync level of the video signal.

TACHOMETER LOCK A VTR record or playback condition where the head wheel is in phase and frequency lock with a station reference (i.e. mains, station vertical sync or input video vertical sync) from a comparison of the reference with the head position pulse.

TACH PULSE A pulse derived optically, magnetically or mechanically from the rotation of a controlled motor.

*TAKE-UP REEL** A reel on to which the tape is wound during the forward movement of the tape.

*TAPE** *Magnetic* A tape consisting of a flexible base material usually coated on one side with a thin magnetisable layer.

TAPE GUIDES Rollers or posts to position the tape correctly along its path on the tape transport.

*TAPE INPUT GUIDE** The last guiding element encountered by the tape before the vacuum guide.

*TAPE LEADER** (*magnetic*) The section of tape, usually recorded ahead of the programme material, which contains engineering alignment signals and production information.

*TAPE NEUTRAL PLANE** A plane located and defined by the tape input guide and tape output guide in which the tape would lie if it were undeflected by the vacuum guide.

*TAPE OUTPUT GUIDE** The first guiding element encountered by the tape after the vacuum guide.

299

*TAPE SPEED** The linear rate of travel of the undeformed recording medium past any stationary portion of a transport.

*TIME BASE ERROR** A timing error between an off-tape video signal and a stable station source.

Tone-wheel pulse, see TACH PULSE

Tracking control signal, see CONTROL TRACK SIGNAL

Tip engagement, see TIP PENETRATION

Tip height, see TIP PROJECTION

*TIP PENETRATION** The momentary radial deflection of the tape in the vacuum guide caused by the passage of a video head pole tip.

*TIP PROJECTION** The measured radial difference between the pole tip and the head wheel rim.

Tip protrusion, see TIP PROJECTION

Television magnetic recording, see VIDEOTAPE RECORDING.

TENSION SERVO A servomechanism controlling the longitudinal tension of the tape either keeping it constant or by maintaining minimum time base error.

*TRACK** An area on the tape containing a record.

*TRACK-CURVATURE** The deviation from straightness of a single video track record

TRACKING Adjustment of the tape playback position to phase the video tracks to the rotating head.

*TRAILING EDGE, VIDEO TRACK** The upstream edge of the video track.

*TRANSVERSE** Pertaining to dimensions or motions perpendicular to the tape travel.

Transverse Recording, see QUADRUPLEX RECORDING.

*UPSTREAM** Pertaining to locations on the tape longitudinally displaced from a given reference point, in a direction opposite to tape travel.

*VACUUM GUIDE** The part of the video head assembly used to maintain the tape in the correct position relative to the head wheel by means of a suction system.

VELOCITY ERROR The rate of change of time base error, often expressed in time base error change per TV line.

Velocity error compensator (VEC) A device that reduces the time base error changes during the line period.

VERTICAL LOCK A VTR playback condition where the vertical sync of the playback video is in synchronism with station vertical sync.

*VIDEO DUB**

    1. To dub by rerecording the video signal recovered from the tape being copied.
    2. A copy made by this process.

Video Head optimiser (VHO) see RECORD CURRENT OPTIMISER

*VIDEO TAPE** Magnetic recording tape intended for recording and playback of television signals.

VIDEOTAPE RECORDING A term normally refering to all forms of magnetic tape recording of video signals sometimes abbreviated to VTR.

WHITELEVEL FREQUENCY The frequency of the *FM* signal corresponding to the peak white level of the video signal.

Index

A.F.C., 99
Audio:
    record, 25
    playback, 28
Auto:
    editing, 241
    equalisation, 116
    frequency control, 99
    servo mode, 139
    tension, 167
    tracking, 142
Axial Displacement, 149
Azimuth, 35, 148, 254

Back Gap, 26, 256
Beat Frequency Oscillator, 96
Bias, 37
Blanking Switcher, 108
Burst Locked Oscillator, 199

Capstan:
    helical: playback mode, 146
            record mode, 145
    quadruplex: record mode, 132
                playback mode, 134
                vertical mode, 135
Cartridge, 213
Cassette:
    helical, 211
    quadruplex, 208
Channel Amplifiers, 103
Chroma Pilot, 91, 186, 204
Coercivity, 20, 22
Colour Error, 156

Colour Correction:
    disc, 247
    stabilisation, 197
    tape, 181, 193, 194
Compatibility, 159
Control Track:
    helical, 74
    quadruplex, 60, 132
Cosine Equaliser, 105, 273
Cue Track:
    address codes, 234
    cue tones, 239
    general, 58

Decode-Encode, 200
De-emphasis, 39, 93
Degaussing, 51
Delay Line:
    analogue, 172
    binary, 175
    quantised, 180
Demagnetisation, 33, 51
Demodulation, 112
Deviation, 83
Disc, 243
Discriminator, 124
Distortion:
    frequency modulation, 84
    tape, 36
Drop-Out:
    compensation, 115
    description, 49
Dumping, 185

Eddy Current:
  brake, 120
  loss, 33
Editing:
  automatic, 241
  electronic, 217
  physical helical, 215
  physical quadruplex, 216
Electronic Editing:
  address codes, 231
  assemble, 218
  automatic, 241
  colour, 228
  cue tones, 229
  helical, 219
  insert, 218
  quadruplex, 224
  record phase, 227
Equaliser, 104, 273
Equalisation (Audio):
  parameters, 40
  standards, 41
Erase, 24
Error Detection, 176

F.A.M., 195
Fast Motion, 253
Field Sync:
  alignment, 259
  position, 61
  waveform, 247
Fluctuating Error, 171
Flying Erase, 219
Formats:
  Ampex 1 inch, 73
  IVC 1 inch, 73, 264
  EIAJ ½ inch, 265
  Phillips VCR, 68, 266
  quadruplex, 59
  IVC/Rank 2 inch, 267
Forward/Backward Counter, 123
Fourth Power Law, 177
Frame Pulse, 138
Frequency Losses, 31
Frequency Modulation:
  deviation, 83
  distortion, 84
  modulators, 95, 276
  moire, 87, 271
  standards, 82
Friction, 165, 280
Front Porch Switch, 111

Gap Effect, 31, 257
Geometry Errors (Helical):
  adjustments, 157
  environment, 162

Geometry Errors (Helical) contd.—
  head position, 157
  interchange, 158
Geometry Errors (Quadruplex):
  cause, 147
  correction, 171
  environment, 156
  guide radius, 150, 279
  velocity, 186, 280
Guide Errors:
  calculations, 277
  cause, 147

Head Response, 103
Head Wheel:
  dimensions, 56
  logic, 140
  modes, 140
  servo, 138
Helical Scan:
  adjustments, 157
  alpha wrap, 70
  conical wrap, 71, 269
  interchange, 158
  omega wrap, 68
  stop motion, 75
  tape path, 71
Heterodyne, 201
High Band, 82
Horizontal:
  comparator, 140
  mode, 139
  synchronism, 141
Hysteresis, 19

Instability (Helical), 146
Interchange, 158

Logic Symbols, 195
Longitudinal:
  helical, 75
  quadruplex, 58

Magnetophone, 16
Memory Store, 188
Modulator (FM):
  a-stable, 97, 276
  reactance, 98
Moire:
  calculation, 271
  causes, 87
Motor Control:
  d.c., 130
  frequency, 126
  pulse width, 129

Noise (Modulation), 86

Optimisation, 52, 101
Overlap, 58

Phase Comparator:
  logic, 141
  types, 122
Pilot Tone, 91, 198, 204
Pre-emphasis, 39, 93
Processor, 48

Quadrature Displacement, 149
Quadruplex:
  deck, 63
  format data, 59
  general, 61
Quantised Gate, 179
Quartz Delay Line, 174

Record Driver, 100
Retentivity, 20, 23
Ring Counter, 126

Secam, 194
Sequential Coding, 196
Servo-mechanism:
  capstan (helical), 145
  capstan (quad), 47, 134
  drum scanner, 144
  general, 119
  head wheel, 47, 132
  modes, 140
Sheared Hysteresis, 22
Shelf Working, 91
Signal System, 47, 95
Spacing Loss, 32
Slow Motion:
  disc, 243
  helical, 75
Stabilisation, 197
Standards:
  organisations, 283
  specifications, 286
Static Error, 171
Switcher, 107
Sync Feedback, 184
Sync Line-up, 74
Sync Subcarrier Lock, 185

Tangent, 34
Tape:
  care, 48
  characteristics, 41
  checking, 49
  signal distortion, 36
  tension, 156, 165
Temperature Coefficient, 162
Tension (Tape):
  auto, 167
  helical, 165
  quadruplex, 156
Thickness Loss, 33
Tilt, 34
Time Base Error:
  calculation, 277
  detection, 176
  general, 171
  helical, 162
  quadruplex, 147
Time Base Error Correction:
  analogue, 172
  colour, 181
  digital, 180
  monochrome, 171
  velocity, 186
Tip Projection, 51, 56
Tracking, 56
  auto, 142
  control, 134
  mistracking, 34, 160
Transport (Tape):
  helical, 47, 71
  quadruplex, 47, 63

Vacuum Chamber, 63
Varactor Diode, 97, 172
Velocity Control, 119
Velocity Error:
  calculation, 280
  cause, 153
  correction, 186
  typical errors, 156
Vertical:
  mode, 138
  synchronism, 142
Vera, 17